Steel Boat, Iron Hearts

A U-boat Crewman's
Life aboard U-505

Hans Jacob Goebeler
with John Vanzo

Steel Boat, Iron Hearts

A U-boat Crewman's
Life aboard U-505

Savas Beatie
SB

Cataloging-in-Publication Data is available from the Library of Congress.

First Savas Beatie hardcover edition 2005

This book was originally published in a privately distributed paper edition as *Steel Boats, Iron Hearts: The Wartime Saga of Hans Goebeler and the U-505* (Wagnerian Publications, 1999)

ISBN 978-1-932714-31-9
First trade paper edition, third printing

SB
Published by
Savas Beatie LLC
989 Governor Drive, Suite 102
El Dorado Hills, CA 95762

Phone: 916-941-6896
E-mail: sales@savasbeatie.com

Savas Beatie titles are available at special discounts for bulk purchases in the United States by corporations, institutions, and other organizations. For more details, please contact Special Sales, P.O. Box 4527, El Dorado Hills, CA 95762, or you may e-mail us at sales@savasbeatie.com. Please visit our website at www.savasbeatie.com for additional information.

Printed in the United States of America

This book is dedicated to Axel-Olaf Lowe,
first skipper of *U-505*

and

To my wife Erika: I was, I am, and will stay as long as I live,
even after my death, at your side.

Author Hans Jacob Goebeler as a member
of the Kriegsmarine in 1942.

Contents

Contents (continued)

Maps and Photographs

*   *   *

Frontis: Author Hans Goebeler in the Kriegsmarine

Additional photographs have been placed throughout
the text for the convenience of the reader.

Preface

Out of the approximately 37,000 trained U-boat crewmembers in World War II, only about 6,000 survived the war to return safely to their homes in Germany, This represented the greatest percentage loss of any military service in our history. From the 1,000 or so German submarines in action during the war, only a handful remained after 1945. As unbelievable as it seems, the story of the U-boat men's sacrifice has never been truthfully and completely told in Germany. Only now, as logbooks and war diaries are being released from British custody, is a objective source of facts being made available to journalists and historians.

My friend and comrade Hans Göbeler has succeeded in describing in his book *Steel Boat, Iron Hearts* the day-to-day life of a wartime U-boat crewmember. The comradeship, the worries and fears, and the many unforgettable moments aboard his boat are all honestly portrayed in his autobiography. Many books have been written about the U-boat service, nearly all by the commander of the boat about his thoughts and decisions. What makes Hans's book invaluable is that it is written from the perspective of an ordinary crewmember. As a member of the control room crew, he had the best opportunity to experience the real atmosphere on board a frontline U-boat.

Unfortunately, Hans did not live to see the publication of this honest (and what is sure to be popular) portrayal of the German Navy in the

Second World War. Hans Göbeler passed away on February 15, 1999, after enduring a long period of severe illness.

Horst Einbrot
Oberleutnant zur See
Crewmember, *U-351*

Commander's Note

Hans collected material and worked on his memoir for many years before it was finally published. This letter was written to Hans from his former commander shortly before Lowe died in December 1984.

*I*n a highly praiseworthy manner Hans Goebeler, former crewmember of the *U-505*, has researched and gathered together facts about the boat and his crew to be published in the form of a book. May the purpose of this book, to bring together all those that can still be found in one single willing act of comradeship, be fulfilled.

I put the *U-505* into commission on the 26th of August, 1941, and in 1942 carried out three operations, including the trip to Lorient. At the commissioning, only two men had frontline U-boat experience, but the crew was brought to such a high level of professionalism that the boat was successful in the first year. The crew was, until the day I left and also thereafter, a first class crew in which no serious fall-outs occurred.

And so, my words should be a salute to all the men who sailed on the *U-505*, who did their duties and lived in comradeship on the boat, through happy and difficult times.

Axel Löwe
Former Korvettenkapitän
and the first commander of U-505

Introduction

$\mathcal{E}$ver since that first day he stepped foot on her decks as a young recruit in 1942, Hans Göbeler's life and soul revolved around *U-505*. During the war, he sent hundreds of photos and mementos of his experiences aboard the submarine back to his parents for safekeeping. After the war, he meticulously collected every article or passing reference written about her. This book is entirely the result of his efforts to memorialize his beloved boat.

Hans was never shy about expressing his pride about *U-505*, and about the U-boat service in general. In the climate of harsh political-correctness that dominated postwar Germany, he was often made to suffer because of his refusal to demonstrate the expected shame or repentance. He would have none of that, he said, because none was called for. Till the very end of his life, Hans steadfastly defended the bravery and devotion of his comrades in the German Navy—no matter what the personal cost was to him or his career. "I'm no chameleon!" he was proud of saying.

When *U-505* was enshrined as a monument at Chicago's Museum of Science and Industry in 1954, Hans vowed to move near her one day. True to his word, when he retired 30 years later, Hans moved his family from Germany to a suburb of Chicago. Once there, Hans organized the first reunions of the crews of *U-505* and the American ships that had captured her on June 4, 1944. Unbeknowst to many, he had also been gathering materials and writing his memoirs of life about *U-505*.

Hans was generally satisfied with the published accounts of his boat's history. During the 1950s, Daniel V. Gallery, commander of the task force that captured *U-505*, wrote a detailed history of the incident titled *Twenty Thousand Tons Under the Sea*. Gallery's version is generally accurate, though Hans disputed his conclusion that the crew on *U-505* was suffering from low morale. Hans was also pleased with the short memoir written by his friend and fellow crewmate Hans Joachim Decker, whose account was published as an article for the *U.S. Naval Institute Proceedings* entitled "404 Days! The War Patrol Life of the German *U-505*."

All of this changed, however, with the apperance in 1986 of a book by Lawrence Cortesi called *U-505 Victory*. In Hans's opinion, the book was filled with one egregious factual error after another. Horrified at what he perceived to be a perversion of his boat's historical record, he accelerated the pace of work on his own autobiography to correct the historical record. Supplementing his remarkable memory with a copy of *U-505*'s logbook and interviews with many of his fellow crewmates, Hans produced a 300-page manuscript of his wartime adventures aboard the boat.

For ten years Hans painstakingly penned his memoir. In the meantime, he had moved south to central Florida because of his wife's health. And that is where we met in early 1996. Hans allowed me to interview him for an article that appeared in the July 1997 issue of *World War II* magazine. The piece was very well received and prompted Hans to seek my help in writing his autobiography in preparation for publication. I was honored to do so.

Throughout the re-writing of his manuscript, I stayed utterly loyal to Hans's uncompromising demand that this book be a completely factual account of his wartime adventures. Throughout our collaboration, he steadfastly refused every temptation to censor or romanticize his experiences. I warned Hans that he sometimes came across in the narrative as a less-than-sympathetic character. No matter, he insisted, the book must be true to his experiences—blemishes and all.

What emerged is an authentic slice of life, a unique perspective on a critical point in history that has rarely been allowed to be expressed fully or honestly. It is a complex depiction, one that may displease those who seek to portray the German fighting man as either an inhuman monster or heroic superman. At its core, Hans's story is the tale of an ordinary young man's reactions to extraordinary circumstances. In its own way, it reflects the experiences of an entire generation of youngsters sent to war, regardless of nationality.

Sadly, Hans Göbeler's 75 years of life on this earth ended on the morning of February 14, 1999. Cancer and the noxious brew of chemicals doctors called a cure had whittled his once muscular body to a pitifully frail shell. On that chilly winter morning, his weakened heart finally gave out. His wife carried him to the living room couch, where he momentarily regained consciousness. Lying cradled in Erika's loving arms, Hans's eyes suddenly grew large and wide, as if staring at an incredible sight hovering over him.

"No, not yet. Not yet." he begged. A moment later, he was gone.

No one who knew Göbeler thought his last words were an expression of fear. Hans had faced death many times, always unflinchingly. No, he was not afraid of dying. His words conveyed his anxiety that the writing of this book was not yet complete. In his later years, "setting the record straight" about *U-505* and the men who served on her was his one and only ambition in life. My great sadness is that he did not live long enough to see this book in print. *Steel Boat, Iron Hearts* offers the most complete and accurate account of *U-505*, the first enemy ship captured on the high seas by the United States Navy since the War of 1812.

I think Hans would be pleased.

John P. Vanzo, Ph.D.
Bainbridge College

P.S. to Hans:

Auf Wiedersehen, my old friend. Wherever in the cosmos your spirit sails, may you always have a hand's breadth of water under your keel!

Foreword

$\mathcal{I}$ met Hans Göbeler in 1989 during the early months of my employment at the Museum of Science and Industry in Chicago. At that time I was but a lowly assistant to the then-Registrar and Collections Manager and working to finish the restoration project of *U-505* in 1988-89. To celebrate the completion of that restoration—the most aggressive since the arrival of *U-505* in 1954—a re-dedication was planned and Navy veterans from both sides were invited to attend. Because I was a recent arrival at the museum, I was not directly invited to attend the reunion. However, my interest in military history in general, and *U-505* in particular, drove me to crash the party anyway with the promise I would not interfere with the gathering!

My most vivid recollection of that day was how impressed I was that former enemies (language barriers notwithstanding) could meet again under less deadly circumstances and freely discuss their experiences. They were genuinely happy to see each other. Some talked of the boat, some spoke of their individual roles on the morning of June 4, 1944, and others were just happy to be among friends old and new. One of these men at this reunion was Hans Göbeler.

It was there I learned what an amazing man Hans was. Although he had been a "lowly" control room mate (and thus not an officer), he played a key role in organizing the reunion of *U-505's* crew. Inside his 5' 6" tall frame (an ideal height for a World War II submariner) was a much larger presence that impressed me each time we met until his death in the late 1990s. The former 65-year old Kriegsmarine member lifted weights to stay in shape, a routine that helped him maintain his youthful heavily muscled chest. He had an air of confidence and a devilish smile that naturally drew people to him. His eyes sparkled with humor and good cheer. Hans told me about the success he enjoyed as a student and entry into the U-boat service, and how the former paved the way for the latter. We shared many jokes over the years, and he was always ready to tell a good story about his time on "the old boat."

After several visits from Hans and many phone calls, I realized his stories were important to record for posterity. Passing them on to the tour guides working on *U-505,* so they could share them with visitors was one thing, but the recollections would eventually be lost or changed unless they were written down. In addition to his firsthand stories, Hans himself added a unique dimension to the *U-505* experience. Whenever he stopped by, Hans loved to give informal tours to visitors. He became part of the exhibit for a day, standing in the control room talking about a piece of equipment or a particular experience to anyone who had an interest. Inevitably, a tour group would pass through and somehow its members would sense Hans had a direct connection with the boat. Perhaps it was his accent, or simply his obvious expertise, but once the cat was out of the bag, the only thing to do was to step back and watch.

Touring *U-505* with a former crewmember is both a rare and unforgettable experience. And for Hans, it was very satisfying. I always enjoyed watching the absolute attention he could command from the visitors as he spoke about life aboard *U-505* while standing at his former duty station. The visitors, as one might imagine, were in total awe. Many took the opportunity to ask some tough questions about what it meant to be a German submariner in WWII, what was life on board like, how he felt at the time of the capture, and how he feels about it now so many decades later.

I think all of this attention and outpouring of gratitude helped Hans flesh out and finish his memoir. I was relieved to learn he had been thinking for some time about penning his recollections, and had been gathering information from former comrades and checking his facts with them and through other sources. Hans wanted to be sure to tell his own story as well as he could, but also to represent the point of view of a common sailor. Fortunately for us Hans was more amused than deterred by any potential critics of his efforts, which likely made him more determined to complete his book. Unlike so many memoirs of service, Hans found a way to present his own personal experiences within the broader context of World War II very well. His recollections, which will be especially valuable to generations yet unborn, outline his path into the U-boats, his service on *U-505* (Hans made every combat patrol aboard that single U-boat), shore leave, the capture of the boat on June 4, 1944, and his interesting life as a POW. I particularly enjoy the stories of life at sea and tales of the POW experience of the crew, which help breathe life into the 750-ton *U-505* exhibit.

In 1998, the Museum of Science and Industry began planning an important oral history project. Its purpose was to interview as many German crewmembers as possible, as well as the key players from CTG 22.3—Dan Gallery's task group that captured *U-505*. The project was well organized and underway the following year, and we had identified the people we believed needed to be interviewed for posterity. Hans cheerfully offered his assistance. He helped contact several of his comrades on our behalf and, naturally enough, agreed to provide an interview.

And then tragedy struck. About this time Hans was diagnosed with the lung cancer that would take his life. He was optimistic throughout his battle with the terrible disease and encouraged us to wait until after his next treatment before we came to see him, for he was confident he would beat the cancer. I spoke with him on the phone shortly before he died, and by that time we all knew he was losing his battle with cancer. Erika, Hans' wife, told us he did not look well enough to be on camera, and it was clear from his voice the disease had sapped his strength; he no longer had enough energy even for an interview. We were all deeply saddened when the news of his passing arrived. We also knew we had missed a valuable opportunity to preserve his legacy on film; thankfully, I had the foresight to made audio recordings of many of our conversations. Hans was the last living *U-505* crewmember in the United States. When he died, there were eleven men left alive; today, the number stands at ten.

Hans' death was a great lost to both his family, the museum staff, and the U-boat community. Thankfully, however, Hans had worked tirelessly during the months leading up to his death to complete his memoir, which was originally published in a small-run private paperback printing shortly after he died.

I know how proud Hans would today if he could see his "old boat." *U-505* has been moved indoors to a new protective underground environment and restored with her wartime paint (both inside and out). I am particularly proud to know that the long conversations with Hans and the expertise that only a former crewmember can provide are part of the experience every visitor will enjoy during the walk through the boat.

Through his personal visits and recorded conversations, Hans helped the museum and its patrons understand the submarine's complexity and intricacies. His posthumous memoir *Steel Boat, Iron Hearts: A U-boat Crewman's Life aboard U-505* helps all of us understand and appreciate what it must have been like to serve aboard *U-505*.

Keith Gill
Curator, *U-505*
Museum of Science and Industry

Chapter 1

My Destiny is Fulfilled

*J*une 4, 1944, was the worst day of my life. My crewmates and I were being held captive in a steel cage on an American aircraft carrier. Searing heat from the ship's engines turned the already stifling tropical air in the cage into a virtual blast furnace. Worst of all, far worst of all, we could see our proud boat, the German submarine *U-505*, being towed behind us like some wounded gray wolf being dragged into captivity. Despite my best attempt to scuttle her, she had fallen into American hands intact; the first enemy vessel captured on the high seas by the United States Navy since the War of 1812.

Fifty-five years later, however, the shock and shame of that day has mellowed to a nostalgic pride in our lucky old boat. Today, *U-505* can be seen high and dry on display at Chicago's Museum of Science and Industry. According to its commemorative plaque, the submarine stands as a monument to the sacrifice of American seamen during World War II. But for us crewmen of *U-505*, the boat also symbolizes the hardships and sacrifices that we endured for two years of bloody warfare against overwhelming odds. The saga of our boat's wartime adventures is big enough to accommodate both interpretations.

Over the years, I have organized several reunions of the American and German veterans involved in her capture. Today, the hatreds and misunderstandings that once separated our peoples have vanished. We veterans embrace each other, much as our nations have, focusing on our similarities rather than our differences. We now understand that during the war, whether we were hunting or being hunted, we were all just young boys doing what we saw as our patriotic duty. The only arguing now is over who will pay for the next round of drinks.

This book has been written to tell the full and true story of our life aboard *U-505*, as I experienced it firsthand. I have withheld or exaggerated nothing. My only concession has been to conceal a few names of some of our crew members in deference to the feelings of their families. My hope is that by explaining what life was like aboard a frontline U-boat during World War II, a fuller and more balanced understanding of military history and human behavior will result. The final judgment of our nation, and of ourselves, must be left to future generations.

*   *   *

My decision as a young man to join the German navy, rather than the *Luftwaffe* or *Panzers*, was totally my choice. But there was never any doubt that when the time came, I would enlist to defend my country in one service or another. After all, I came from a family with a proud military tradition.

I was born Hans Jacob Göbeler on November 9, 1923, in the little Hessian farming village of Bottendorf, near Marburg. As a young boy, I spent many an hour on the knee of my grandfather Mathias, who had fought in that most splendid of German conflicts, the Franco-Prussian War. His service in that war, which culminated in the capture of the capital of our ancient enemy the French, instilled in my young mind visions of the heroic glories of combat.

The dark, inhumane side of war I learned from my father Heinrich's experiences in the First World War. Father enlisted in the German Army at the age of 18. He fought on the Eastern Front, where he participated in the great early battles of maneuver against the Russians. On November 20, 1914, he was captured and spent the next several years in terrifying conditions of captivity in the Katskoye slave labor camp in Siberia. Of the 20,000 men in his group captured by the Russians, 18,000 died that first year from exhaustion and malnutrition. It was only through the intervention of a famous Swedish nurse that the International Red Cross found out about the labor camp and caused conditions to improve.

Once the war ended, the surviving camp inmates were caught up in the Bolshevik Revolution. Over the course of the next three years, my father and his comrades slowly fought their way westward, sometimes skirmishing with both Red and White armies on the same day. During their trek, my father witnessed unspeakable atrocities committed by the Communists on the Russian people. A steely determination grew in his soul to never to allow the scourge of Communism to take hold in our homeland.

In November 1921, a full seven years after his capture, my father finally arrived home. To his horror, he discovered that the infection of Communism had indeed spread to Germany. Revolutionary councils had been set up in many cities, and the political system from top to bottom was in total chaos. The Reds were especially strong in the trade unions. My father had resumed his old civilian job as a local official in the railroads, but eventually his honorable service in the military and his refusal to swear allegiance to the Communist Party resulted in him being fired. Blacklisted by the Red unions, my father spent five agonizing years trying to find steady work to support our family.

The situation worsened when the national economy collapsed. Readers should remember that the Great Depression began in Germany, and had its severest effects there. Money became worthless and famine was rampant. I have many haunting memories of the hunger and poverty my family endured during this period. Riots and revolution were everywhere. German society, once the most prosperous and cultured in all of Europe, was disintegrating.

It was at this time a politician appeared who promised to solve our nation's problems; give food and work to the unemployed, regain our lost territory, reestablish safety in the streets, and restore dignity and honor to our people. We would have voted for such a man if his name were Schmidt or Meyer; his name just happened to be Hitler.

Whatever else may be said about the National Socialists, no one can say they didn't fulfill their early promises to the German people. Despite the qualms many people had about the Nazis, all doubts were quickly swept away by the flood of reforms and improvements they brought to our nation. Today, many people say we Germans made a Faustian deal with the devil, but at the time it seemed the only way out of a national nightmare. No one regretted the passing of our short, ineffectual experiment with democracy, the Weimar Republic.

For my family, the election of Hitler as Chancellor had very concrete benefits. The Communists were thrown out of the railroad unions and my father was rehired as an official in the new *Reichbahn* national rail system. As for me, I joined the Hitler Youth movement. I was an enthusiastic member, becoming for a short time the youngest *Deutsches Jungvolk* leader in the country. I still have my *DJ* Leader's identity book, and a photo of me and my much older and taller troop members, as mementos. The Hitler Youth's emphasis on patriotism, loyalty, and sacrifice fit in perfectly with the values my father instilled in me. Little did we suspect that these same qualities would compel our nation to follow Hitler over the precipice to disaster.

Meanwhile, I did well in school. When not studying for exams, I immersed myself in reading military histories of the First World War. The exploits of our submarines—the U-boats—especially fascinated me. In my view, victory over the British Empire could only be won at sea. Since Germany could never challenge the British Fleet directly, our submarines would have to be the key to victory. As the international situation worsened in the late thirties, my thoughts were increasingly preoccupied with joining the military.

War seemed imminent in the summer of 1939, so I attempted to join the Navy. To my horror (and my mother's immeasurable relief), I was rejected on grounds that I was only fifteen years old, and because of a mistaken diagnosis of color blindness. A quick examination by our family doctor dispelled the mistaken diagnosis regarding my vision, but still the recruiters would not have me.

"Complete your schooling," they advised me, "and learn a trade that will make you valuable to the *Kriegsmarine*. Then, perhaps, we will consider you."

A few weeks later, war broke out in Europe. Rather than continue with higher education by entering the *Gymnasium*, I chose to follow the recruiter's advice and learn a technical trade that I knew would make me of value to the Navy. I attacked my studies with a vengeance. I was absolutely determined to get into the war before it was over. Due to my obsessive efforts and the war emergency, I was able to complete the Master Motor Mechanics course in only two years—half the normal time. I also earned a driver's license which, back in those days, was a very

Hans Goebeler dressed in an infantry uniform during
naval basic training in 1941. *Author's Collection*

rare thing for a teenager to have. The only remnant of non-technical subjects I allowed in my life was my interest in learning English. Learning to speak the language of our enemy was seen as mildly unpatriotic, so I quietly studied an English textbook in my spare time.

In August of 1941, at the ripe age of seventeen, I reapplied for enlistment in the *Kriegsmarine*. This time I was immediately accepted. Naturally, my departure from home was an emotional affair. My mother Elizabeth and two sisters Anna Marie and Käti were especially distraught. My mother gave me a small black Bible to read, and reminded me to be a good boy and say my prayers every day. My father did his best to retain his composure, but the mix of pride and concern in his glistening eyes was unmistakable.

My naval basic training took place at the big Luitspold Barracks in Beverloo, occupied Belgium. To my infinite disappointment, we were issued green uniforms, steel helmets, and *Mauser* rifles just like ordinary army soldiers. Indeed, our training was identical to the *Wehrmacht's* basic infantry training.

They chased us like dogs at that camp! The only skill I learned was how to crawl like a snake on my belly through the mud. I was quite a bit smaller than most of the recruits, but I wouldn't let that stop me from passing all the tests. After three and a half months of grueling training, we were physically tough and mentally conditioned to instantly obey any order.

Unbeknownst to us, each one of us had been very carefully watched and evaluated by recruiters from the U-boat service. Looking back on the recruiters' decision, I suppose they were impressed by my enthusiasm, not to mention the fact that the cramped conditions inside a sub was one place where my small size would be an advantage. At any rate, at the end of the training my name appeared on a list of those graduates being offered a chance to go to submarine school. Naturally, I jumped at the chance to join this elite service. Only 10% of naval recruits were offered this honor.

My next destination was the main naval base at Wilhelmshaven on the North Sea. I was proud as a peacock as I boarded the train back to Germany. I was especially satisfied to be wearing the sharp-looking blue dress uniform of a sailor instead of the rough woolen tunic of a foot soldier. My orders and travel pass listed a false destination in order to camouflage the fact that I was headed to U-boat training. Once in

Wilhelmshaven, we underwent an extensive series of medical exams and written tests, which I passed without any problem.

After one month, I left for basic submarine physical training at a base in Neustadt on the Baltic Sea. We spent three torturous weeks in various pressurized chambers and deep diving tanks. The main point of this training was to accustom us to the pressure changes inside a submarine and to teach us how to escape from a sinking boat using artificial lungs. After it was all over, a group of about 80 or 90 of us were ordered to the *1st U-bootschule* (Submarine School) at Pillau in East Prussia for advanced technical training.

If any of us thought the hardest part of submarine training was over, we were sadly mistaken. It seemed as if the school instructors at Pillau were deliberately trying to make as many of us "wash-out" as possible. And it worked. For one thing, the physical conditioning became ever more brutal. Every day, despite knee-deep snow, we were forced to march several kilometers dressed in nothing more than a pair of sports shorts. Morning calisthenics were performed under the same conditions. After a couple minutes, our arms and legs became numb from the cold, but there was never any question of complaining. We also went on long forced marches designed to improve our endurance. The worst torture was running up and down sand dunes on the coast while wearing our gas masks. The slightest bit of slacking or complaining resulted in even more of the same.

Some of the physical training contained obvious psychological components. For instance, we were ordered to jump over walls not knowing what was on the other side, and to jump off platforms not knowing how high they were or what awaited us at the bottom of our fall. Trainees who couldn't bring themselves to jump were given one more chance; those who hesitated a second time were immediately expelled from the *U-bootschule*. We were also given boxing gloves and purposely matched with opponents who would challenge our courage. My opponents were always taller than me, sometimes over a foot taller, but I always stood my ground and tried to give as good as I got. Through it all, I forced myself to never hesitate at performing these tests because we knew that every little reaction of ours was being very carefully recorded.

When they weren't toughening us up, they were teaching us new technical skills. I was a little disappointed when they assigned me to study electric motors instead of the diesel engines that were already my specialty. I soon learned that the U-boat service expected us to have multiple skills so that we could take over the duties of other crewmen who might be injured while at sea. Inside the classroom, the instructors demanded the same unhesitating performance that they did on the athletic field. If asked a question, we shot up out of our seat and snapped to attention, automatically shouting out the full answer without a moment's delay.

In the end, only about nine or ten out of every hundred candidates graduated from the school. The ones who did not pass were assigned to other parts of the Navy. When I received word that I had successfully graduated, I was ecstatic. It was the proudest day in my life.

The top-ranked graduates were assigned directly to a frontline U-boat crew. The graduates who had performed less well were sent to the shipyards to witness the final construction of their submarine; in this way they would get reinforced in their familiarization with the structure and functions of their future boat. Once again, I was gratified to learn that I had done very well. The sleeve insignia on my uniform now designated me as a *Maschinengefreiter* (Machinist Second Class). After a short furlough home, I was given orders to report for active duty to the *Second U-boat Flotilla* located in Lorient, France.

I was floating on wings of joy as the train rumbled its way to Lorient. For a long time I stared at my reflection in the window, my familiar face in the unfamiliar uniform forming a transparent, ghostly image flying past the French countryside. It was as if powerful winds of fate had swept me up and were guiding me to the very eye of the great storm of events engulfing the world. Our U-boats were littering the ocean bottom with the hulks of dozens of enemy vessels every month, and I was actually going to participate in the glory! I was sure that it would be just like the heroic war stories I had read in my history books. Excitement and pride filled my soul as the train brought me closer to what I felt was my destiny.

I tried hard to see some remnants of battle from our amazing victory over the Anglo-French armies the previous year, but I only managed to glimpse one or two rusty enemy tanks knocked-out during the fighting. For the most part, there were very few outward hints of last year's campaign. Except in the train stations where one saw clusters of signs in German pointing the way to various military installations in the area, there was little to indicate that France had even fought, much less lost, a major war.

After 18 hours of exhausting travel, I finally arrived in Lorient. This picturesque seaport on Brittany's Atlantic coast was the site of the first German U-boat base built to take advantage of our conquest of France. Compared to our old Baltic and North Sea bases, Lorient would allow our boats to sail directly into the Atlantic without hazarding the long and dangerous trip around the British Isles. Giant concrete bunkers had been built in the harbor to protect our boats from air attack. Similar U-boat sally bases were constructed in Brest, LaRochelle, St. Nazaire, and Bordeaux.

I spent my first few days in Lorient dealing with the hundreds of annoying little administrative details required by the military bureaucracy to fight a war. After what seemed an eternity, I was finally given a boat assignment: *U-105*. She was a veteran old war horse under the command of *Kapitänleutnant* (Navy Lieutenant) Georg Schewe. I had barely settled-in, however, when I was notified that I was being transferred to a new boat: *U-505*.

That afternoon, I walked over to the bombproof slip where *U-505* was being berthed. I could tell by her condition that she was fresh out of the shipyards, with the light gray factory paint job with dark gray trim typical of those early war years. A handsome insignia featuring a rampaging lion wielding an ax graced the conning tower. A dockworker told me the emblem signified the skipper of the boat, whose name meant "Lion" in German. She was a beautiful boat. If *U-505* had been a woman, you could have called it love at first sight.

Unlike the medium-sized Type VII boats which formed the majority of Germany's submarine fleet during the war, *U-505* was one of the larger Type IX boats designed to operate independently on long-range patrols on the periphery of the Atlantic. The bigger displacement was utilized to carry more fuel and torpedoes, making it superior in range and armament to its smaller cousin. Unfortunately, the Type IX's significantly longer length and heavier weight made it less maneuverable and slower to dive than the medium boats, characteristics which made the Type IX especially vulnerable to surprise attack from the air. They were also three times as expensive to build than the Type VIIs. Because of these factors, the Type IXs never comprised more than 25% of Germany's wartime submarine fleet.

U-505's keel had been laid on June 12, 1940, at the *Deutsche-Werft* submarine yards in Hamburg. She was one of the first of the Model C subtypes built, a 1,232-ton version incorporating the latest improvements based on wartime experience. She was 252 feet in length and 15.25 feet wide at her middle section. The height between her keel and the tip of her periscope was 44.5 feet, giving her a periscope depth of 14 meters, in the European method of calculation. Reflecting the almost leisurely pace of German industrial production in the early war years, it took well over a year before her construction was complete.

The layout of *U-505* was typical of submarines of that era. Starting at the bow, the first main compartment was the forward torpedo room. The four torpedo launching tubes located here formed our boat's main anti-shipping armament. Aside from the four torpedoes loaded in the tubes, there were four additional torpedoes stowed here as reloads. When not in combat, the room doubled as the forward crew quarters. There were not enough bunks for everyone in the crew, so someone slept in your bed while you were on duty. The bunks folded-up out of the way whenever we needed to fire or reload the torpedoes.

Moving back from the forward torpedo room, you passed through a heavy waterproof hatch into the Petty officers' quarters. Their quarters were just as crowded as ours, but at least they didn't have to share their bunks with anyone.

Just behind the petty officers' bunks was the tiny galley where meals were prepared. Food was heated by three hot plates and two small ovens, all powered with electricity. There was also a small refrigerator and food locker there. Since the galley was so small, fresh food had to be stored throughout the boat. Only as a war patrol progressed and we consumed the food, did we have even the slightest bit of free space on board. However, no matter how much fresh food we tried to cram aboard before a departure (usually about four tons), we always suffered from symptoms of an unhealthy diet by the time we returned.

The next compartments were the officer's wardroom and the radio/underwater sounding station. To add a bit of opulence to the officers' accommodations, the bulkheads of the wardroom were decorated with oak veneer paneling. When not being slept in, the lower bunks could be folded up in order to form a sort of conference room or recreation area. Their quarters also featured the luxury of their own washbasin. Unfortunately, since our boat's water distillation unit only produced about 64 gallons of fresh water each day, there was only enough water for cooking, drinking, and replacement water for the

The bunk Hans shared on *U-505* with another sailor.

Author's Collection

batteries. That left the officers' prized washbasin largely a symbolic amenity.

The radio/underwater sounding station was also popular as an entertainment area, especially when the technicians tuned-in a favorite radio broadcast or played records on the gramophone. Opposite from the radio station was the captain's quarters. Like the officer's quarters, this tiny room was paneled in oak and featured its own washbasin. When not in use, a folding top covered the washbasin, transforming it into a small writing desk.

The next compartment, located amidships directly beneath the conning tower, was the control room. This was the operational heart of a U-boat. Hundreds of levers, valves, cranks, gauges, and wheels covered virtually every inch of the compartment. My first duty station as a control room mate was at the forward end of this room, controlling the hydraulic lift for the periscope. During an attack, the skipper operated the periscope from the conning tower above us. After a while, I was moved to the forward port corner of the control room. There, I took on much more responsibility: handling the approximately three dozen hand wheels that controlled the opening and closing of various diving and trim tank valves.

Beyond the control room, through another watertight hatch, was the diesel engine room. The two huge engines, which we nicknamed "the Jumbos," were nine-cylinder M.A.N. diesels capable of producing 2,200 horsepower each. With a standard load of 208 tons of diesel fuel, they gave us a range of approximately 13,000 nautical miles. Top speed with the diesels was just a little over 18 knots. Of course, since the Jumbos were air-breathers, they could only be operated when our boat was on the surface. Only later in the war were U-boats built with the *Schnorkel* device, which allowed our subs to run on diesels while at periscope depth.

We had a lot of sympathy for the grease and soot-covered men in the diesel room, whom we nicknamed "the black crew." The compartment was always filled with terrific noise and choking fumes whenever the Jumbos were running. Even worse, if a young seaman in the control room made a mistake by closing a valve or hatch at the wrong time, the diesels would suck the air out of the compartment, creating a vacuum very painful to the diesel crew's ears.

For underwater travel, we had two battery-powered Siemens electric motors, giving us a top cruising speed of seven knots and a range of about 63 nautical miles. The long banks of 110-volt D.C. batteries, located beneath the deck plates, needed to be recharged after about ten hours of operation. It took about seven hours of running the diesels to fully recharge the batteries. Cruising on the surface for seven hours was usually no problem early in the war. But later on, after Allied carrier task forces made their appearance, planes often prevented us from recharging our batteries. This made us unable to escape underwater and literally turned us into sitting ducks for the enemy. The electric motor room was located just aft of the diesel engine room. The electric motor control board, rudder controls, and air compressors were also located here.

The last compartment was the aft torpedo room. There were only two torpedo launching tubes here, as well as eight bunks for 16 crewmen. An auxiliary steering wheel was located at the far aft end of the room for use in case the normal steering controls failed.

All of these compartments were enclosed within one large cigar-shaped enclosure called the pressure hull. The walls of the pressure hull were constructed of a thick steel alloy specially designed to withstand the immense water pressure exerted against it when submerged. Our maximum depth published in the manuals was 100 meters (about 330 feet), but in an emergency we could dive to twice that depth—or more. Attached to the outside of the pressure hull were various other tanks. Some of these were diving tanks, which were flooded with seawater or pumped-out with air in order to submerge or surface, respectively. Smaller trim tanks were used to more precisely control our depth. Other tanks held our supply of diesel fuel. Enclosing the entire vessel was the exterior hull, constructed of much thinner steel plate.

The flat top surface of the exterior hull was called our upper deck. Wooden planks covering the upper deck gave us some measure of traction when walking around up there. At first glance, the upper deck of our boat appeared rather barren. Hidden below the wooden planks, however, were pressurized storage tubes for ten more spare torpedoes. U-505 was originally armed with a large 105mm deck gun mounted on the upper deck just forward of the conning tower. Later in the war, when surface attacks became impractical, the deck gun was removed and replaced with anti-aircraft weapons.

Built on top of the upper deck, right above the control room, was the superstructure of the sub. The bulk of the superstructure was taken up by the conning tower, which functioned as the skipper's command station during battle at periscope depth. The open-topped bridge was located above the conning tower. Platforms for our various anti-aircraft weapons were located aft of the bridge. Obviously, the bridge and anti-aircraft stations could only be manned when the boat was surfaced. Towering above everything were the periscope masts.

When she was built, U-505 was a state-of-the-art weapon of war. But it is most important to remember that technically speaking, she was only a "submersible." That is, like all so-called submarines of the period, she was primarily a surface craft that had the additional ability to submerge for short periods. True submarines, designed to spend most of their time underwater, were not developed until later in the war when our magnificent Type XXI submarine made its appearance.

The next morning I reported to my new skipper, commander of U-505, Kapitänleutnant Axel Olaf Löwe. He was of medium height, with a head of thick, dark, unruly hair. My first impression of him was not favorable. He seemed very casual in both dress and demeanor. He addressed me in an informal, almost familiar manner, which was quite a change from the authoritarian tone of our instructors in Submarine School. This was not the image of a U-boat commander that I had gotten from my adventure books!

I soon found, however, that his quiet, casual demeanor was based on a firm foundation of first-rate professionalism and ability. As my future crewmates were quick to tell me, the very best officers don't need to throw their rank around, but rather lead by example. Löwe was just this sort of officer.

The skipper sat me down in his little cabin and asked me about my family, my training, and my attitudes about service aboard a U-boat. Throughout our small talk, I could see his quick, penetrating eyes gauging my responses. After a few minutes, he got around to the point. His deep, soft voice suddenly took on a business-like tone.

"Göbeler, I see from your records that they trained you in electrical motors, even though you had a Master's certificate in diesel engines. The Navy wanted two-in-one. Well, I want three-in-one. If you agree to the assignment, I will appoint you to duty in the *Zentrale* (control room). It's complex work, and one small mistake can sink a boat, but I think you can handle it. If it doesn't work out, you can always go back to duty in the diesel room. What do you say?"

I didn't even hesitate before accepting the skipper's proposal. A big smile spread across Löwe's face signifying, I thought, that his evaluation of me had been correct. We shook hands in agreement. Then I snapped to attention, saluted, and left to stow my gear aboard my new boat.

I spent the next few days settling into the routine of a frontline U-boat crewman. I was expecting some jealousy from the other crewmen because of my assignment to the control room, but I was mistaken. The skipper had already established a reputation for assigning men to do the job they fit best, rather than what the regulation book said. There were even a couple of lads in the crew who had gotten in trouble with the police. No other captain would have them on their boat, but Löwe was happy to accept them as long as they did their job well. In fact, he said, if they used the same resourcefulness in keeping our boat alive that they used to stay out of jail, so much the better!

The reason there were slots to fill in the *U-505* crew in the first place was because a few of the original crewmen didn't fit-in during the cruise from Germany to Lorient. Our skipper was using his skills in assessing

Kapitänleutnant Axel Olaf Löwe, *U-505's*
beloved first commander. *Author's Collection*

men to consciously build a crew that could operate effectively as a team. This was an important lesson we learned from *Kapitänleutnant* Löwe: that rank and decorations didn't matter a thing aboard a U-boat; what mattered was how well one performed his duties as part of a team.

Over time, we learned what special strengths and weaknesses each one of us had, and organized ourselves accordingly. For instance, one of my good friends was a perfect seaman during normal conditions. I mean, he was <u>absolutely</u> perfect, and was a great asset to our crew. But as soon as the depth charges began exploding, he became totally useless. We all knew this, so someone automatically took over his duties when things got rough. I think it was this intimate knowledge of each other's individual capabilities that helped us survive the challenges we met later on, even under different skippers.

*   *   *

I spent the daylight hours learning the intricacies of my control room duties. My main job would be to maintain the periscope's hydraulic pump and operate it during action. My other main duty was to pass-on commands from the conning tower above us to the control room crew. I was reminded again and again that one improperly communicated order could finish us all. I soon demonstrated mastery of these duties.

During our off-duty hours, I read technical manuals and traded scuttlebutt with the rest of the crew. I heard about *U-505*'s initial shakedown cruise and her voyage from the Kiel naval base to Lorient. Rather than taking the shorter but much more dangerous route through the English Channel, *U-505* had sailed north around the British Isles, then southeast down toward Lorient. A couple of times they had encountered British destroyers en route, but the rough seas prevented either side from launching any attacks. My crewmates warned me about seasickness, the "final exam" for any sailor.

By early February, final preparations were made for departure on our maiden war patrol. But first, a virtual mountain of supplies had to be loaded on board. The interior of our submarine looked more like a grocer's storeroom than a weapon of war by the time we were finished.

I found it difficult to sleep those last few days before our sailing. While others in the crew enjoyed one last taste of Lorient's nightlife, I stayed awake in my bunk reading and re-reading training manuals. I also found solace in the Bible my mother had given me. I prayed that my conduct in battle would be worthy of my family, nation, and God.

Chapter 2

My First War Patrol

$\mathcal{M}$y wartime adventure aboard *U-505* began on February 11, 1942, with a rather ceremonious departure from Lorient. The crew members who were not on watch assembled in narrow parade formation on the upper deck. The rest of us manned our maneuver stations below. I was desperate not to make a mistake on the beginning of this, our boat's first true combat patrol. The skipper and the men on watch stood clustered on the bridge, the top of which was decorated with garlands of flowers for the occasion. A wave of excitement washed over us all when *Kapitänleutnant* Löwe shouted the order to cast-off lines.

The removal of the mooring ropes was the Navy band's cue to begin a farewell serenade of military marches. Three loud cheers of "Hurrah!" erupted from the dockside audience and echoed off the walls of the dimly lit bunker. With that, at precisely 1800 hours, our boat began to slowly back out of the black oily waters of the submarine pen into Lorient harbor.

Once clear of our berth, we were joined by *U-68* for the trip to the departure point. In the outer harbor we met our escort, a small minesweeper. The music and cheers gradually faded into silence as our little flotilla made its way to Port Louis, the last cusp of friendly land we would see for quite a while.

Kapitänleutnant Löwe turned to the Executive Officer and said, "Nollau, throw the flowers overboard."

"It will be a hard life—have no illusions about that. But with a well-disciplined crew, we'll have our successes." So spoke *U-505's* first commander *Kplt.* Axel- Olaf Löwe during the boat's commissioning ceremony on August 26, 1941. NA

According to old German naval tradition, it was bad luck to carry flowers out of sight of land. *Oberleutnant* (Lieutenant j.g.) Nollau nodded in agreement and over the side the flowers went. No one wanted to offend Old King Neptune on our first sortie against the enemy!

When the ocean depth reached 200 meters, we made our final deep test dive, a precautionary procedure performed by all submarines departing on a war patrol. After a successful test, we re-surfaced and signaled to our escorts: "Everything O.K."

They signaled back: "Safe return and good hunting!" before turning back toward the harbor. We were now on our own.

Our diesels roared up to flank speed and *U-505's* bow began cutting its way through the choppy waters of the Bay of Biscay. The afternoon departure time had been calculated to give us maximum cover of darkness to traverse the Bay. The Brits maintained constant surface and air patrols designed to catch departing or returning submarines moving through the area. We would soon come to call the place "the U-boat Graveyard" because of all of the unfortunate subs sunk here. By the end of the war, most U-boats never got a chance to engage the enemy before they were snared by the Allies' cordon of death around our submarine sally ports. Despite our fears regarding what awaited us in the Battle of the Atlantic, we were determined not to be caught here and sunk before we had drawn blood.

Not long after our escort disappeared, we heard the click of the intercom. Everyone cocked their ear towards the nearest speaker to better hear the message over the reverberating clamor of the diesels.

"This is the *Kapitänleutnant*. We have been ordered to hunt along the West African coast. Our operational area will be the Allies' convoy assembly point off Freetown Harbor. We will be going up against fast ships and it certainly won't be easy. In the meantime, keep your eyes open and be alert! That is all."

Few of us in the crew had ever heard of Freetown. We were told it was a port in Sierra Leone and that it was a major refueling point for Allied supply convoys headed towards the North African front. We were pleased to learn we would be taking a direct role in helping Rommel and his *Afrika Korps* fight against the Tommies.

Just then, we received a *FT* (radio-telegraph message) ordering us to turn around and assist one of our sister boats that had just been heavily damaged in an air attack off the Spanish coast. Some of us younger crew members seethed in frustration; we wanted to be warriors, not nursemaids or ambulance drivers! Only later, with experience and maturity, did we learn that one who saves lives is as heroic as one who kills the enemy. The whole matter blew over, however, when a little later the news reached us that the damaged U-boat had safely reached a Spanish port under its own power. We resumed our course for the West African coast.

We had a number of "Alarm Dives" during our transit through the Bay of Biscay because of approaching enemy aircraft. This was the true test of any submarine crew: to plunge the boat beneath the waves to a safe depth before the diving enemy bombers had a chance to drop their deadly loads. Our hearts pounded louder than our diesels during the first few encounters we had with those buzzards, but in a surprisingly short time these dives became absolutely routine. Occasionally, we heard the detonation of depth charges exploding over our heads, but they were never close enough to cause us serious worry or damage.

Once we cleared the Bay of Biscay, things loosened up a bit. After we passed the Azores, we shut down one diesel and ran at half-speed in order to conserve fuel. The *Kapitänleutnant* even allowed three men at a time to join the bridge watch and have a smoke. What a joy it was to stand on the bridge with a good cigarette and the warm African breeze in one's face! Back home in Germany our families would still be huddled around the fireplace at this time of year.

Before long, however, the warmth turned from a blessing into a curse. As we crossed the Tropic of Cancer, the boat began to heat-up like a furnace during the daytime. German submarines were not equipped with air conditioners, so we used every imaginable excuse to get out onto the deck and escape the roasting temperature inside the hull. When we dived, the ocean water cooled the pressure hull, causing drops of condensation to rain down upon us. We switched to a very casual tropical uniform: khaki canvas shorts and no shirt. We donned a broad-brimmed pith helmet when we were topside. Soon we all had skin as brown as African natives.

The tropical heat began to make our food stores spoil much sooner than expected. For example, upon our departure from Lorient, we had taken on 3,000 eggs. In the chilly waters of the North Atlantic, eggs could be counted on to last two or three months before getting rotten. In this torrid climate however, the eggs began to rot after only a couple of weeks. The skipper decided that we should try to consume them as quickly as possible and announced that we could eat as many of them as we wished every mealtime. Well, some of the boys on board really liked eggs and began eating literally dozens of them daily. After a few days, though, no one could even stand the sight of the little white devils. For many of us, the mere smell of eggs was repulsive for a many years afterward.

Those were lazy days as we slowly plodded southward. During the cool clear nights, we would sit on the deck and stare at the Southern Cross, telling every story from our civilian lives we could remember. At first it all seemed very idyllic to be sailing under these strange constellations towards our unknown fate. But after three weeks out of Lorient, the boring routine began to grate on my nerves. The unending cycles of watch, trying to read with condensation water dripping on the pages of my English language textbook, someone telling his old story for the tenth time, the same phonograph record playing for the one hundredth time. For young guys like us, this inactivity was a kind of slow psychological torture.

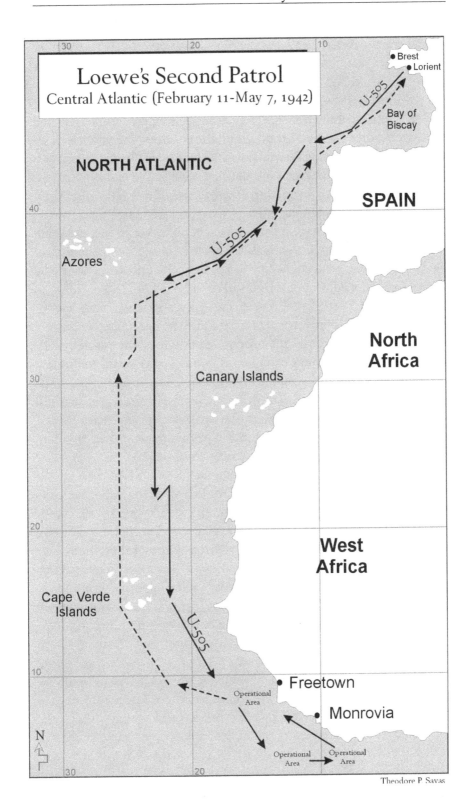

Loewe's Second Patrol
Central Atlantic (February 11–May 7, 1942)

NORTH ATLANTIC

Azores

SPAIN

Brest
Lorient
Bay of
Biscay

U-505

North
Africa

Canary Islands

West
Africa

Cape Verde
Islands

U-505

Freetown

Monrovia

Operational
Area

Operational
Area

Operational
Area

N

Theodore P. Savas

Of course, torture can be of the physical variety, too. I was smaller and younger than most of the others, and therefore had to take my fair share of teasing and hazing before being fully accepted as one of the crew. I was also less experienced than they were because I had missed *U-505*'s initial journey from Kiel to Lorient. The biggest challenge to me was gaining my "sea legs." During storms, the boat would often rock 60 degrees from side to side. In situations like that, even if you were deathly seasick, you had to perform your duties perfectly. We were well aware that some boats never returned to base because of one little mistake by someone in the control room. In a way, I was lucky that first patrol was so rough, because if you learn the hard way, it becomes easier later on. Some men never got used to the motions and pressure changes of a submarine. One Petty Officer reluctantly returned to duty on destroyers because he simply could not adjust to the rigors of submarine life.

At any rate, after a few weeks at sea, I got a promotion in my control room duties. The skipper moved me from the periscope pump operator's position to the diving manifold operator's position a few feet away. My new duties were much more complex, as I was responsible for controlling the water level in the numerous diving tanks. The tanks needed to be blown out with air or filled with water in a precisely timed sequence lest the boat lose pitch control. Except for occasional emergencies when I assisted the diesel engine crew make repairs, this was to be my duty position for the rest of my wartime career aboard *U-505*.

During our transit to the Freetown operational area, we had several sightings of smoke plumes from enemy convoys. Naturally, we gave chase. However, patrolling British aircraft, usually one of the big 4-engined Sunderland flying boats, always managed to spot us before we got into firing range. Once we were forced to emergency dive, it was easy for the enemy ships to slip away because *U-505*'s electric motors gave us a cruising speed of only seven knots underwater. Unless we were already perfectly positioned in the path of a convoy, this was far too slow to catch up with a target and conduct an attack. *Kapitänleutnant* Löwe would be left watching through the periscope, muttering in frustration as the convoy disappeared into the distance.

A couple of times aircraft didn't spot us, which allowed us to stay on the surface and use our faster diesel engines to chase a target. But even at top speed, we were only a few knots faster than most convoys. Therefore, we would try to maneuver in front of their anticipated course in order to intercept them. A few times we ran the diesels at dangerously high speeds in order to catch a convoy, but a fortuitous change of direction always saved the enemy ships from an attack.

You cannot imagine the excitement we crewmen felt during these chases. "Finally," we thought, "we will get our first hit!"

But eventually we would hear the roaring diesels reduce to normal speed again and the skipper would apologize to us over the intercom for guessing the convoy's course wrong. At those moments the crew's mood barometer would drop to zero and all of the built-up frustrations and petty feuds of the past few weeks would come flooding back. Suddenly, once again you became conscious of the heat and the noise and the stench of whatever shit our cook was preparing for dinner. With such a young, green crew on his hands, *Kapitänleutnant* Löwe knew we needed a kill—as much for crew morale as for the war effort.

In an attempt to provide us with some diversion, the skipper began to organize our off-duty hobbies into ship-wide tournaments. Chess and card games were the most popular contests. My favorites were the trivia games where we would try to name the capitals of foreign countries or answer history questions. Winners were allowed to skip a watch duty or given an extra scoop of dessert as a reward. These games helped a lot, but everyone from the skipper on down knew there was no cure for morale problems like a few victory pennants flying from the conning tower.

As we entered our operational area off the West African coast, Allied air activity stepped up considerably. The planes buzzed over our heads like swarms of hornets. They forced us to emergency dive uncounted times, but no one cared about the increased danger as long as it meant we had a better chance to sink some enemy ships. On the morning of March 8, 1942, we finally arrived at our patrol station off Sierra Leone. Now, we thought, it is them or us.

We searched in vain all day for signs of the enemy. Then, at 1836 hours, one of the sharp-eyed boys on bridge watch spotted something on the horizon. It was an enemy freighter piled high with cargo heading on a general course for Freetown. She was running at 12 knots, zigzagging with lights dimmed. It took us four full hours to finally catch up with her and maneuver into attack position.

The tension inside the control room was excruciating as we made the final preparations for firing. My own heart was beating wildly with excitement as I adjusted the boat's trim to compensate for the flooding of the torpedo tubes. After all the training and hard work, after all the tedious waiting, at long last we were going to strike against the enemy!

We all strained to hear the whispers of the firing crew as they calculated range and speed. Finally, at a range of 600 Meters, we heard *Kapitänleutnant* Löwe's deep voice boom out the words, "*Torpedoes los!*" (Torpedoes away!). With a hiss and a shudder, two torpedoes leapt from their tubes. We waited breathlessly as the seconds ticked by to the estimated time of impact. Then . . . nothing! For some reason, both torpedoes missed the target.

The skipper didn't give us time to get depressed. We felt an abrupt change of course and heard the diesels once again rev up to flank speed. There was heavy phosphorescence in the sea, our churning propellers leaving a huge curving trail of eerie green light in our wake. Our nerves were as taut as violin strings. Anger now joined the medley of other emotions sweeping through our hearts. Caution be damned, we MUST get that freighter!

The sudden ringing of the machine telegraph bell made a few of us jump. The ringing meant new orders were being transmitted for course and speed, new numbers being dialed in for the torpedo data computer. No one talked; our emotions were communicated to each other though our eyes.

The hammering clamor of the diesels seemed to fade to silence as the firing commands were given: "Tube 2, distance 400 meters, depth 3 meters . . . *Torpedo los!*"

We all joined in to chant the torpedo timing count: ". . . 15. . . 16. . . 17. . . 18. . . 19. . ." Boom! The explosion! The torpedo hit the steamer amidships, stopping her dead in her tracks. Lifeboats were lowered and a large night beacon buoy was deployed. A brave radioman still on board the steamer started broadcasting a frantic S-O-S. From his message we discovered the ship was the British freighter *Ben Mohr*, 5,920 tons.

The *Ben Mohr* was settling into the water, but very slowly. Once all men had left the ship and the lifeboats had cleared the area, Löwe ordered another torpedo to be used for the *coup de grace*. The "eel," which was our slang word for torpedo, was fired point-blank from a distance of 300 meters. It hit directly under the bridge and the freighter began to break in two.

By 2347 hours, there was nothing left floating on the surface except the lifeboats and a curious assortment of debris. We were so close to our target that we could plainly see the survivors huddled in the boats. We were relieved that no one appeared to be injured. It may seem strange, but despite our countries being traditional enemies, we felt no hatred toward the British seamen. We were fascinated by the awesome destruction we had wrought, but we had no desire to see our brother sailors harmed. In a way, it was like watching an automobile race: one loves to see a good crash, but at the same time hopes that no one gets hurt.

But there was no time to contemplate our first victory for the moon was bright and we had to make good our escape. Satisfied the Brits were all right, Löwe ordered us out of the area at top speed. We were very busy at our duty stations, but everyone was jubilant. All of the trials and frustrations we experienced earlier in the mission were forgotten. Sinking a fully loaded freighter on our first mission, we decided, was a good omen.

The very next morning, we sighted another smoke plume drifting leeward over the horizon. The sudden appearance overhead of a British Sunderland interrupted our chase, but a few hours later we spotted the smoke again. Dead ahead, emerging from a heavy rain squall, was a large tanker running zigzags at 10 knots. Her general course was the same as the freighter from yesterday. She was not flying a flag, but a quick glance at the recognition book revealed her to be a British *Confidence* class tanker, approximately 8,000 tons. Best of all, she was lying low in the water, fully loaded with oil destined for the enemy's forces in North Africa.

We positioned ourselves for attack and submerged, waiting for our prey to come to us. By the time *Kapitänleutnant* Löwe raised the attack periscope, we were so close (less than 200 meters away) that only 1/3 of the target could be seen in the scope's field of vision. We had to hurry before the tanker got so close that we would be endangered by our own torpedo's explosion.

"Torpedo depth 4 meters, bearing 130."

The forward torpedo control room mate flooded the tubes and we adjusted the boat's trim for the shift in weight. In the drama of the moment, everything seemed to be moving in slow motion. I envisioned the torpedo officer's fist raised over the red firing button, like a guillotine blade hanging over the head of a condemned man. We all held our breath waiting for the inevitable order to fire. The tension was unbearable; what the hell were they waiting for?

Then, at last, the order: "Torpedo 5 . . . los! Torpedo 6 . . . los!"

With a loud hiss of air pressure, the long, black "eels" shot out of the tubes on their mission of destruction. Time, 1131 hours. At this range, we couldn't miss, could we?

Again, we began counting down the seconds until impact: " . . . 7 . . .8 . . .9." A sharp explosion was followed immediately by a deafening roar. A moment later, a gigantic shock wave hit us, knocking us off our feet and rocking the boat like a baby's cradle. Huge waves blocked the periscope's vision for almost two minutes.

When the periscope view finally cleared, all that could be seen was an enormous plume of white smoke. The tanker, which had evidently been loaded with gasoline, had exploded like a bomb when the torpedoes hit. Inside the sub we could still hear low, rumbling explosions several minutes after the first detonation.

The blast wave caused some minor damage to our diesel clutch. Repairs were accomplished quickly and *Kapitänleutnant* Löwe ordered "Battle stations, surface."

As soon as the conning tower cleared the surface, the skipper and the rest of the watch crew popped open the hatch and clambered out on to the bridge. All that could be seen was scattered debris and a huge, quickly spreading oil slick where the tanker had once been. Then, incredibly, the bridge watch spotted some survivors! There were about twenty of them, thickly covered in oil, paddling toward us in a lifeboat and two rafts.

Löwe maneuvered our boat closer to render aid to the dazed survivors, many of whom had suffered burns. We gave them fresh water, food, medicine, and bandages. The grateful sailors told us that the tanker was the *Sydhav*, bound for Freetown.

We had no sooner found out the name of the tanker when another Sunderland was spotted approaching from the east, range about 8,000 meters. Satisfied that we had done all we could for the survivors, we made good our escape. After the war we found out the aircraft had somehow missed seeing both our boat and the giant oil slick, but at the time we had to assume we had been detected.

The next two days were spent in a fruitless search for more targets. We were repeatedly forced to dive to escape from approaching aircraft. Our two sinkings had obviously disturbed a hornet's nest, and now an angry swarm of enemy planes blackened the skies above us. A fierce tropical storm finally grounded our tormentors, giving us a brief respite to surface and reload torpedoes into the forward tubes. Torrential showers and a heavy swell hindered our work, but the main problem was a faulty upper deck plate built in Lorient. It was our first experience with sabotage by the shipyard workers of Lorient, a problem that would become much more frequent and serious as the war progressed.

After two hours of backbreaking labor, we finished loading the torpedoes and slipped into relative safety under the waves. It was just plain good luck that no aircraft had seen us. Only one year later, with increased Allied air activity, being stranded on the surface for two hours like that would have meant certain destruction.

Our first two kills had whetted our appetite for combat, but we had become victims of our own success: Allied merchant traffic was scared away from the area. Occasionally we would encounter a neutral ship or Allied destroyers on patrol, but no freighters or tankers that we were in a position to attack. Radio messages from *Fregattenkapitän* (Navy Commander) Karl Merten's *U-68*, which was also operating in the Freetown area, reported a similar situation: no targets.

Eventually, our frustrated skipper radioed the headquarters of Admiral Dönitz, the commander of all U-boat forces, asking permission to sail across the narrow waist of the Atlantic to strike at shipping coming out of South America. Löwe's request was refused, however, due to the delicate political situation there. So, we were left to ply the steamy African waters in a vain attempt to locate enemy ships.

Unfortunately, there was never a shortage of enemy aircraft. Several times a day we were forced to emergency dive to escape from the damned planes. The sheer physical and emotional effort expended by so many crash dives began to wear us down.

Submariners of today cannot imagine the complex operations required of a crew to emergency dive in a World War II boat. When the "Alarm" signal was received over the machine telegraph, many dozens of hand wheels and valves had to be sequentially operated, all to a precise degree. In the hot, crowded control room of our boat, you had to push and shove each other out of the way to make hasty adjustments of the instruments. There was no time for emotions or apologies—just get your job done, and get it done right the first time! There wasn't even time to fully explain orders; usually a hand signal or a single word had to suffice. Only the Lord in Heaven knows how many boats went down for the last time because of a simple mistake or misunderstanding.

For the next several days we had zero success. We spotted a few distant ships moving at high speed, and once we even managed to fire a couple of torpedoes at long range, but failed to score a hit. We continued on a generally southern course along the coast of Africa. The days began to blur in our minds into one unending, steaming hell.

*   *   *

It was during this time that we experienced our first real baptism of fire . . . on the receiving end. In the very early morning hours of March 29th, we spotted a suspicious shadow lurking in a rain squall. The vessel turned out to a freighter, but with an unusual silhouette. Löwe decided to play it safe and pursue the ship underwater.

We chased the zig-zagging target for more than four hours, but with our slow electric motors, we could not close the distance between us. At 0550 hours the bright moon set, giving us a short window of opportunity to make a surface attack before the sun rose.

We surfaced and started the diesels when, suddenly, an aircraft appeared, illuminating our general vicinity with blindingly bright searchlights. A moment later, another aircraft appeared 300 meters to our starboard, flying parallel to our course. The second aircraft began signaling to the ship with recognition lights. Then, both the steamship and the airplane made abrupt turns, heading directly toward us.

This was more than enough for Löwe, who knew a trap when he saw one. We immediately alarm dived and made evasive maneuvers. After twenty minutes of silence, we rose to periscope depth to take a look. If the planes were gone, perhaps we could still make an underwater attack on the suspicious freighter. No sooner had the periscope broken the surface, however, than we all heard the unmistakable "pings" of a warship's *Asdic* underwater detection device. Well, *Asdic* pings are like a woman's labor pains; the shorter the interval between them, the closer the moment of truth. These pings were getting closer—and at a very alarming rate!

The skipper immediately ordered a crash dive to 100 meters. We had barely passed the 40-meter depth point when four gigantic explosions rocked the boat. Now we really understood what a depth charge sounded like at close range! After 10 minutes of maneuvering, the pings began to gradually fade into the distance. We concluded the ship was a

U-Bootfalle, one of the heavily armed merchant "Q-Ships" used as decoys by the British to ambush our subs.

After we were sure of our safety, the intercom clicked on and Löwe made an announcement. "At this moment, I wish to compliment the crew on their performance during our boat's baptism of fire. Sometimes in war," he reminded us, "the hunters are successful. But other times they themselves get hunted. We will head farther south . . . *U-505* has caused enough turbulence in this area! That is all."

Surviving our close shave with the Q-Ship was a relief, but it galled us that we had been chased from the area without us being able to fire even one shot. To us younger members of the crew, the incident just added insult to injury for the past three weeks without a victory. Emergency diving several times a day to escape from aircraft caused fatigue and frustrations, which also began to tear at our nerves. With no success to show for all of our labors, our crowded boat became a pressure cooker of emotions. Off-duty personnel began to succumb to *Blechkoller* . . . the so-called "tin can disease." A psychological condition caused by prolonged confinement, its classic symptoms were the outbreak of "baloney-quarrels" between boys who argue and fight over nothing.

Situations like these separate a real leader from a mere giver of orders, and *Kapitänleutnant* Löwe now showed himself to be a commander of the first rank. He sensed the mood of the crew and decided to create a little mental diversion during this lull in the action.

Stretching his orders a bit, Löwe ordered *U-505* south of our official operational area. On April 1, we crossed the Equator, an occasion requiring the crew to undergo the ancient baptism rituals of Neptune.

The ceremony was celebrated on the upper deck of the boat with the entire crew in attendance. After an appropriate fanfare, King Neptune appeared on the bridge to preside over the rituals, complete with flowing beard and trident. An extra touch of hilarity was provided by our baby-faced ensign, who had the embarrassing task of portraying Neptune's lovely mermaid wife.

The other veteran sea dogs in the crew, also dressed in makeshift costumes, took devilish delight in subjecting us first-timers to a wide variety of elaborate rituals and good-natured tortures. Quite a lot of water and rough scrubbing was required to wash the dirt of the Northern Hemisphere off our skins before we could enter the southern half of King Neptune's empire!

Of course, we were told, it was also necessary to be cleaned-out on the inside, too. Depending on how many "bad points" one had collected, we were each required to eat a certain number of specially prepared laxative balls made of flour and caster oil. Pepper and other evil-tasting spices were added to the mixture to enhance the entertainment. If we couldn't swallow the golf ball-sized pills without chewing, we were assisted in the endeavor by a water hose in the mouth. Then, we would pull down our shorts and crawl out onto a long plank extending from the side of the boat. There, we sat on a large hole drilled through the plank until the caster oil provided the final amusement.

Without a doubt, it was the most foolish and memorable April 1st any of us would ever experience. When it was all over, we each received an award document from King Neptune, attesting to our accomplishment. It may sound strange, but getting that silly little piece of paper did much to fulfill the *Kapitänleutnant's* very serious purpose of raising our morale.

*   *   *

The morning after the ceremony was a quiet one. We spent the hours test diving and setting the trim while we recovered from our digestive distress. Except for an alarm dive around noon caused by the appearance of a Sunderland, nothing happened until that evening.

At 1622 hours we spotted a steamer to the west, headed on a generally southern bearing. The appearance of an escort vessel in its company, however, convinced our skipper that a night attack would be the safest course of action.

At 2150 hours we fired two torpedoes at the target, range 1,000 meters. Both torpedoes either missed or failed to explode. For the next ten hours we tried to line-up another attack, but heavy squalls limited our visibility to less than 100 meters. Eventually we lost contact. This situation, as we used to say, was about as productive as milking mice.

The *Kapitänleutnant* placed us on a curving search pattern for the target. The next morning we re-acquired the elusive steamer and moved into a firing position in front of her. Just as we submerged to make the attack, however, another steamer appeared, sailing in the opposite direction. Unfortunately, the second steamer was flanked by two escort vessels. Nevertheless, Löwe decided to go for the more heavily protected newcomer because it had a more favorable firing angle. Besides, he reasoned, such a heavily guarded ship might be carrying a more valuable cargo.

At 2100 hours we lined up for a surface attack on the steamer with the two escorts. They were steering directly toward us; indeed, one of the escorts was actually on a collision course with us. Löwe, with his nerves of steel, waited until the escort was only 400 meters away before he swung our boat sharply to the right and let loose with two torpedoes at the merchantman.

According to our timing count, the first torpedo missed, but the second struck home with a thundering explosion. A tall column of water, gleaming white in the moonlight, sprouted from the waterline just forward of the bridge. Damage must have been massive because the ship immediately began to sink, bow first. The steamer broadcasted a short S-O-S message from which we learned its name: *West Irmo* (5,775 tons). With two angry escorts looking for revenge, this clearly was no place to loiter. We promptly turned-tail and made good our escape. The stricken steamer quickly disappeared into the darkness, but in the distance we could plainly hear the dull booms of her boilers exploding on her way to the bottom.

Our sinking of the *West Irmo* once and for all ended morale problems aboard our boat. It felt like someone had lifted a heavy weight from our chest. Especially satisfying was the way we had sunk the ship right under the noses of the escorts, escaping without so much as one shot being fired against us. We felt we had erased the Q-ship's insult and were as proud as roosters.

Kapitänleutnant Löwe had a hunch there was other prey in the area. Sure enough, at 1407 hours the very next day, our eagle-eyed boys on the bridge spotted a smudge of smoke far to the south of us. The ship had a 25 nautical mile lead on us, but our entire crew, without exception, had full confidence this would be another success.

It was getting late by the time we caught her, so the skipper decided to use the same sort of night surface attack tactics that had served us so well the day before. We trailed the steamer just outside of her sight range, careful to keep the bow of *U-505* constantly pointed towards our target so as to present the narrowest possible silhouette.

At 2100 hours we heard the click of the intercom, heralding the announcement we had been so eagerly anticipating. Löwe's deep, steady voice ordered *"Auf Gefechtsstationen!"* ("Battle Stations!"), sending a thrill deep through each of our souls.

Our hearts swelled with unbounded pride and confidence in our skipper . . . and ourselves. Somehow, the shared labors, dangers, triumphs, and even the silliness of the Neptune ceremony, had combined in a mysterious alchemy to produce a mature and professional crew committed to enduring any hardship or danger in the service of our country. It was a magical process, one that we were not fully conscious of. But at that moment, we all felt it.

With the diesels running full speed, we caught up with the ship in less than 30 minutes. A single torpedo was fired from a distance of 800 meters, hitting the ship slightly astern. The steamer sank quickly, her bow hanging high in the air as she slipped under the waves.

Löwe maneuvered our boat close to the lifeboats to render aid. We found out from the survivors that the ship was a Dutch merchantman named the *Alphacca*, 5,759 tons, carrying wool from Capetown to Freetown. The survivors had escaped from the sinking ship without casualties, and their lifeboats were well provisioned with supplies. Our skipper's conversation with the survivors, in English and German, was remarkably cordial given the circumstances. The Dutch crew thanked us for our help, and even wished us farewell and *bon voyage*! As we left the area, we pondered the irony of fate that had pitted our country against such a friendly people who spoke our own language.

We departed the scene of the sinking headed on a fake course. Once out of the survivors' sight range, we resumed our generally northern track. Since the *Alphacca* did not have time to send a distress signal over her wireless, our skipper believed that Allied merchant traffic in the area might still be unaware of our presence. The next couple of days were spent quietly, another transfer of torpedoes from the storage tubes into the bow torpedo room being the only event worthy of note.

On the morning of April 6, however, we all got quite a scare. We were cruising on the surface when, suddenly, the bridge watch shouted the aircraft alarm, *"Flieger!"*

A Sunderland was flying a course directly toward us. Löwe ordered us to dive, but the air relief valve for one of the diving tanks refused to open. The stuck valve not only prohibited us from submerging, but also caused a dramatic imbalance of weight within the sub. Within seconds, *U-505* was stranded on the surface with its bow buried deep underwater and its stern sticking high up into the air at a 40-degree angle! We were absolutely helpless to escape from the approaching Sunderland.

Lightning fast reactions by Chief Engineering Officer Fritz Förster managed to temporarily free the valve. Meanwhile, the skipper ordered all crewmen to run to the stern end of the boat to help even the imbalance of weight. We all held our breath as the stern slowly began to descend back into the water, wondering when the Sunderland would attack. Luckily, it did not attack before we had a chance to escape.

We resurfaced at 1430 hours. All sorts of gallows humor enlivened our work as we repaired the relief valve. The best joke was that the English pilot failed to attack because he thought *U-505* was an ostrich, with its head buried in the water and its tail sticking up into the air. The grim humor masked the fact that we came very close to being killed, either by the Sunderland or by an uncontrolled plunge to the bottom of the ocean. The incident also served to increase our respect for our Engineering Officer's technical skill and *Kapitänleutnant* Löwe's cool self-control. Not once during the entire emergency did the skipper raise his voice in either anger or fear.

Things quieted down considerably for the rest of the patrol. We made a few more sightings of ships, but were usually unable to catch them. When we did catch them, they turned out to be either neutrals or British destroyers, which *Kapitänleutnant* Löwe discretely declined to challenge. Of course, there was no let-up of the harassment from the air. Alarm dives were a daily affair, sometimes involving very narrow escapes from bombs or depth charges. On April 18, one of the Sunderland "Big Birds" laid an egg close enough to cause us some minor damage.

By the end of April, our boat and crew were both showing signs of exhaustion. The diesel engines were badly in need of an overhaul and fuel was getting critically low. Indeed, we did not even have sufficient fuel reserves to give chase to any more targets without endangering our ability to return to base. Also, some of the crew were displaying skin eruptions and symptoms of scurvy because of the lack of fresh food on board. It was clearly time to head home.

By the beginning of May, our generally northern course had brought us back to the entrance of the Bay of Biscay. Having survived thus far, Löwe was playing it very safe for this last leg of our journey. He ordered the bridge watches to be doubled whenever we were surfaced because of the increased chances of air attack. We also took care to avoid being spotted by the French fishing fleet, who, we suspected, reported the presence of U-boats to the British.

Sometimes, Löwe seemed to have an uncanny ability to sense danger before it made its presence known. For instance, on the afternoon of May 5 while we were peacefully cruising on the surface, for no apparent reason the *Kapitänleutnant* ordered the diving tanks to be partially filled with water. This precaution, he explained, would minimize the time needed for an emergency dive. Exactly four minutes later, a two-engined land-based bomber swooped down at us from nowhere and dropped nine bombs. Though we escaped without damage, some of the bombs landed close enough for us to find bomb splinters on the bridge when we later resurfaced. The skipper's precaution, based solely on his premonition of danger, had made the difference between life and death for us. From then on, we traveled mostly underwater during the day, surfacing only at night to recharge the batteries.

During the night of May 5, we received a *FT* radio telegram from *Second U-boat Flotilla* headquarters with details of our rendezvous with the harbor escort craft. Until they met us, our radio directional finder and arc lamp searchlight beams from Lorient would guide us in for the final stretch.

On the evening of May 7, we sighted *Ile de Groix*, a small island near the mouth of Lorient Harbor. A few moments later, our escort arrived to guide us to our berth. With four victory pennants fluttering over our heads, we proudly sailed the last few miles back to base.

Chapter 3

Lorient

*A*n escort ship from Lorient harbor met us at the prearranged rendezvous point just as dawn broke over the horizon. The morning sun warmed our happy faces as we followed the craft back to our armored nest. The anticipation was unbearable as we rumbled those last few miles back into port. Our spirits leaped even higher when we spied the reception awaiting us.

The pier was crowded with hundreds of spectators, all cheering and waving. The naval band was also there, their martial music adding pomp to the festivities. After the lines were secured to the dock, we were given the command to assemble in formation on the top deck. After almost three months at sea without a proper bath or shave, we must have been quite a sight to the spectators (fortunately, they weren't close enough to smell us!). We tried to maintain a posture of strict attention, but most of us could not refrain from breaking into wide smiles and stealing glances at the four victory pennants fluttering from our bridge.

From the dockside we heard, "Three cheers to *U-505* and her brave and successful crew . . . Hurrah! . . . Hurrah! . . . Hurrah!" It was a wonderful feeling to be cheered by the crowd, especially once we noticed all the attractive nurses and female office workers in attendance.

The entire command staff of the Second U-boat Flotilla came on board to shake hands with our officers. *Kapitänleutnant* Victor Schütze, Flotilla Commander and winner of the Knight's Cross with Oak Leaves, made a fine speech praising our accomplishments. The Second U-boat Flotilla was the most successful submarine command in the German Navy, and its members really knew how to welcome their men back into the fold. My God, how our hearts swelled with pride at the Flotilla Commander's words! Standing there before him, gazing at the gorgeous medal hanging from his throat, I was already dreaming of returning to sea and earning a similar medal for our skipper. But in the back of my mind, I was also relieved to know that we were once again safe, protected from enemy air attacks by the massive 22-foot thick reinforced concrete roofs of the submarine bunkers.

After another half-hour of ritual, we were finally allowed to disembark and step once again onto dry land. We walked like old salts for the next day or two, experiencing the strange sensation of our "sea legs" adjusting to land that was not constantly pitching back and forth like the motions of our boat.

After our long ordeal at sea, we had only four thoughts in mind: a hot bath, good food, mail from home, and . . .well, satisfying the all-too-human lust for female companionship that every sailor feels after a long sea voyage.

Unfortunately, we had no choice as to the order in which our desires would be met. We were first led to the dining hall, where we found the postman waiting for us. We felt like children being visited by Saint Nicholas at Christmas as he opened his big bags of mail and began distributing the parcels. Shouts of our names followed by an eager "Here!" echoed out hundreds of times as we received our precious letters and packages from home. What followed was an indescribable hour during which three months of compressed emotions were released in one gigantic flood. This one had a new baby . . . that one's brother had fallen in Russia . . . every conceivable reaction resonated simultaneously through the hall. Some men were laughing; others shook with anger. Most of us just sat alone, quietly trying to read the letters through misty eyes.

We then checked into our barracks. After a luxuriously long and hot shower, we hit the bunks for a bit of rest before the evening's festivities. The banquet that night was truly memorable. As a reward for our efforts, we were provided all manners of foods totally unavailable to the other fighting men of the *Wehrmacht*. Juicy sausages, white bread, fresh vegetables, ripe fruits, and sweet French delicacies for dessert all graced our tables. Best of all, there was beer! Not the horrible ersatz beer that was normally available to the other services, but real bottles of *Becks* and *Falstaff*. Some of the boys, unaccustomed to the rich food and alcohol, became sick. But as soon as they were able, they were back at the table, enjoying what we all knew might be our last chance to enjoy such a feast.

Once the food was gone, we began to pay serious attention to the bottles of beer and strong French wine. Glasses were raised and drained in toast after toast. The hall quickly filled with a blue haze of pipe and cigarette smoke as we leaned back and digested the marvelous food. Our more basic needs filled, conversation began to turn to other, less gentlemanly interests of sailors on leave. The crew members with wives or sweethearts scoffed at us, but stories of the exotic pleasures awaiting us in the entertainment district of Lorient fired the imagination of us young bachelors. Our service in the *Kriegsmarine* would make us a man in more ways than one!

The next day was spent preparing *U-505* for its transport into the dry dock inside the armored bunkers. Hundreds of little maintenance duties had to be accomplished before she could be moved and overhauled. Once these chores were completed, the shipyard workers took over. With our major responsibilities on the boat finished, the first train tickets to home were passed out to the crew. Half of us would go on furlough while the other half would perform watch and training duties onboard *U-505*. A week later, the other half of the crew would have their chance for leave.

I felt that a few days of leave wasn't sufficient for a proper visit to my parents, so I stayed the entire period before our next war patrol in Lorient. The first couple of days were spent cleaning and performing some minor maintenance duties aboard *U-505*. Once our boat had been hoisted into its armored dry dock, the real work began. We changed the oils, overhauled the engines, tested the controls, and dozens of other tasks. There was also more training to keep us current on the latest tactics and operational routines.

The nights, however, were usually free of duty and we were able to enjoy some well-earned recreation. Our main destination was the *U-bootsheim*, the "U-boat Sailor's Home" in Lorient, where we could watch the latest German movies, play cards, mail letters, buy cheap beer and snacks, and generally just relax and converse with fellow sailors.

Despite the best efforts of the Navy to provide wholesome entertainment for us, the civilian entertainment district drew us toward it like a magnet. For boys like me, who had spent their entire lives in small agricultural villages, the streets of Lorient were like a dreamland. One would have never guessed from the gaiety of the nightlife on the streets that France was a defeated country, much less that there was a war going on anywhere.

Our favorite street was nicknamed *"Der Strasse der Bewegung"* (The Street of Movement) because of the constant buzz of activity. Music and laughter poured from almost every window. French love songs, German sailor ditties, and even American jazz music, officially frowned-upon as decadent, combined in a crazy jumble of sound.

The sweet scents of perfume also filled the night air with its hypnotic magic. There were certain houses renowned for the beautiful girls who, for a small fee, gave comfort and entertainment to lonely sailors. Glamorous mademoiselles with fancy dresses and flowers in their hair beckoned from the doorways. Speaking both German and French, the lovely sirens would tempt us to enter. "Come in, sailor! Good music, *beaucoup dance*, good drink, *amour.* . . ."

Once inside the establishments (*etablissements*), the Madam would personally greet us. "Hello, boys! How have you been? Just come back from the sea?"

Taking our caps and leather coats, she would fuss over our newly won medals while the ladies came forward with bottles of wine and Anisette. The drinks were twice as expensive as in a regular bar, but who cares when a beautiful young girl is sitting in your lap? If all the girls were busy, we could pass the time watching motion picture films of the French art of love. Since most of us had never been with a girl before, these "training films" gave us plenty of ideas of what to do when our turn with the ladies finally came. After a few hours we would stagger back to our barracks, our faces covered with telltale traces of lipstick and rouge.

In time, we developed a personal relationship with our favorite Madam. She would greet us by name when we entered and tell us when our pet girls were available. After a few weeks, when our money began running low, she would make sure that our drinks were "on the house."

We showed the same largesse to our comrades in the Navy. At the beginning of our leave, when we had lots of money, we would buy drinks for crewmen from other boats. A few weeks later, when we were broke and the time before our next patrol was running short, they would buy drinks for us. This reciprocal generosity built a sense of comradeship between us sailors. The comradeship sometimes even extended between us and the Army soldiers stationed in the area. For instance, I became good friends with a soldier from a nearby *Panzer* unit. I would share with him food and drink unavailable to Army troops' he, in return, would take me for rides on some of the armored vehicles. One time later in the war I got to ride on top of a giant Tiger tank. It was great fun to roar about the maneuver area, smashing down small trees.

Of course, it wasn't all love and kisses during our leave time; we also enjoyed an occasional fight. Sometimes another U-boat crew would have a few too many beers and start bragging about how they had the best boat or the cleverest skipper. In cases like that, we had no choice but to knock some sense into their heads! We also didn't like the administrative troops who somehow managed to drape their uniforms with medals for doing nothing more than pushing paper all day. While we were out on war patrol, these desk-sailing heroes would be safely back at base enjoying all that Lorient had to offer. There was nothing more satisfying than to let off some steam by throwing a scare into the little worms.

The greatest object of our scorn, however, was the *Feldgendarmerie*, the military police. We called them "Chained Dogs" because of the big metal police gorget they wore suspended around their necks on a chain. They usually looked the other way and allowed us to go about our business when we first returned from a patrol. But after a couple of days, they would lose their patience and start to break up our fun. It was serious business to be arrested by the military police! If we saw the Chained Dogs coming, we would give a certain alarm whistle and our whole gang would split up into small groups and run in different directions. Later, we would rendezvous at our favorite bar and the fun would start all over again. Usually we didn't want any trouble from the military police, but sometimes we were in the right mood to have a brawl with them, despite the risks.

I know it must be difficult for someone who has never served aboard submarines to understand our desire to get drunk, cavort with prostitutes, and fight with the police. Our nation's armed forces certainly didn't have a reputation for tolerating these irresponsible kinds of behavior! But after being crammed into a steel cigar for three months with constant hard work and danger, a man must be allowed to let off steam. Luckily for us, the U-boat command understood this. Navy doctors regularly inspected the girls in the *etablissements* for diseases. The *U-bootwaffe* (Submarine

Service) also gave us the finest food and drink available, and later in the war, would even send us on crew vacations to ski resorts. And when we did get in trouble, our skippers tried their best to intervene with the police on our behalf. I'm certainly not proud of everything we did in those days, but when you consider the fact that of the 38,000 men who served on U-boats during the war, more than 30,000 lost their lives, our behavior may seem a bit more forgivable.

When I first arrived in Lorient, I spent most of my time walking up and down *Der Strasse der Bewegung*, sampling as many different girls as I could. Having so many beautiful women open to one's advances was something I had never experienced before. Back in my little hometown of Bottendorf, most girls were careful not to get a bad reputation by sleeping with men. Such behavior, however, would earn a girl a very good reputation among us sailors in Lorient!

Nevertheless, in time I developed a special relationship with one of the French girls I met. Her name was Jeanette and she worked in one of the *etablissements* officially approved by the U-boat service for visits by their crewmen. She was a pretty girl, with a slender figure and soft, light-brown hair. I liked her from the first moment I met her. I found myself going to her more and more often.

Well, after one of our trysts one day, she asked me if I would like to accompany her to the *coiffeur* to have her hair cut. I was surprised by her request, but immediately accepted. I must admit that, contrary to my expectations, I thoroughly enjoyed the experience. It was quite amusing to sit there waiting for Jeanette while the other French women in the place clucked their tongues and gossiped about us.

Afterward, we went to a bistro and ate dinner. We spent a long time there, talking and laughing and learning about each other. I don't know how or why it happened, but sometime during that dinner we realized that we had developed a deep affection for each other. We dared not call it love because of the hopelessness of our situations. After all, she was a young woman of the night having an affair with an enemy sailor, and I was a crew member of a U-boat with very little chance of surviving the war. Perhaps we felt close to each other because we both had such uncertain futures.

Anyway, after we left the bistro, we were walking down the sidewalk when she abruptly stopped in front of a jewelry store. "Oh heavens," I thought, "she wants me to buy her a ring!" But instead, she darted into the shop and a moment later emerged with a beautiful little St. Christopher pendant on a chain.

"Here," she said, "I want you to have this. St. Christopher is the protector of all sailors and travelers; he will bring you safely back to me."

When she handed it to me, I could see it was solid gold. I protested that the present was far too expensive, but she would hear none of it. After all, she said with a sly smile, it was my money that she had spent, anyway.

After that evening, we grew very close. But it was a strange, complex relationship. We had a deep emotional bond between us, though we still took care not to use the word "love." We still retained the "business" aspect of our relationship when I first returned from a patrol with plenty of money to spend. But after a few weeks when my money ran low, it was she who would pay for things. Indeed, she usually spent far more on me than I was ever able to spend on her. Sometimes, when I was laying in my bunk on a war patrol, I dared dream of a future for us.

*   *   *

The following weeks passed quickly as final preparations were completed for *U-505*'s next war patrol. We had clocked 13,253 nautical miles on our previous voyage, and the diesel engines had been badly in need of an overhaul. Once that was accomplished, we began the task of loading torpedoes and other stores aboard the boat. Unlike our first war patrol, this time we did not mind the overcrowding due to the storage of foodstuffs. We all remembered the gastronomic monotony and health hazards we experienced after running out of fresh food on our last trip. By the time we were finished, our control room looked like a restaurant pantry.

We had also learned the layout of the boat well enough so that each of us had secret little hiding places where we stashed a few special, personal items. The nature of these items, of course, varied according to individual tastes. Tiny stockpiles of chocolate, cigarettes, liqueur, and little *Souvenir* booklets with pictures of women in scandalous poses were squirreled away throughout *U-505*.

Before we left, Admiral Karl Dönitz, Commander-in-Chief of all U-boat forces, paid us a visit. Dönitz made it his policy to personally acquaint himself with his submarine skippers, and we crewmen were thrilled to see him cross the gangplank and board our boat. After conferring with *Kapitänleutnant* Löwe, Admiral Dönitz wrote in *U-505*'s war diary, "First mission of Captain with new boat, well and thoughtfully carried out. Despite long time in operations area, lack of traffic did not permit greater success."

The visit of the tall, distinguished Admiral to our sub made an everlasting impression on me. We U-boat men had unbounded confidence and respect for both his abilities and devotion to duty. It was for good reason that we called him "the Great Lion." Many readers may not realize that in the final days of the war, Dönitz became Germany's official head of state after Hitler's death. After the war, despite the Allies' intense desire for revenge, Dönitz (and the U-boat service in general) was absolved of any war crime guilt during the Nuremberg Trials, primarily due to the courageous testimony by the American Admiral Chester Nimitz.

I never lost my admiration for Admiral Dönitz. In 1980, I attended his 89th birthday celebration at the Dönitz family's ancestral home in Aumühle, Germany. In a short speech he delivered before we toasted the memory of our missing comrades, the Great Lion expressed his heartfelt gratitude for the loyalty and sacrifice made by his men in the U-boat service. It was a deeply emotional experience for all of us. Later that year, I received a personally signed letter from him, one of the last letters he ever wrote. Calling me *Kamerad*, he warmly acknowledged my efforts to organize a reunion for *U-505* veterans. Finally, on January 6, 1981, I had the sad honor of attending his funeral. *Großadmiral* Karl Dönitz will be forever remembered, by both friend and foe, as a master strategist and a true gentleman.

*   *   *

By early June, *U-505* was ready for another war patrol. This time, lack of targets was not expected to be a problem: Admiral Dönitz had decided to send our boat to the fertile hunting grounds of the Caribbean Sea. Of course, the "officially neutral" United States had been aggressively attacking our U-boats since September of 1941, a full three months before her declaration of war on Germany. We were eager to get revenge for what we regarded as Roosevelt's underhanded war against us. The Americans had made dramatic improvements in their anti-submarine operations since the early days of hostilities, but even so, it was expected that there would still be plenty of under-protected targets for us to sink.

As far as we crew members were concerned, our next mission couldn't begin soon enough. Despite the varied entertainment available to us, we had become fed-up with life on base. And, despite all its hardships and dangers, we yearned to return to the sea. Salt water, so to speak, was now in our blood. We also knew the war was entering a critical phase. The fighting was reaching a crescendo in Africa and in Russia, and we were eager to do our fair share for the war effort.

So it was, on June 7, 1942, *U-505* slipped out of Lorient harbor and we embarked on our second war patrol.

This remarkable image was taken aboard *U-505* on June 29, 1942, during a war patrol in the Caribbean. It shows the *Thomas McKean*, a new 7,400-ton freighter, burning a few hundred yards away. *Author's Collection*

Chapter 4

Caribbean Cruise

*B*y 2030 Hours, we had cleared Lorient harbor and were heading for open waters. Our initial destination for this leg of the voyage was Grid Square DD50. Once there, the skipper opened his sealed orders to reveal our destination: the Caribbean Sea. Our mission was to prowl the western Caribbean and intercept traffic coming through the Panama Canal. A thrill ran through us when we heard we would be sailing across the Atlantic, for American waters were still rich hunting grounds for our U-boats at that stage of the war.

The waters of the Bay of Biscay were being whipped by summer storms, so for the next several days we ran about one-third of the distance submerged in order to save wear and tear on our boat and crew.

On June 11, we received several short *FT* radio telegrams from one of our sister boats from Lorient, *Kapitänleutnant* Heinrich Schuch's *U-105*. The frantic messages reported that she had been attacked by aircraft and her situation was critical: she was leaking seriously and unable to submerge. The broadcasts ceased a few minutes later. We then received orders from Admiral Dönitz's headquarters to speed to *U-105*'s last reported position to render assistance. Before we reached her, however, we were ordered to resume our previous course. We all knew what that probably meant.

When we returned to base after this patrol, we were relieved to learn *U-105* had not sunk, but at the time we were all heartsick over what we assumed had happened to our comrades. I felt especially bad because I had been originally assigned to *U-105* during my first month in Lorient. If not for a lucky transfer to *U-505*, I mused, I would be sharing that watery grave with my old friends right now. Of course, life goes on and I had to stay alert as ever at my duty station in the control room. But sometimes, when all was quiet except for the monotone rumble of the diesels, I would get lost in thought and imagine the faces of those boys sealed in their steel tomb at the bottom of the sea.

Unfortunately, *U-105*'s good luck was the exception rather than the rule. Almost all of our comrades from that early period were eventually lost during the course of the war. The death of so many friends and family members caused some of us to become morose or frightened. Not me. As our casualties mounted, I became angry and more determined than ever to defeat our nation's enemies. Perhaps I was just too young and idealistic to read the writing on the wall, but I believed—right up until the very end—Germany would triumph in the war.

The next couple of weeks passed quietly. We are able to run most of the time on the surface, making good time in our transit across the Atlantic. My favorite moments were passed on bridge watch, especially during the relatively cool nights. Blazing stars filled the summer heavens, the whole universe seemingly dipping and swaying with the gentle rocking of our boat. Around midnight, Anton "Toni" Kern our boat's cook, would come to the bridge with his steaming pot of *Mittelwächter,* a welcomed mixture of very strong coffee laced with rum. He had to guard the pot like a hawk since the tasty black brew was very much desired by everyone in the crew, whether on watch or not.

Toni and I became good friends. I remember the first time he tried to make a big pot of hot tea for the crew. Most Germans are coffee drinkers, so Toni had not been trained how to make tea during his four-week cooking course in U-boat School. In his ignorance, he used the same measure of tea leaves as one would use for coffee. He boiled the leaves until the tea was as black as old motor oil. The stuff tasted bitter as poison when we tried to drink it. *Kapitänleutnant* Löwe's mother was Dutch, so the skipper was a big tea drinker. Naturally, he demanded it be properly brewed. It was very amusing to watch the skipper hovering over the stove like a patient old aunt, instructing a very embarrassed Toni on the intricacies of tea making.

The balance of our voyage across the Atlantic was a fine one. The weather was quite calm and we escaped serious attention from the enemy. At one point we even felt confident enough to set up a table on the upper deck and enjoy our lunch *alfresco*. It was to be the last time in the war that we would be able to travel so far on the surface without molestation from the air.

Sometimes we were visited by schools of friendly dolphins that jumped and danced next to their big and noisy new playmate. It was marvelous to watch the powerful, playful creatures enjoy their carefree lives, blissfully unaware of the deadly contest being waged by their human cousins. Once, Executive Officer Nollau tried to catch one of the sleek mammals so he could ride on its back. Luckily for the dolphin, and probably for Nollau too, he did not succeed in catching one.

After three weeks of peaceful cruising, we had nearly completed our transit of the Atlantic. Thus far on our journey we had encountered only a scattering of neutral ships. But on the afternoon of June 28, we spotted a distant ship running a fast straight course toward the southeast. We identified her as a heavily-armed American freighter, *Robin Hood* type, approximately 7,000 tons. Löwe's order to action stations sent us into a frenzy of activity, our excited heartbeats rising in tempo with the increased RPMs of the diesels. A fault in our gyrocompass made us fall behind, but after seven hours of racing at top speed, we caught-up to the steamer and moved into firing position. The high-speed sprint had been costly in fuel, but we considered it an investment in victory.

At exactly 1800 Hours we heard the diving klaxon ring, followed by the humming song of our Siemens electric motors as we slipped down to periscope depth. After another hour of stalking, we were in perfect position for attack. We control room operators busied ourselves with fine adjustments to the boat's trim as we quietly waited for the freighter to cross our path.

Löwe's low, steady voice came over the intercom, breaking the silent tension. "We are starting the attack. Torpedoes . . . tubes one and two set on three-meter depth, distance 800 meters. Ready . . . FIRE!"

The sound room reported the torpedoes running hot and true. The seconds ticked by . . . 22 . . . 23 . . . 24 . . . Boom! The first torpedo hit just forward of the bridge, sending up a column of water as tall as the mast. An eye blink later, the second exploded just behind the bridge. A perfect set of shots.

The freighter began slowly sinking, bow first. Lifeboats were being lowered, but Löwe ordered that we remain submerged. The reason was clear from one peek through the attack periscope: in an admirable display of discipline, the enemy gun crews were still manning their battle stations at the ship's big 4-inch forward deck gun and aft 40mm anti-aircraft weapon. After another hour, the brave gun crews finally abandoned their posts and took to the lifeboats.

When the hundred or so survivors had moved sufficiently away from the ship, we fired another torpedo, this time set at four-meter depth. It hit in the same spot as the first torpedo and the ship began sinking fast. What a magnificent sight the ship was with its deck crowded with more than 20 twin-engine airplanes, the American flag still flying defiantly as she slipped beneath the waves! Years later I found out that the valiant freighter was the *Seathrush*, 6,900 tons.

We spent the better part of the next day reloading spare torpedoes from the racks into the empty torpedo tubes, a difficult and arduous procedure that required the participation of half the crew. Even those not involved in the operation could get no rest because their bunks had to be moved to allow clearance for the 23-foot long black eels. Once that was accomplished, most of our attention centered on the making of the small canvas victory pennant signifying our fifth success.

Our mood of enthusiasm and pride was so distracting that we off-duty crewmen lying in our bunks failed at first to notice the change in diesel RPMs. We had already begun our chase after another victim! A big, very heavily-armed merchantman had been sighted in the bright moonlight, making sharp zig-zags on a generally southerly course. The ship was a fast one, and it took us several anxious hours before we could maneuver into firing position. To our great joy, the intercom finally crackled with *Kapitänleutnant* Löwe's order to dive for the firing run.

We heard the forward tubes hiss and felt the boat gently shudder as two torpedoes were sent speeding toward their target, range 1,200 meters. Then . . . Whomm! One of the eels hit the ship's stern and she came to an immediate stop. Once again, brave American Navy gunners refused to leave their battle stations until all other personnel had abandoned ship.

This grainy images depicts a lifeboat from the 7,400-ton *Thomas McKean*, which had been steaming on her maiden voyage from New York to Trinidad when *U-505* found her. *Author's Collection*

Once the lifeboats were clear of the ship, Löwe brought our boat to the surface to assist any survivors. At first, the men in the lifeboats ducked, thinking we would machine gun them. When they saw we meant them no harm, they pulled along side, nervous but clearly curious about us "ruthless Nazi submariners."

We gave medical supplies and some of our precious fresh water to the wounded men in the lifeboats. Our skipper, speaking in English, learned from them that the ship was the brand-new 7,400 ton *Thomas McKean*, sailing on her maiden voyage from New York to Trinidad. Like the *Seathrush*, her deck was also crammed with about two dozen large aircraft, all eventually bound for the Soviet port of Baku. It gave us enormous satisfaction knowing those bombers would never reach the Communists fighting against our boys on the Eastern Front.

Although the *Thomas McKean* had developed a heavy list to port, she stubbornly refused to sink. Rather than waste another torpedo, the skipper ordered our deck gun crew to finish her off with cannon fire. The gun crew aimed at the waterline, but the slowly listing ship kept lifting the shell holes above the water. It took 80 rounds from our powerful 105mm gun before the flaming ship finally rolled over and sank. Löwe was a former gunnery officer, and he was obviously frustrated with the number of shells it took to sink her.

The skipper allowed everyone off duty to come out to the upper deck and watch the bittersweet drama of the handsome new ship being sunk. Ironically, it was virtually the only time most of us were able to personally view any of our sinkings. It was quite a fireworks show, and someone snapped a picture of the burning ship.

After she slipped under the waves, several of the bombers on her deck bobbed up to the surface. Löwe said we needed to make sure the planes sank, so he personally opened fire on them with our little 20mm flak gun. He explained that we needed to remove the evidence of her sinking so we couldn't be located, but we suspected all the cannon fire had given the old gunnery officer an itchy trigger finger. We certainly didn't begrudge him his fun, for we had added another victory pennant to our periscope and our spirits were as high as heaven. Once the skipper had satisfied himself, we went back below decks and cleared the area.

Fifty years after the end of the war, I met one of the survivors of the *Thomas McKean* at a naval veterans' reunion in Tampa, Florida. Charles Sanderson was one of the crew members responsible for the maintenance of those 25 aircraft bound for the Soviet Union. The high point of the evening was when he recognized himself in one of the photographs we had taken at the time of the sinking. Sure enough, there was the young Sanderson, with a hat on his head and an oar in his hands, sitting in one of the lifeboats we were rendering aid to. There was no acrimony between the Americans and us Germans at the reunion. We respected their bravery and valor, while they were grateful for our humanity in aiding the survivors. Naturally, I gave Charles a copy of the photo and we have been friends ever since.

*   *   *

The day after the sinking was spent much as the previous one: loading more torpedoes into the forward tubes and constructing another victory pennant. In the evening we watched a cutter approach the area where the *Thomas McKean* went down, apparently to rescue survivors. Löwe gave the ship a wide berth.

During the next week we spotted absolutely nothing. Our double success had obviously scared all other traffic out of the area. As we prowled the waters north of Puerto Rico, the crew took advantage of the lull to go topside and get some fresh air. Some of the boys stayed in the sun a bit too long and got a painful sunburn.

On July 4, 1942, we entered the Caribbean Sea. The water temperature was 29 degrees Celsius (84 Fahrenheit) and felt like warm bath water. Conditions inside the boat became unbearably hot, especially during the day. I tried to ignore the heat by reading my English language novel by John Knittel, but the dripping condensation soaked the pages until they dissolved into paste. Adding insult to injury, the weather started getting rough. As we passed through the western end of the Caribbean, the weather deteriorated even further. We began to feel like an American Wild West rodeo rider as giant, rolling waves tossed our boat up and down. We rated the conditions as Sea State six-point-four. Löwe radioed headquarters that he was moving closer to the South American coast in order to intercept traffic passing through the Panama Canal.

As we approached the Colombian coast, air activity increased dramatically, but still we did not encounter any merchant sea traffic. By the second week of July, air alarms became so frequent we could not even

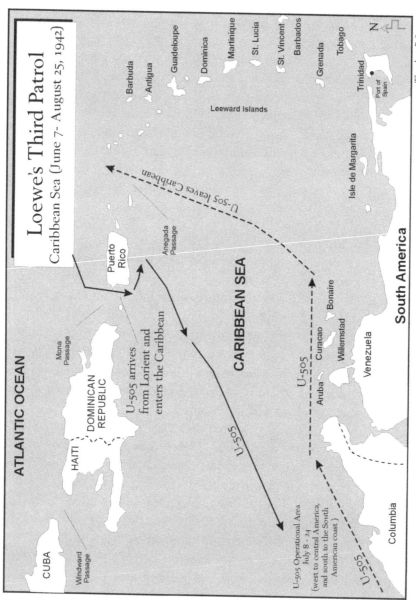

Loewe's Third Patrol
Caribbean Sea (June 7- August 25, 1942)

ATLANTIC OCEAN

CUBA

Windward Passage

HAITI

DOMINICAN REPUBLIC

Mona Passage

Puerto Rico

U-505 arrives from Lorient and enters the Caribbean

Anegada Passage

U-505 leaves Caribbean

Barbuda

Antigua

Guadeloupe

Dominica

Martinique

St. Lucia

St. Vincent

Barbados

Grenada

Tobago

Leeward Islands

Isle de Margarita

Trinidad

Port of Spain

N

CARIBBEAN SEA

U-505

U-505

U-505 Operational Area July 8 - 24 (west to central America, and south to the South American coast)

U-505

Aruba

Curacao

Bonaire

Willemstad

Venezuela

South America

Columbia

Theodore P. Savas

stay surfaced long enough to fully charge our compressed air tanks. The alarms took an especially hard toll on the crew, as we were continually deprived of sleep. I distinctly remember one occasion I was enjoying a particularly pleasant dream about Jeanette when the alarm went off. I awoke with a start and my lovely dream was suddenly replaced with the steaming, stinking reality of our existence. I wanted to scream. The alarm had sounded because we had begun chasing a target, but our prey escaped into a thunderstorm and it was all for naught.

The miserable routine of thunderstorms and air alerts continued for two more weeks. Even the cloak of darkness failed to protect us from the ever-present enemy vultures hovering over our heads. The warm seas were often highly phosphorescent, making our wake shimmer with a glow that could be spotted miles away from the air.

The situation became worse with the appearance of American "Consolidated" flying boats, which somehow had the ability to spot us in total darkness, even with no phosphorescence. The speed and accuracy with which the aircraft were able to find us caused us to suspect that the enemy planes had been fitted with airborne radar devices. Several times we were surprised in the middle of the night by the blossoming of giant flares that illuminated us as brightly as the noonday sun. When this happened, we had mere seconds to crash dive before the plane circled back for his bombing run. A couple of times we were very nearly sunk by their bombs and depth charges. Over time, we got to be quite expert in the roller coaster game of evading aircraft, but as a result of the constant exertion and stain, our morale and health began deteriorating fast.

On the afternoon of July 22, we got a bit of diversion that was to have far-reaching consequences. We were lying off the coast of a small island called Courtown Cays when a large three-masted schooner with a luxury car lashed to its deck was spotted 30 degrees off our starboard bow. The beautiful sailing ship was not flying a flag and was making violent zig-zags—the type a ship makes to avoid torpedoes rather than to tack against the wind. The unusual ship excited Löwe's curiosity, so he ordered surface battle stations.

The deck gun crew went through their well-practiced drill for preparing the 105mm cannon for action. In less than 30 seconds, the gun was loaded and ready to fire. The skipper shouted to Gunnery Officer Stolzenburg to send a warning shot over the sailing ship's bow to halt the craft and identify them. Either the gun crew misunderstood the order, or they just plain missed, because the first shot took off the ship's mainmast. The handsome windjammer looked like a mess, with its mast and sails draping over her elegant decks like a giant tent.

Despite the damage, the ship refused to stop. *Kapitänleutnant* Löwe ordered another couple of warning shots to be fired. The ship ran up the Colombian flag but still refused to heave-to. Did they really believe that a de-masted sailing ship could outrun a submarine? We moved our boat into the path of the schooner, whereupon she once again turned to avoid inspection. From the stern of the boat we could see her name: the *Roamar* out of Cartagena.

Löwe's face showed he was struggling with a hard decision. After a moment more of thought, our skipper made a judgment call he would profoundly regret for the rest of his life.

"Sink her, Stolzenberg, but make it quick."

The first round into the ship's hull was all the convincing the Spanish-speaking crew needed to abandon ship. We waited until the near-hysterical crew was well clear of the ship, then opened fire for effect. It took only a few minutes for our deck gun to make matchsticks out of the 400-ton schooner. It was great fun for our gun crew, but Löwe sensed this was a big mistake. We immediately departed the area, assuming the sailing ship had ample time to radio a report of our presence.

We all believed we had good reasons for sinking the schooner. Technically, we were totally within our rights to sink a ship in a declared war zone that had refused orders to heave to and allow her cargo to be inspected. Legalities aside, once the first warning shot had de-masted her, we really had no practical choice but to erase the evidence of our presence by sinking her.

Löwe, however, could not shake the feeling that he had made a tremendous mistake. The *Kapitänleutnant*, usually a paragon of steely calm, began to show signs of nervous distress. His physical condition worsened dramatically during the next few days and it began to affect his performance. He seemed to be literally worrying himself sick. More and more, our Executive Officer Herbert Nollau began to perform the day-to-day duties of the skipper. (NOTE: Based on his competency during this emergency, Nollau was promoted and became the commanding officer of his own boat, *U-534*, which was sunk May 5, 1945, by a British Liberator. In 1993, a commercial salvage group raised Nollau's boat in the Kattegat, out of Denmark. She was taken over by the Warship Preservation Trust, hauled to England in May of 1996, and is now on display at the Nautilus Maritime Museum in Birkenhead, near Liverpool. Thus, in a stunning bit of coincidence, Nollau served on two of the three U-boats that survive today.)

*   *   *

The remainder of July was spent in a fruitless back-and-forth search of the South American coast for shipping. We suspected that, somehow, the Allies were constantly aware of our position and were directing traffic around us. As it turned out, our suspicions were fully justified. Unbeknownst to us, the Allies were not only triangulating our positions through radio direction finders, they had also cracked our top secret *Enigma* code and were deciphering our most sensitive messages to and from headquarters.

Meanwhile, our troubles continued to multiply. The skipper's face grew more pale by the day and he rarely talked. Nollau continued as he had been, assuming more of the captain's duties. The seas were also extremely rough: Sea State seven. The boat rolled so much that literally everything on board had to be tied down or it would fall to the floor. The battering of the waves was so severe that one of our forward torpedo tube covers was damaged. As far as we crew members were concerned, it took our constant effort to avoid being thrown to the deck, even when trying to sleep. At least the terrible weather was keeping the Allied aircraft grounded.

On the last night of July we had a memorable encounter with "St. Elmo's Fire," a freak atmospheric condition caused by an electrical charging of the air. The entire conning tower and upper deck was lit in the most miraculous manner with a halo of blue light. By wetting one's hand, you could even make your fingers glow. Such a phenomenon is grand entertainment if one is sailing on a cruise ship in peacetime, but we only worried about being spotted by our "friends" in the air. Off duty, we heard many old sailors' superstitions about the meaning of this magical experience.

Löwe's condition, meanwhile, continued to deteriorate. Only with the greatest physical exertion and force of will could he manage to perform his duties. It began to become clear that there was physically something very wrong with him—far beyond mere worry over the schooner incident. On August 1, we radioed U-boat Headquarters that we were returning to base due to our commander's health. Naturally, we were disappointed we would be returning with only three victory pennants, but our main thoughts were to save the life of our beloved skipper.

On the afternoon of August 3, we were once again forced to crash dive due to an attacking aircraft. The big plane swooped down so close we could hear the roar of its engines from inside the sub as we dived. Clearly, the bridge watch had been caught totally unprepared. We were surprised to see *Kapitänleutnant* Löwe, the color temporarily returned to his face, struggle out of his cabin to address the crew. He remained calm, but using a voice that could not be misunderstood, he reminded us of the need to stay vigilant. No one was punished, though Löwe's quiet disappointment was penalty enough for us. The sailor whose inattention to duty was primarily responsible for the close call was transferred to another boat before our next patrol, but with no black mark against his record.

I'm not ashamed to admit that our brush with death threw a real scare into us. The loud rumbling sound of the diesels, which had so often annoyed me, now seemed like a beautiful song announcing our return to base. East of the Antilles we rendezvoused with *U-463* in order to take on more diesel fuel. *U-463*, commanded by First World War submarine veteran Leo Wolfbauer, was one of the "Milk Cow" submarines specially designed to replenish U-boats on the high seas with fuel, torpedoes, and other supplies. Luckily for us, the sea was smooth as a mirror and there was no difficulty in making the diesel fuel hose connection.

After taking on 25 cubic meters of precious fuel, we bid a hearty farewell to our big-bellied benefactor. We were relieved no aircraft had shown up to torment us; several U-boats had already been sunk by air attacks conducted while docked together in the vulnerable refueling position. *U-463* was eventually caught on the surface by a British Halifax bomber and sunk with all hands in May 1943. We were greatly saddened to hear of her loss, considering how crucial she had been to our own safe return.

East of the Azores, we had another rendezvous with a outgoing U-boat, this time *U-214*. This was strictly a social visit between two lone wolves, one returning from the war zone, the other heading toward it.

Kapitänleutnant Günther Reeder, the skipper of *U-214*, asked in his heavy Frisian accent if we had any tea to spare. We still had plenty because, despite the skipper's best attempts to instill in us a taste for tea, we all much preferred coffee. We transferred two tins of the stuff to Reeder while the officers shouted gossip back and forth. We wished each other good luck and continued on our way. As they disappeared into the distance, we wondered whether our little mid-ocean "tea party" with the crew of *U-214* would be the last time we would ever see them.

As we approached the Bay of Biscay, we began getting more and more attention from British air patrols. Air-dropped depth charge attacks became so frequent that we were forced to run the entire length of the Bay underwater, surfacing only long enough to recharge our air and batteries. It was during this leg of our journey that we began having severe navigational difficulties. Our gyrocompass began giving us trouble again, and to make matters even worse, magnetic anomalies were simultaneously interfering with our magnetic compass. Meanwhile, the air threat prevented us from getting proper fixes on the stars with the sextant. As a result, we could only estimate our course within a margin of error of five degrees.

On the night of August 24, we were finally close enough to Lorient to surface and ask for a radio-directional beam to guide us in the rest of the way. To our immense relief, the beam came in loud and clear on our direction finder and we were able to adjust our course. Early the next morning, we encountered a small fleet of French fishing boats. The vessels immediately lit their navigation lights. A friendly greeting or a betrayal of our position to the British? To be on the safe side, we ducked below the waves until we were well out of sight.

That afternoon, we met our escort boats at Rendezvous Point *Luci-2*. Within a few hours we were safely tied to our pier in Lorient harbor. Once again we were greeted by the military band and our Flotilla Commander Schütze. There was also a large, noisy crowd of admirers, this time including quite a number of French girls waiting to reunite with their *Beaus*. My heart began to race when I spotted Jeanette's beaming face in the crowd. She looked more beautiful than ever.

Of course, we were very happy to be back in port. But somehow, as we stood assembled in formation on the upper deck, the cheers and hurrahs seemed a little hollow. After all, we had managed to make only two good kills this mission and there was a dark cloud of uncertainty hanging over our skipper. This patrol, which had begun so auspiciously, ended in frustration.

After the ceremonies concluded, we hurried to complete the necessary duties on board before walking with stiff, unsteady legs onto dry land. As before, we received our mail and enjoyed a luxurious banquet. After the feast we stumbled to our barracks, without the energy to even remove our uniforms before falling into our bunks. We were so physically and emotionally drained we slept like mummies until late the next day.

A smiling Hans Goebeler,
happy to be once more ashore.

Chapter 5

A New Skipper

We spent the next few days unloading *U-505* and preparing her for the move to a berth in the armored bunkers. Once the boat and our personal possessions had been safely stowed, we were finally granted liberty to leave the barracks. Naturally, we spent most of our free time paying visits to our favorite haunts in Lorient's entertainment district. Upon leaving our barracks, however, we were shocked to see how much things had changed during our absence. The British had been hitting the city with heavier and heavier bombing raids. Luckily for us, most of the damage was confined to the port area; our favorite streets were still relatively intact. Many other parts of the city, however, were scenes of utter devastation.

The ladies of Lorient were very happy to see us again, especially since we had everything they longed for: cigarettes, chocolate, and even a little spending money. Of course, in the back of my mind I tried to believe that Jeanette loved me because she considered me handsome and charming . . . but a couple of nice presents never hurt! At any rate, it was wonderful to be back on land again. Even the military police were good to us, looking the other way as we staggered from pub to pub in search of "just one more drink." In time, we discovered a way through the perimeter wire that allowed us to sneak back into the barracks after hours. After that, our opportunities for recreation were only limited by our capacity to perform duties the next day.

Despite our fun, however, the fate of our skipper hung like a dark cloud over our heads. It turned out that *Kapitänleutnant* Löwe had been suffering from a severe case of appendicitis. Prompt medical attention alleviated the threat to his life, but the physical pain he had endured was nothing compared to the emotional anguish he was to experience over the sinking of the damned three-masted schooner. Löwe's instincts were correct, for the sinking was a colossal mistake.

We soon learned the 400-ton *Roamar* was the property of a Colombian diplomat. Its sinking, though technically-speaking perfectly legal, provided the political grounds for Colombia to declare war against Germany! Of course, at that point in the war, Colombia's declaration of war had about as much effect on us as the howling of a dog has on the moon. But the effect on Löwe's career was catastrophic: he was relieved of command of *U-505* and assigned to shore duty. Admiral Dönitz, however, recognized our skipper's talents and arranged to have Löwe put on his staff. Löwe's assignment to the Great Lion's staff would have been the envy of most naval officers, but it broke our skipper's heart to have to give up frontline sea duty.

News of Löwe's transfer was an occasion of great sadness for us all. We had tremendous affection for him, and unbounded respect for the way that he had handled our boat. Even in the most dangerous moments, our *Kapitänleutnant* had never lost his head. How many times the mere sound of his deep, steady voice had calmed us young crew members during emergencies! A green crew is sensitive to little things like that, and is reassured by them. Löwe also had a sort of intuitive ability to sense danger. The survival lessons he taught us would be ignored in the future only at great cost. Most importantly, Löwe was a natural leader with a keen understanding of how to deal with men in the pressure cooker environment of a submarine at war. He always treated us with respect, was never demeaning and never abused his authority. Rather, he led us by personal example. It's not an exaggeration to say that Axel Olaf Löwe was like a father to us. Quite a few of us were moved to tears during his farewell speech.

* * *

After the first group of crew members had departed for furlough, we met our new skipper, *Kapitänleutnant* Peter Zschech. Young, handsome,

Peter Zschech, U-505's second commander. *NA*

and cultured, he appeared to be a perfect example of the new breed of U-boat commander that the Propaganda Ministry liked to portray in magazines and films. Rumored to be the son of an Admiral, Zschech came to our boat with the very highest of reputations. His previous assignment was as Executive Officer on *U-124*, U-boat ace Jochen Mohr's famous "Edelweiss Boat." Our first personal impression of him was that he was intelligent, self-confident, but a little aloof . . . like an aristocrat. Almost immediately, however, we found out that his aloofness hid an explosive temper. His sudden fits of anger and general moodiness contrasted sharply with Löwe's calm approach to command.

Zschech also seemed very eager, perhaps a bit too eager, to get at the enemy. He actually had the cheek to criticize his mentor Jochen Mohr for being too timid! This we took with a grain of salt since Mohr was universally regarded as one of our greatest U-boat commanders. We suspected Zschech had a bad case of *Halsschmerzen*, or the "sore throat," a condition common to many young officers and one that could only be cured by wearing a Knight's Cross around the neck.

Because Zschech was a newly-promoted skipper, we passed his braggadocio off as youthful exuberance. Despite a few misgivings about his inexperience, Zschech had an excellent recommendation and we were hoping some of *U-124*'s great success (more than 100,000 tons sunk) would rub off on our boat.

To replace our departing Executive Officer Nollau, who was being transferred to take command of his own boat, came *Oberleutnant* Thilo Bode. Bode was Zschech's close personal friend and had graduated with him in the naval officer class of 1936. Right from the beginning he seemed very arrogant. His attitude was one of utter contempt toward us, and he even refused to introduce himself to his new crew! The nature of his "friendship" with Zschech also began to make us a bit uncomfortable. Bode and Zschech would spend long hours alone together and would sometimes even hold hands in the presence of the crew. I had deep misgivings regarding our new Exec right from the beginning, but most of the crew remained optimistic that any problems would be worked-out during our next war patrol.

The one new officer about whom we had absolutely no doubts was *Oberleutnant* Josef Hauser. This swaggering, baby-faced engineering officer acted as though he knew everything about a U-boat, but it was immediately apparent that he knew almost nothing. Our Chief Engineering Officer Fritz Förster had to teach Hauser virtually everything about his job. On one of the first crash dives Hauser supervised, he came close to killing us all by diving *U-505*'s nose into the sea floor. Only quick action by Förster saved us from certain doom.

I witnessed Förster lecturing the new engineering officer in no uncertain terms: "This submarine is not your toy! Always keep in mind that there are 49 other human beings on this boat and that they want to return to their homes after this patrol."

I remember muttering to myself, "Amen to that!"

As a matter of fact, this new crop of officers soon had quite a few of us crewmen muttering to ourselves. The officers acted as though fear was a better motivator than respect. How different this was from Löwe, who always said that on a submarine, rank mattered nothing compared to how well a person did his job!

Of course, anyone who has served in the military knows that a new commander always tries to "shake things up" in his unit in order to establish his authority over his men. In the case of these three new officers, however, we thought they were going way too far. Even our veteran officers Förster and Stolzenburg agreed. Our new skipper and his friends seemed to resent any advice from our old officers, even when presented in the most friendly and deferential manner. They seemed especially hostile towards Förster, who, although functioning as Chief Engineering Officer, was actually more senior in rank than *Kapitänleutnant* Zschech. In the end, they had to leave Förster pretty much alone in engineering matters because of his great wealth of experience.

The discomfort of our old officers was nothing compared to what we crewmen experienced. Zschech's first order was that we would undergo, of all things, infantry training! We were issued brand new *Mauser 98k* rifles and immediately began a course of tactical ground combat training. We got used to the actual training fairly quickly, though the chore of keeping our weapons and uniforms clean was a constant annoyance. We all wondered what the hell any of this had to do with serving on a submarine. More and more of us began to grumble about our new skipper, but the majority of the crew still withheld judgment, optimistic that Zschech would prove his worth at sea.

*   *   *

While we played soldiers in the mud, *U-505* was undergoing repairs and modifications. To reduce the need for at-sea replenishment by the "Milk Cows," our diesel fuel capacity was increased. This alteration was actually designed by our old skipper *Kapitänleutnant* Löwe. More importantly, we were equipped with one of the first versions of the new *Metox* radar early warning devices. This crude-looking contraption, consisting of a cross-shaped wooden frame wrapped with wires, operated much like the modern radar detectors now mounted on many automobiles. It was hoped this apparatus would eliminate any nasty surprises, especially from the increasingly deadly air attacks. In time, the *Metox* device was nicknamed the "Biscay Cross" because of its antenna's cruciform shape and its critical importance in helping us survive the dangerous trip across the Bay of Biscay.

We also had several additions to our boat, including two crewmen from *U-124*, Zschech's old boat. The two boatswain mates were tight-lipped regarding our new skipper, but it was clear to us that, despite the excellent reputation of their former boat, these men were not up to our standards in the performance of their duties. One of them made the adjustment and happily served aboard *U-505* until our capture in 1944. The other one, however, requested transfer back to his former boat at the end of the next war patrol. Later, we heard he went down with the rest of the crew of *U-124* when she was sunk in the Atlantic in 1943.

Two new Petty Officers also came aboard. One was a diesel specialist and the other was an electric engine specialist, both fresh out of submarine school. These two fellows had a lot to learn about life on board a frontline U-boat. For instance, on their very first day, they began chewing out us crewmen for failing to salute them in the corridor of our boat! They learned very quickly they were no longer in basic training. Their biggest mistake was trying to curry favor with Zschech by ordering us to do infantry drills and calisthenics at sea during our next war patrol. This crazy idea caused a lot of hard feelings among the men, but we eventually got our revenge when we returned to port. Luckily for everyone concerned, once we got our revenge, they fit in perfectly with the rest of the crew.

*   *   *

Work on our boat was completed by the end of September. The change in skippers brought with it a brand new emblem. *Kapitänleutnant* Löwe's ax-wielding lion was removed and a new emblem—a large set of Olympic rings—was painted on the front of the conning tower. The rings symbolized Zschech's friendship with several other U-boat commanders who were fellow classmates of his from the Naval Academy class of 1936 (the year of the Olympics). There were five or six skippers in this little clique who chose the Olympic rings as their vessel's symbol. But in a concession to the great affection we still felt toward our former skipper,

U-505 leaves Lorient under the command of Peter Zschech. The boat's former emblem—the battle ax—is visible on the port side of the conning tower. Zschech left it there as a token of continuity between the two commanders. *Author's Collection*

Zschech allowed us to retain the ax from Löwe's emblem on the sides of the conning tower as a token of continuity between the two captains.

The arduous chore of loading the boat with supplies and munitions began in early October. Our mood during this time was a complicated one. On the one hand, we had very mixed feelings about Löwe's replacement by Zschech. Opinions were sharply divided as to whether our new skipper was a move in the right direction. On the other hand, we were all committed to erasing from our record the stigma of the schooner incident. Chief of Western U-boat Operations Eberhard Godt, on behalf of Admiral Dönitz, had entered a stinging entry into our boat's log: "Because of sickness, commanding officer interrupted war patrol before the proper time. Few chances for attack existed because of stopped traffic in the area. The sinking of the Colombian sailing ship would have been better left undone. No further remarks." New skipper or not, we were determined to redeem ourselves on this next war patrol.

We departed for our third war patrol at exactly 1800 hours on the 4th of October 1942. Our transit out of Lorient harbor had a new wrinkle: all non-essential personnel had to assemble on the upper deck until we cleared the breakwaters. A red buoy in the channel marked the spot where, just a few weeks before, a returning U-boat had struck a mine laid by enemy aircraft the previous night. The boat sank in full view of the horrified spectators. Only two members of the crew survived, even though the water was only about ten meters (33 feet) deep. Apparently, the concussion of the mine had broken the backs of many of the men. As a result, all departing and returning boats were now under orders to assemble non-essential crewmen on the upper deck wearing life jackets. Furthermore, we were required to kneel, because it was believed this precaution would prevent our legs from being driven into our spines by the concussion.

As a control room operator, it was my duty to stay inside the sub during almost all of these harbor transits. I didn't worry much because my attitude was one of complete fatalism. I think my point of view was common among young sailors—especially in a dangerous business like the U-boat service. We didn't spend too much time thinking about what would happen tomorrow; we just tried to live life day-to-day. Death might come today, or tomorrow, or it might never come. I just wanted to get my share of the good things in life and would meet my fate when it came. As the French say, *C'est la vie*!

* * *

Less than an hour out of Lorient harbor, we got a taste of what life at sea with *Kapitänleutnant* Zschech would be like. As usual, our conning tower and bridge were festooned with flowers for our departure ceremony. In our customary precaution against bad luck, the bridge watch began throwing the flowers overboard before we lost sight of Brittany's rocky shore. Zschech saw what was happening and literally screamed at them to stop. Second Watch Officer Stolzenburg tried to cover the crewmen by explaining to the skipper it was our custom to do so, but he was cut-off in mid-sentence by an angry, red-faced Zschech.

"*Kapitänleutnant* Löwe is no longer in command of this boat!" He yelled. "This is my boat and I am the only one giving orders from now on. I want everybody to understand that!"

Stolzenburg and the men were perplexed and embarrassed by the outburst. None of them ever dreamed of questioning Zschech's authority. Why had he reacted in such a manner?

From then on, Zschech made sure that everyone was absolutely certain, as we used to say, "which way the wind was blowing." During the next few days, virtually the entire crew was personally treated to the skipper's wrath. There were only two exceptions. The first was our Executive Officer, whose "personal" relationship with Zschech overrode professional considerations. The second exception was our Chief Engineering Officer Förster. He technically outranked Zschech, though as skipper, Zschech was still in command of the boat. In deference to his rank and mechanical expertise, Zschech left Förster pretty much alone, at least at the beginning. As for the rest of us, we began praying to Heaven that Zschech would prove as bothersome to the enemy as he was to his own crew.

We continued sailing westward, battering our way forward through heavy rolling swells. On the night of October 6, the new *Metox* radar-warning device proved its worth by alerting us to an approaching Allied aircraft. We were able to crash dive safely before the buzzard ever came into sight. The next night we received a *FT* radio-telegram from Dönitz's U-boat Command advising us of our preliminary destination: Sea Square ED99. We would once again be hunting for prey in the Caribbean, this time off the coast of Trinidad.

In the morning, our port diesel engine failed. While we sat submerged to effect repairs, our sound man reported a detonation and faint propeller noises to the west. *Kapitänleutnant* Zschech decided to take a look around and brought *U-505* up to periscope depth. We saw nothing, but a few minutes later we received a radio message from another U-boat reporting a small Allied convoy approximately fifty nautical miles away. At least a dozen enemy ships were just waiting to feel the sting of our torpedoes, but we couldn't get there because one of our engines was dead! We sat frustrated and helpless as our sound man reported more detonations. Some of the crew blamed our wretched luck on the flowers. I don't think anyone really believed in that superstition, but it was the topic of more grumbling among the crew.

Our duties for the next few hours were dominated with the need to get that damn diesel going. Since the engines had just been overhauled, speculation centered on whether it was a defective part or if it was sabotage by one of the mechanics back in Lorient. We tried to make ourselves believe this wasn't another bad omen.

As dawn broke on October 11, we sighted sails to the west. We crept up at periscope depth to investigate. The deck of the ship, which was apparently Portuguese, was stacked with a load of cork balls for fishing nets. After the *Roamar* affair, we had no appetite for another encounter with a sailing ship. We left the boat alone without checking her cargo for contraband.

By the end of the second week, we were clear of the Bay of Biscay danger zone and well on our way across the Atlantic. In our wake trailed heavy phosphorescence, but our trusty *Metox* device allowed us to relax a bit more than in former days.

On the morning of the 15th, I was assigned to one of the least pleasant duties a control room operator has ever had: picking rotten potatoes out of the bags of provisions that still littered virtually every spare inch of the control room. The stench of the black mushy potatoes mixed with the aromas of rotten eggs, diesel fuel fumes, exhaust gas, and bilge water to create a hellish perfume I shall never forget. After a few weeks, one usually got used to these repulsive smells, but getting covered up to the elbows by the stuff was truly disgusting.

I tried to forget the stench by going up onto the bridge and enjoying a smoke, but there was only one type of cigarette available on board: the horrible-tasting *Jan Maat* brand. Back in Lorient, we could get all sorts of good brands like *Atikah*, *Memphis*, and *Gold Dollar*. But for some reason, you couldn't taste the tobacco when you smoked the good stuff at sea. Perhaps the changes in pressure or exposure to salt spray affected the better quality tobacco; we didn't know. All we did know was that, after a couple of weeks at sea, the vile little *Jan Maat*s were the only cigarette that still retained any taste. The trouble was, it was a terrible taste! One had to pull a bit of tobacco out of the smoking end (cigarettes didn't have filters in those days) and pinch it between your thumb and index finger in order to tolerate the literally nauseating smoke. It was a toss-up as to which smell was worse: the *Jan Maat*s or the rotten potatoes.

It must seem very petty to a reader to hear of our preoccupation with such little things like flower superstitions and the smell of cigarettes, but during the long lulls between attacks, you didn't have much else on a U-boat to occupy your mind. When you take 50 men, crowd them without privacy into a long sardine can and totally isolate them from the rest of the world, minor matters such as these become very important. Like gossip in a small town, even insignificant things became the focus of intense interest. Stories made their way back and forth throughout the boat like an echo in a cave, bouncing fore and aft and gaining intensity with every telling. A tiny pleasure like smoking a good-tasting cigarette seemed like the most important thing in the world to a lonely young sailor in the middle of the ocean. Only when the alarm klaxon rang and we went into action did all of these inconsequential matters shrink back to their proper proportions.

On October 20, we received an *FT* radio-telegram that must have been good news to *Kapitänleutnant* Zschech, but which was devastating to the rest of the crew: our Chief Engineering Officer Förster was ordered to transfer at sea to another U-boat. The last of the senior officers from *Kapitänleutnant* Löwe's old crew was being removed. Two days later, just after sunset, we rendezvoused with *U-514* to effect the transfer. Förster's departure was an emotional one, though none of us dared to make the full depth of our feelings known to Zschech's clique of officers. An hour and a half later, *U-514* disappeared from sight, eliminating what *Kapitänleutnant* Zschech must have regarded as the last remnant of resistance to his authority on board our boat. The sea became rough in the next few days, as if Neptune was displeased with the latest turn of events.

With Förster gone, Zschech and his Exec, Thilo Bode, became even more tyrannical in their behavior toward us. We didn't mind so much the constant practice drills; after all, proficiency in one's duties has always been the best guarantor of success and survival in war. Soon we broke our previous records for the quickness of completing drills, and we were rightly proud of that. But Zschech never seemed to be satisfied, nor even to acknowledge our prowess. Instead, the harassment increased. It was no longer enough to be proficient at one's job, one also had to deal with an endless stream of other duties, most of which seemed like unnecessary "busy work."

The most infuriating duty I experienced during this time was serving the officers during their mess. One would have thought they were dining at a fancy restaurant in Paris given the way they would haughtily return the food to the galley as unsatisfactory. You had to listen to their constant, sneering complaints and say nothing but, "*Jawohl, Herr So-and-So.*" And woe be to the sailor who did not stand sufficiently rigid at attention while they ate their meals! A couple of times I found myself down in the bowels of the boat cleaning out the bilge for committing such a serious infraction. What made it all so aggravating was that we, and sometimes even our cook Toni Kern, would miss our own meals and have to go to sleep hungry because of all of these extra waiter duties.

* * *

By the beginning of November, we arrived at our patrol station off the South American coast. Our orders were to prowl the narrow strait between Trinidad and the coast of Venezuela, concentrating our efforts on any tankers bringing oil out from the mouth of the Orinico River. Remembering the gigantic explosions and fires that resulted from our previous attack on a tanker, we were hoping to put on a good fireworks show for the native villagers we saw living on the beaches.

Even though it was late autumn, the sea and air temperatures were still unbearably hot. Condensation water dripping on our heads was our only relief from the heat. Between the sauna-like conditions inside the boat and the constant torment from the officers, our nerves frayed and tempers once again began to flare. Men would get into a shouting match,

Escaping the heat. While a watch scans the horizon, a handful of *U-505's* crew rest above decks, grateful for the chance to escape the oppressive heat inside the hull. Author Hans Goebeler is standing in the center of rear line. Hunter-killer groups would soon made these relaxing days above deck impossible. *Author's Collection*

usually for little or no reason, and then the fists would fly. Usually it would be over in a matter of seconds, with the men ending up laughing and agreeing to forget the whole idiotic episode. It was clear we needed to get back into action in order to get our minds off our troubles. Contrary to expectations, however, there was no enemy traffic coming through the strait. For days we sat in our iron pressure cooker, waiting for targets that never came.

My favorite pastime during this lull in the action was to secretly watch our newly-promoted Chief Engineering Officer Hauser preen himself in the officers' quarters. We soon nicknamed him "the Raccoon" because of his constant fussing over his facial hair. For hours on end he would sit there in front of the mirror, trimming, pulling, and plucking at his thin little beard, trying desperately to make himself look like a seasoned mariner. Once he was satisfied that his beard was perfect, he would practice various scowls and other authoritarian poses in front of the mirror. Of course, he was unaware anyone could see him through the control room hatchway.

We didn't have much respect for this fellow. Naturally, he was far less technically knowledgeable than old Förster, but the main thing that irked us was the Raccoon's neurotic obsession with his beard. Any member of the engineering crew who had the audacity to grow a thicker beard than his was given a very rough time. The Raccoon loved to punish crewmen for even the slightest of infractions by subtracting days from their next furlough.

But the biggest pest, besides Zschech himself of course, remained our Executive Officer Thilo Bode. He was a thoroughly unpleasant character, with a disposition that grew steadily worse as our lack of success began to frustrate him. The Exec always spoke to us in a very nasty tone, continually belittling us as lazy and incompetent. As far as we were concerned, it was he who was incompetent. His favorite punishment was to assign us to long periods of extra watch duty, often for doing nothing more than humming a tune while working.

Of course, the German military man has traditionally been accustomed to strict discipline and hard training, but there is always an underlying respect between officer and men, based on the understanding that the hardships are for the good of the unit. But these officers went far beyond what was reasonable, hurting our morale and even our physical ability to do our jobs.

I remember very clearly one encounter I had with the Exec. It was after midnight and I was trying to get some sleep during my six-hour rest period. I was shaken awake and told Bode had ordered me to report immediately to the bridge. In less than a minute, I had dressed and scurried up the ladders to the bridge. As I snapped to attention before him, I wondered what technical emergency had required my immediate presence.

"*Maschinengefreiter* Göbeler here as ordered, Sir!"

"Göbeler, get us some coffee, and HURRY!"

Having an off-duty crewman's all-too-precious sleep interrupted for such a trivial matter seemed incomprehensible to me. *Kapitänleutnant* Löwe would never have tolerated such a self-defeating abuse of authority by one of his officers. By this time, though, we were well accustomed to such treatment by this new group. I ran down to the little corner that served as the galley for our boat and told my friend Toni to make some fresh coffee for Bode. Toni had sensed that Bode was in one of his moods and already had some water boiling. Within a few minutes, I was making my way back to the bridge with some cups and a pot of hot, fresh coffee.

It was quite a trick to get up the two ladders to the bridge with the coffeepot and cups in my hand, but I managed to do so without dropping anything. I reported to Bode and filled the cups with the hot aromatic brew (naturally, the Exec got his cup first). Everything seemed satisfactory, so I began climbing back down the ladder to the control room.

Suddenly, I felt the searing pain of scalding liquid being poured on my head from above. Bode had emptied his cup of newly boiled coffee on me and was now screaming for me to report back to the bridge. Within seconds, I was back on the bridge, rigidly at attention but shaking uncontrollably from the shock and pain.

"You idiot, can't you pay attention? I said fresh coffee, not this stinking bilge water. Get down there and make me some real coffee, immediately!"

"*Jawohl, Herr Oberleutnant!*"

I ran back down to the galley where Toni, having heard every word, was preparing another pot of fresh coffee. While it brewed, Toni warned me not to let Bode make me lose my temper, as any disrespect to an officer would be severely punished—no matter what the provocation. A few moments later, I received another order from the bridge to hurry with the cup of coffee.

"Here, give that asshole his cup of coffee," said Toni, pouring me another cup.

I hurried up to the bridge, holding the cup with one hand and trying to grasp the rails of the ladder with the other. Unfortunately, while climbing one of the ladders, a bit of the coffee spilled out of the cup. When I reported to Bode, he looked at the cup and once again exploded into anger.

"I gave the order for one cup . . . one FULL cup! Rush down there and get me another one, this time filled to the top. HURRY!"

The other members of the watch just stood there, frozen in fear and wide-eyed disbelief. Once again I ran down to the galley for more coffee.

My buddy Toni gave me a conspiratorial look and whispered to me, "This is what you have to do, Hans. Fill your mouth with coffee until you are on the last couple of steps of the ladder. Then spit enough coffee back into the cup until it is filled right up to the top. You'll see how he likes that cup of 'fresh' coffee!"

So, up I went for the third time. Once again, a bit sloshed out of the cup as I climbed up the ladder, but I refilled the cup exactly as Toni had instructed me to. Sure enough, Bode was satisfied with this cup, asking me why I didn't do it right like this the first time.

I had to get off the bridge as quickly as possible to avoid breaking out in laughter. I stopped by the galley to thank Toni for his advice and then went directly to my bunk. The Exec's fun and games had cost me an hour of precious sleep, but at least I had gotten the last laugh.

*   *   *

We had still not found any enemy ships as the month of October came to a close. Our only neighbors in the empty ocean were some friendly dolphins who danced and jumped along side our boat like little children playing next to their mother's skirt.

Once we encountered a gigantic school of flying fish. Hundreds of them would leap simultaneously into the air, sailing for 50 or even 100 meters at a time. Then, as if on signal, they would all dive back into the water, disappearing back under the blue-green waves. Some of the more superstitious among our crew took it to be a good omen, claiming we would always be able to dive in time to escape danger.

Conditions within the boat were getting unbearable. The heat was unrelenting. Constant drills and training exercises ordered by *Kapitänleutnant* Zschech made the crew's mood barometer drop below zero. The total lack of enemy merchant traffic only exacerbated our frustrations. The only comic relief from this routine was a visit from the Radio Petty Officer who, doubling as our boat's medic, appeared in the control room one afternoon holding a crew roster and a big magnifying glass. He was on the hunt for the little pests we called "Luftwaffe Antelopes." One by one, he called our names and we dropped our pants so he could have a close look below our belt line for any tiny hitchhikers that may have jumped aboard our bodies after a rendezvous with a *Mademoiselle*. Despite our infrequent opportunities to bathe at sea, most of us were pronounced clean and shipshape. Those sailors found to be infested were treated with medicine by the medic, and given a good teasing by the rest of us.

Unfortunately, there were other health concerns aboard the boat. Heat and exposure to diesel fumes had affected the engine room crew, as well as all the men assigned to the aft crew quarters. Their eyelids had turned red from the fumes and many were suffering from infections. Despite these problems, Zschech would not diverge from his strict policy of allowing only two men at a time to get fresh air topside.

On November 1, we received orders from U-boat Headquarters to move towards Trinidad via Barbados. It was hoped this new operational area would put us in the middle of some enemy naval traffic. The only traffic we encountered, however, was air traffic. We were repeatedly forced to dive as the *Metox* device gave us warning of approaching Allied planes.

I spent most of my free time with my nose buried in an English language textbook, repeating word definitions and grammar. Many of my boat mates asked me why I was studying English.

"They are the ones who will have to learn German!" they said.

I was sure they were right. But, I thought, it is always good to know more than one language—even though we would win the war.

*   *   *

Around midnight on November 7, we were shaken from our slumber by a sudden increase in the hammering roar of our Jumbos. Running the diesels at such high RPMs meant only one thing: we were chasing a target! We jumped into action without waiting for the klaxon to ring.

It was exciting to feel our boat running at top speed again. The bow heaved upwards by the crests of the long, rolling waves, then crashed downwards into the deep troughs. The diesels' thirst for air was pulling in a cool, stiff breeze throughout the length of the boat. The combination of the ear-splitting noise, violent bucking of the bow, and sudden gust of clean fresh air thrilled us all to our very souls. We were finally on the hunt again!

Alfred Reinig, our Chief Navigator, went topside to get a fix on our position by "shooting the stars" with his sextant. I was asked to assist him. He would shout out the names of the various stars and I would record the minutes and seconds for him to calculate. That was one thing about being assigned to the control room of a U-boat: you always had a variety of tasks to perform, from the most interesting to the most mundane.

We raced on the surface like that for nearly an hour until we heard the command to take our battle stations. Another suspense-filled hour passed before we heard the orders to ready the torpedo tubes.

"Target position ninety degrees, speed 11 knots. Distance 1,500 meters. Torpedoes ready to fire. . . . Torpedoes in tubes one and two . . . Ready . . . FIRE!"

The stopwatch ticked off the seconds as we all held our breaths. After an adequate number of seconds had passed, I moved over to where I could see Zschech through the hatch to the conning tower. His face had turned red and he was hissing something under his breath. I couldn't understand exactly what he had said, but I knew what it meant: the torpedoes had missed. We found out later that he had misjudged the speed of the target by a wide margin.

Zschech barked a command to the engine room and once again our boat was filled with the roar of the diesels. The target had increased the distance between us; our last chance to score a hit would literally be a long shot . . . 2,000 meters.

At exactly 0400 Hours, tubes three and four unleashed their long black eels. The sound man reported torpedoes running hot and true. The 2,000 meter range of the shots made the countdown until expected impact seem to last forever. First one minute, then two minutes ticked by. Two minutes 33 seconds . . . 34 . . . 35 . . . 36 . . . 37 . . . then, a metallic clang followed immediately by a loud explosion. Four seconds later, another rumbling detonation. The first torpedo had struck the ship directly amidships, sending a geyser of water shooting up as high as the mast. The second torpedo hit between the bridge and the funnel: a perfect spread.

Despite the darkness of the night, we saw no flash of explosions or fires. From lights on the deck of the ship, however, we saw lifeboats being lowered. The bow of the ship settled quickly, causing the stern to rise high into the air. After a moment's hesitation, she slipped forward underneath the waves. Within two minutes, the entire drama was over.

Although we did not detect any radio broadcasts emanating from the stricken ship, Zschech ordered us away from the site without checking on the condition of the survivors. That unsettled me. We all knew how, in the past, enemy propaganda had tarnished the reputation of the German U-boat service. Under *Kapitänleutnant* Löwe, we had done all we could to adhere to the rules of war and common decency. Now, however, under *Kapitänleutnant* Zschech, I felt that we were acting like the heartless hunters the enemy propagandists portrayed us to be. Those were human beings floating in that water, no matter what flag they sailed under. As long as it didn't endanger our own survival, why not render aid to them out of sheer humanity?

Others in our crew disagreed with me. They pointed out that the British had routinely allowed German sailors to drown after sinking our ships in the North Atlantic. The many hundreds of our boys who were purposely left to freeze in the water after the *Bismark* sank was a perfect example of this. Even plainly marked hospital ships and sea rescue craft were fair game to the RAF and Royal Navy. Some of our crew argued forcefully that it would only be fair if we did the same to them. But I wanted to believe that we were fighting this war with more honor than the Brits, and I knew many other men in our crew believed the same way I did. However, no one dared make his opinion known to *Kapitänleutnant* Zschech. We all knew how he reacted whenever someone compared him to our old skipper.

Many years after the war, I found out that the ship we had sent to the bottom was the 7,173-ton *Ocean Justice*. To this day I don't know if it would have mattered if we had rendered aid to the survivors, but I still wish we had.

The memory of the *Ocean Justice* incident came back to me stronger than ever when, just a couple of years ago, I had the opportunity to scuba-dive down to the shipwreck of a vessel sunk by another U-boat just off the coast of Key Largo, Florida. When I saw the big hole in her hull where the torpedo hit, it gave me a very bad feeling. The unknown fate of those poor men on the *Ocean Justice* leapt back into my mind.[1]

In the end, however, Zschech's indifference to life caught up with him, and he faced his own self-imposed form of "ocean justice."

1. *Ocean Justice* was a British steam freighter built in 1942. When she was torpedoed, she was running from Karachi & Durban for Trinidad & New York. There were 56 men aboard, and all were saved. See www.ubootwaffe.net for more details.

Chapter 6

Sillcock

We spent the following night reloading the forward torpedo tubes. This operation was always a difficult one due to the cramped space in the torpedo rooms. The massive 21-inch diameter weapons had to be hoisted up from their tie-down racks and slid forward into the launching tubes. The procedure is easier when the bow is pointed downwards, at least for the forward tubes, so we trimmed the boat to allow gravity to accommodate the process. None of the off-duty crew slept much that night because they had to constantly hold on to their bunks, lest they slide off and land on the floor. The guys who slept in the forward torpedo room couldn't even lay down because their bunks had to be folded up out of the way to allow the torpedoes to be moved forward.

The next afternoon, our bridge watch spotted a smoke plume to the east. We immediately gave chase, but frequent air alarms greatly hindered our pursuit. The enemy must have known we were in the area because the furiously zig-zagging freighter was circled overhead by a continuous air patrol. Finally, after sundown, the buzzards were compelled to return to base. It was now or never. We fired a double salvo of torpedoes, but a fortuitous "zag" taken by the ship at the exact wrong moment caused both to miss. Our prey, speeding along at more than twelve knots, disappeared into the darkness.

We spent another couple of hours during the night once again reloading the empty torpedo tubes. There was also a dangerous leak in the port ballast tank valve that needed to be repaired. And if that wasn't enough, we were repeatedly forced to dive because of air alerts. It was obvious the enemy's airborne radar was now effective enough to deny us our traditional cover of night. The swarm of enemy planes over our heads was so heavy that when running on the surface, we ourselves were forced to steer a zig-zag course in order to lessen the chance of a surprise bomb hit from the air. It was embarrassing to have to zig-zag like a scared little freighter, but better safe than sorry.

Looking back with the advantage of hindsight, it is clear that the Allies were aware of our every move. We didn't fully realize it at the time, but the entire tide of the war in the Atlantic had turned decisively against our U-boats. First of all, the build-up of enemy air forces had made our previous tactics totally ineffective. Gone were the days when we could maneuver primarily on the surface and dive only when conducting an attack or escaping. The *Metox* device still warned us in time to avoid most air attacks, but once we were forced underwater, our speed was insufficient to catch all but the slowest of ships. By forcing us to remain submerged, the Allies had turned our U-boats into little more than slow-moving minefields; dangerous to their ships only if they happened to blunder across our path. Given the enemy's elaborate radio direction finding efforts, it was easy for the Allies to re-route their convoys around us. Once the convoys were safe, the bombers and destroyers would descend upon us like packs of jackals.

As important as the technological race was, however, it wasn't the only factor. Once the Allies cracked our top secret *Enigma* cipher system, they were able to read almost every communication between our boats and headquarters. Another important factor, which we didn't learn about until after long the war, was the treachery of Admiral Canaris, the head of our nation's military intelligence service. Canaris, one of the greatest traitors of WWII, was responsible for sending many of our comrades to their deaths. Today, I harbor no animosity for our former enemies (the British and Americans), but I can never forgive Canaris for his bloody-handed betrayal of his fellow countrymen.

With knowledge of our operational orders, combined with their burgeoning numbers, the enemy gradually moved from the strategic defense to the strategic offense in the Battle of the Atlantic. Our massed wolfpack attacks against enemy convoys, which should have reaped us tremendous harvests of tonnage, became instead opportunities for the enemy to overwhelm and sink our boats. Of course, we had no way of knowing any of this at the time, but one thing was crystal clear: the "Happy Time" for Germany's U-boats was over.

*   *   *

Our experience in *U-505* was mirroring the wider strategic picture. Because of the intense air activity over our heads, *Kapitänleutnant* Zschech decided to flee from the area as quickly as feasible. As soon as repairs on our ballast tank were complete, we attempted to make a run for it. We didn't get far. Virtually every time we surfaced to use our diesels, the *Metox* device would sound the alarm that a radar-equipped enemy plane was stalking us. All day long we played the old roller coaster game of surfacing to run the diesels and recharge batteries, only to find that we must once again dive to escape air attack. In this regard, the *Metox* was proving to be a mixed blessing. True, it protected us from surprise, but because the mechanism was unable to measure the distance of enemy signals, we could not distinguish between attacking aircraft from those merely passing by at long range. As a result, every enemy radar contact forced us to emergency dive. The constant alarms jangled our nerves, exhausted our bodies, and prevented our boat from fully replenishing our air supply and recharging our battery power.

During this period, on the night of November 9th to be specific, I was on duty in the control room of *U-505*, bemoaning the fact that the air alerts had once again robbed me of my chance to eat supper. At exactly midnight, our Chief Navigator Alfred Reinig crawled through the control room hatch and walked over to my station. He stopped in front of me, grabbed my hand, and began shaking it vigorously.

"Congratulations, Hans! Today you are nineteen, right?"

I had forgotten it was my birthday! "*Jawohl, Herr Obersteuermann,*" I stammered.

"Come on, Hans, stop calling me Chief! Especially since we've been working so well together for the past year. Besides, who knows where we will be in another year."

With a broad smile and a pat on my back, Reinig retreated back through the hatch to his bunk. I wished he had never reminded me about my birthday. Homesickness washed over me like a big green ocean wave. The calendar might say that I was a year older, but I felt more childlike and lonely at that moment than at any time in my life.

Another *Metox* alarm shook me from my reverie. I wanted to scream, laugh, and cry, all at the same time. Eventually, anger won out. I sat at my station, sullenly going through the diving operations, blaming the British for robbing us of our chance to enjoy a normal life.

To my great annoyance, word soon spread throughout the boat that it was my birthday. More backslaps and handshakes. My birthday present from the officers on this special day was permission to stand watch on the bridge for an hour to get some fresh air. My friend Toni found a bottle of *Beck*'s beer, which had "mistakenly" been loaded with the ship's galley stores. We shared it together. I was grateful for such good friends, but I couldn't stop thinking about what the navigator had said: "Who knows where we will be in another year."

*   *   *

The uninterrupted cycle of surfacing to recharge batteries, only to immediately dive again to escape an attack from the air, continued throughout the next day. In desperation, Zschech resorted to a full-speed underwater run in an attempt to shake loose from our airborne tormentors.

Around noon we finally got a break from the buzzards and were able to surface without molestation. To the west was the coast of Trinidad, so close we could smell the sweet, spicy fragrance of tropical flowers in bloom. Above us, a thick layer of clouds obscured the sun, bathing us in cool shadows. The gorgeous turquoise water gently lapped against our hull. It was the quiet before the storm.

Second Watch Officer Stolzenburg, standing watch on the bridge with the skipper, was worried. It was suspicious enough that the swarm of enemy airplanes, which had been so numerous the previous day, had mysteriously disappeared. What made it worse was the blanket of dark gray clouds, so low they seemed to be scraping the top of his cap. Conditions like these were what *Kapitänleutnant* Löwe used to call "perfect air attack weather." Zschech had been even grouchier than usual these past few days, but Stolzenburg could not restrain himself any longer. Something in the back of his head told him we were in danger.

"Sir, may I suggest that we double the bridge watch in order to guard against surprise air attack?"

Zschech turned to the Watch Officer and gave him a disdainful smirk. "No need to get nervous, Stolzenburg, the *Metox* will give us ample warning of any planes."

Despite the icy sarcasm in Zschech's voice, Stolzenburg wasn't ready to give up. "Sir, don't you think we should at least trim down the boat so we can make an alarm dive quicker? *Kapitänleutnant* Löwe used to say . . ."

At the mere mention of our previous skipper's name, Zschech exploded into one of his famous rages, reminding the stunned Watch Officer at the top of his voice (as if any of us needed reminding) that HE was the skipper now, not Löwe. Satisfied he had reasserted his authority over his inferior, Zschech swaggered off the bridge and returned to his cabin. Within minutes, gossip regarding Zschech's latest temper tantrum was making its rounds throughout the boat. I was on duty in the control room and I spent the next couple of hours trying not to draw attention from any of the officers. They had picked up on the *Kapitänleutnant*'s mood and were trying to imitate it in order to stay out of trouble themselves.

Things remained quiet until about 1514 hours, when suddenly the siren for manning the anti-aircraft guns began to blare. Almost simultaneously, the shrill alarm signaling an emergency dive sounded. We all looked at each other in puzzlement because the orders were contradictory: how could we man the deck guns while at the same time submerge?

Just a few heartbeats later, before we had sorted-out the situation, we heard the unmistakable roar of aircraft engines resonating through the hull of our boat. I unconsciously ducked my head at the sound, instinctively aware of how close the aircraft must be for us to hear its engines above the hammering of our own diesels. Suddenly, a deafening blast, a thousand times louder than a thunderclap, knocked us off our feet. It felt as if a giant fist had slammed the boat down into the water.

A split-second later three more explosions ripped through the air—even louder than the first. Our boat's steel hull rang like a cathedral bell from the concussions. This time the shock waves pushed our boat upward, sending anyone still standing after the first blast sailing through the air.

One of the men who was standing watch on the bridge, a Petty Officer, was blown by the force of the first blast through the top hatch and down into the conning tower. The second set of blasts rolled his bloody, unconscious body down through the control room hatch, where he fell and landed on his head on the steel deck in front of me.

Inside the boat there was pure pandemonium. The lights had gone out and the air was suddenly filled with thick acrid smoke. When the emergency lights finally came on, it unveiled a scene straight from Dante's *Inferno*, complete with screams and burning noxious fumes. Shouts from the aft end of the boat told us that there was a large breach in the hull. A thick jet of seawater was pouring into the boat, filling the diesel bilge and flooding the engine room. Someone reported that the depth meter indicated that water was weighing the boat down. Translation: we were sinking!

I cannot possibly begin to describe what it was like inside the boat at that moment. Nor can I describe my emotional state. Never in my life had I felt such an irresistible urge to escape—to climb, crawl, and if need be, claw my way up the conning tower ladder to the sun and fresh air of the surface. Something, however, held me back, and I refused to succumb to the animalistic desire within to run. Perhaps it was my training or professional pride. Or perhaps it was just a childish fear of being called a coward. Whatever it was, I somehow overcame the primal desire to escape. Despite our desperate situation, a steely determination to do our duty and fight to save our boat quickly spread unspoken from crewman to crewman. None of us deserted our post.

Not everyone, however, was so determined to stay on board. *Kapitänleutnant* Zschech came running through the control room and clamored up the ladders to the bridge. What he saw must have really scared him because after just a moment topside, he shouted down to the control room the order to abandon ship. We all froze at our posts, unable or unwilling to obey the order.

But when the command to abandon ship reached the next compartment, our Diesel Chief Petty Officer Otto Fricke stormed like a mad bull into the control room. With anger and defiance in his voice, he shouted up to Zschech, "Well, you can do what you want, but the technical crew is staying on board to keep her afloat!"

With a scowl of disgust, Fricke turned around and ran back to the engine room to take command of the damage control effort. The

This photo (and the one that follows on the next page) shows the nearly fatal damage suffered by *U-505* when a Hudson aircraft from Trinidad's RAF 53 Squadron descended from the clouds and dropped a depth charge directly on the boat's aft deck on November 10, 1942. The explosion brought down the low-flying plane, killed its crew, and nearly sank *U-505*. NA

expression on Zschech's face gradually turned from fear to confusion, and then to embarrassment. "All right then, do what you can," he murmured, long after the Chief had left the compartment.

Within a few minutes, the engineering crew had plugged the hole in the hull with a rubber sheet, shored against the water pressure with a long piece of timber. Luckily, the main pump was still working, so despite numerous leaks all along the length of the port diesel engine, the water gradually stopped rising in the engine room. By switching the air supply for the starboard diesel to the interior of the boat, Fricke was able to suck the suffocating smoke out of the boat. We all thanked heaven for our clever Chief and his brave boys in the engineering crew.

With the most immediate danger averted, we were finally able to take a look topside. We couldn't believe the sight that greeted us. Now we realized why Zschech had given the order to abandon ship: our boat had been nearly blown in two by the surprise air attack! The wooden planks of the upper deck aft of the conning tower looked as if a bulldozer had plowed across them. In the center of the damage, an enormous hole gaped half way across the entire topside hull of the boat, exposing a jumble of smashed and broken equipment below. Our 37mm anti-aircraft gun had been blown completely overboard by the force of the blasts, its mounting bolts sheered off as cleanly as if cut by a razor. Fully half of the steel side plates of the conning tower were either gone or hanging limply, clanging against each other in time with the gentle rocking of the waves. One depth charge (or bomb, at that point we weren't sure which) had exploded on the pressurized tubes where the spare torpedoes were stored, completely destroying one of the torpedoes except for the warhead section. If that torpedo warhead had gone off, none of us would have survived.

Despite the enormous damage to the conning tower, *Leutnant* (Ensign) Stolzenburg and the other two men standing watch on the bridge were still alive. They were laying unconscious on the bridge deck, drenched in seawater and their own blood. Stolzenburg was badly wounded and bleeding heavily from shrapnel wounds in his head and back.

The center of the gaping hole (above) once held the 3.7cm cannon, which was blown overboard. Its sturdy mount absorbed the killing force of the blast that would have otherwise sunk *U-505*. The crew worked tirelessly to enable the boat to dive to shallow depths for the trip home. NA

The mystery of why we had not suffered another bombing attack was obvious: floating just 30 meters off our starboard bow was the scattered wreckage of a large enemy aircraft. The mutilated body of one of its crewmen was sprawled lifelessly across the fragment of a wing. After a few moments the wing sank, taking the man's body down with it. The aircraft had been destroyed by the blast of its own depth charges! We didn't have time to think about the death of the enemy flier or our good fortune; we were much too busy fighting to keep ourselves afloat!

Only many years after the attack did I discover exactly what happened to us that day. According to Gaylord Kelshall's excellent book *The U-boat War in the Caribbean*, the aircraft that attacked us was a Lockheed Hudson, number PZ/L, one of the big two-engined bombers the British Coastal Command operated out of Trinidad's Edinburgh airfield on anti-submarine patrols. The pilot of the aircraft was Flight Sergeant Ronald Sillcock, a veteran Australian aviator generally regarded as the top submarine hunter in #53 Squadron.

Sillcock and his seasoned multinational aircrew had already scored hits against two other U-boats in recent weeks. In one attack, he heavily damaged *Kapitänleutnant* Piening's *U-155* off the coast of Martinique. Just a few days later, Sillcock once again demonstrated his superb bombing accuracy by attacking and nearly sinking Schweichel's *U-173*. It was said that Sillcock, using the Hudson's unique depth charge spreading device to maximum effectiveness, had never missed a target.

The Flight Sergeant's fabulous success was based on a bombing tactic he personally developed, one that neatly turned our increasing reliance on the *Metox* radar warning device to his advantage. Over the course of several days, the crafty Sillcock would repeatedly patrol the suspected location of a U-boat using his ASV airborne search radar turned on, pinpointing the sub's position, but not attacking. This lulled the sub into a false sense of security by leading it to believe that its *Metox* would be 100% reliable in warning of any plane in the vicinity. Then, when cloudy conditions limited the ability of German lookouts to spot the approach of his aircraft, Sillcock would patrol the boat's location with his radar turned off. Once his lookouts had visually spotted the U-boat, Sillcock would dive out of the sun with his engines feathered, silently and invisibly gliding down towards his target like a giant hawk. At the last minute, he would turn his engines on again, drop his bomb load, and pull out of the dive.

Sadly for Sillcock and his crew, this time his aim was too perfect. The direct hit on our aft deck directed the force of the depth charge's blast upward, blowing his aircraft to pieces. His tactics had worked perfectly, but the sub-hunting ace became a victim of his own skill.

* * *

During the course of our repair efforts on *U-505*, we found several pieces of bright yellow Duraluminum from Sillcock's aircraft scattered on our deck. Later, our machinist used the scrap metal to make little axes (our boat's symbol ever since our days under *Kapitänleutnant* Löwe) for us crewmen to affix to our caps. This was in no way a demonstration of disrespect for the crew of the aircraft that had nearly killed us. Like so many men during World War II, they had to pay with their lives for doing their duty for their country. We respected them for that, and indeed, were filled with great admiration for their skill and courage.

In 1998, I visited Trinidad and placed flowers at a U-boat memorial there, not only in memory of my fallen comrades in the U-boat service, but also for the brave and able crew of that Hudson. Every year since our encounter with Sillcock, I celebrate my birthday on two days: on my true birthday, and on the anniversary of the day that we so miraculously escaped death at the hands of the courageous Flight Sergeant.

And the little yellow aluminum ax made from Sillcock's plane? I still have it, as a talisman of luck and remembrance.

Chapter 7

The Long Way Home

ith the gaping hole in *U-505*'s hull sealed with nothing more substantial than a rubber bladder, our boat was totally incapable of diving to escape another air attack. We were also virtually defenseless. Our 37mm anti-aircraft gun had been blown overboard, leaving us with only one puny 20mm single-barreled machine gun for air defense. To make matters worse, the sea was absolutely calm, with no white caps to hide our wake. We were also trailing an enormous oil slick from a ruptured fuel bunker. That was especially dangerous, for enemy planes could use it to find us much as hunters follow the blood trail of a wounded animal.

Luckily for us, Sillcock maintained radio silence before his attack in order to mask his presence, and the blasts from his own depth charges ended any chance he had of contacting his base after the attack. That gave us a tiny window of opportunity to escape before the British sent more patrols to the area. We were also lucky because the cloudy weather persisted. King Neptune was evidently looking out for old *U-505*, because the enemy did not spot us during our period of maximum vulnerability.

We spent the next 18 hours plowing as fast as we could through the calm blue-green waters using our one remaining diesel engine, all the while working as feverishly as bees on our repairs. The more we surveyed the damage on our boat, the more we realized how lucky we were to still be alive.

The most immediate problem was patching the hole in our pressure hull. To do that, we needed lots of steel plating. That turned out not to be a problem because the shattered deck and conning tower plates provided all the scrap metal we needed. Some members of the control room crew and I were assigned to clear away the damage on the deck. We spent the next few hours cutting away the bent and torn plates with an acetylene torch. Then, by heating the pieces with the torch and banging away like crazy with sledgehammers, we were able to form the metal into an approximation of the required shapes. With power generated by one of the electric motors, we then arc-welded the steel patches onto the damaged hull. We also tried to repair the ruptured fuel tank, but despite our best efforts, we continued to trail a wide, rainbow-colored oil slick.

Once the larger pieces of deck debris were cleared away, we found that the special steel alloy pressure hull, though punctured and deeply dented by the depth charge concussions, was largely intact. That meant that, theoretically at least, we might eventually be able to dive again. But before we could even consider a dive, dozens of water and air lines which had been smashed flat by the blasts would have to be repaired or replaced. One of the giant mufflers for the diesels also needed to be remounted, and there were many jammed water intakes and exhaust valves that had to be freed. Nevertheless, we tackled each task with a determination borne of desperation. As each problem was solved, optimism grew that we might be able to make it home after all.

We worked like coolies day and night to get our boat back into action. Without proper tools, the work was often frustrating and always back-breakingly hard. But as dawn broke on the 10th, the Chief Engineer felt confident enough to report to Zschech that we could attempt a very shallow test dive. Word of the test dive electrified us all.

The diesel was shut down and we coasted to a stop. The sudden silence accentuated the seriousness of our predicament and multiplied our anxiety. We all knew what was at stake: the failure of one small plate or valve could send us on a one-way trip to the bottom.

The diving alarm rang and startled us with its unaccustomed loudness. The suspense became excruciating as we listened to the gurgling water slowly, very slowly, being let into the diving tanks.

Gradually, only 50 liters at a time, the tanks filled. With each tiny addition of weight, our boat sank lower and lower into the water.

After what seemed an eternity, we heard the announcement we had been waiting for: "Hatch to the bridge is under water."

We had done it! There was still some leaking along the length of the port diesel and around some of our amateurish repairs, but in general everything held together. We all cheered like soccer fans.

But the test wasn't finished. Although we were technically underwater, the top of our conning tower was only a few inches deep and would be plainly visible to any airplane flying overhead. To survive the trip across the Atlantic, especially the heavily patrolled stretch through the Bay of Biscay, we would have to submerge to a depth of at least 35 meters. The skipper gave us the order, "Control room to all compartments: Watch closely for any leaks. All right, then . . . more water!"

Several minutes more ticked by as we sank to periscope depth. Luckily, the front periscope had been shielded from the worst of the bomb blasts by the rear scope and was still partly operational. Zschech used it to take a peek toward the stern. He saw that our boat was still leaking fuel badly, but at least there were no large air leaks to be seen.

We heard the electric motors start to hum and our boat began to slowly crawl forward. As we gained additional depth, some of the plates began to creak and groan. We control room operators exchanged worried glances, but no one said a word. The needle on our damaged depth meter began to vibrate, but it gradually settled down as we neared the 35-meter point. Finally, we leveled off and sat at the desired depth. Our wild exultation was mixed with tears of joy.

We should have expected it, but it still came as a surprise when, at the very moment of our triumph, Zschech and the exec's moods soured. Zschech was pouting because he would be returning from his first war patrol with only one victory pennant flying from the periscope. The Exec was angry that he would have to stand more bridge watches now that poor Stolzenburg was unable to report for duty. Predictably, their depression translated into more torment of us crew members. No matter, they could not dampen our spirits. We had survived the worst the Brits could throw at us and had still stayed afloat. We were proud of ourselves, even if our commanding officer was not.

We stayed underwater during the daylight hours, cruising along at our new maximum depth of 40 meters. We needed to get as far away as possible from the site of Sillcock's attack because we knew his friends would be looking for him—and us. Through the periscope, Zschech could still see a huge oil slick trailing behind us, but there was nothing we could do about that except pray no enemy planes spotted it. The sky remained dark with heavy layers of charcoal gray clouds.

Just after midnight, we surfaced to send a *FT* to U-boat Headquarters describing our situation and giving them a list of our most critical needs. We also requested emergency medical help for our wounded comrades, all three of whom seemed to be on the verge of death. A couple of hours later, we received a reply from Dönitz's Headquarters. Unfortunately, we were told, there were only a couple of U-boats currently operating in the Caribbean with doctors on board. A rendezvous with the nearest one, Engelmann's *U-163*, was ruled out because they themselves had just been heavily damaged by an air attack. Vowe's "Milk Cow" supply submarine *U-462* was also ruled out because of intense air activity in the area. Eventually, U-boat Command directed us to Sea Square EE6680 to meet with Schuch's *U-154*. Schuch's boat didn't have a doctor aboard, but they might be able to give us some assistance.

Headquarters also transmitted some medical advice concerning the care of our wounded: keep them cool and give them good food. Those were things we all could have used! Unfortunately, it was beyond our capability to provide these things to anyone, including our badly injured comrades.

At 1820 hours on November 13, we caught sight of *U-154*. Not only did they not have a doctor aboard, they were also unable to give us any spare parts for our damaged diesel. All we got were 20 ampules of morphine which, for a while at least, provided some relief to the wounded. An hour later, Schuch's boat disappeared into the darkness. Once again, we were on our own.

The morphine, which made the entire boat smell like a hospital, didn't last long. The medicinal stench was soon replaced once again with the unnerving animal-like moaning of our injured comrades. Meanwhile, we were doing some moaning and groaning of our own because of the unending repair work. The most exhausting duty I was assigned to was the removal of some of the damaged spare torpedoes from the pressurized storage tubes located under the upper deck planks. Virtually every torpedo had been damaged. One had been completely blown in half. Others had hundreds of tiny holes and cracks in their bodies caused by flying shrapnel. Sometimes the damage was just inches away from their warheads, each of which contained over 600 pounds of explosive. One by one, the long, unwieldy monsters had to be hoisted out of the storage tubes with block and tackle, then thrown overboard. It was backbreaking, dangerous work that took several days to complete.

Adding insult to injury, Zschech and his bosom buddy Bode continued their abusive behavior toward us. But we crewmen were happy to discover that during this time of emergency, each one of us had particular talents and skills that we could apply to our tasks. As each assignment was completed, we felt prouder and prouder of ourselves. It was as if we were fighting four enemies: the sea, the British, the damaged machinery, and our own officers . . . and we were beating them all! We couldn't help but remind ourselves that U-boat crews were considered the elite of our navy, and through our actions in this emergency, that we were proving ourselves worthy of that reputation. With all we had gone through, we began to think that even within this elite service, we were demonstrating that we were an above average crew.

Of course, all of this remained unspoken. A braggart would have immediately been put in his place. The slogan that made its way around the boat was, "*Alles kleine Fische.*" Literally, it meant, "It's only small fish." The meaning to us was that all the hardships we were experiencing meant nothing in the bigger picture. So stop dreaming, buddy, and let's get back to work so we can bring this boat back home!

*   *   *

A little after midnight on the 14th, we surfaced to send another *FT* to U-boat Headquarters. A few minutes later, we happened to intercept a message from *Kapitänleutnant* Schuch's *U-154* to Headquarters. Schuch reported that soon after departing from our rendezvous the previous day, they had sunk two big freighters in the area.

Spurred by *U-154*'s success, Zschech decided to try to add a few victory pennants to our periscope before returning to base. We considered this decision to be extremely reckless. But when we heard he was planning to sail us into the middle of Trinidad harbor in broad daylight, we thought he had literally gone insane. Even the outer approaches to the harbor were well guarded. Beacon fires burned brightly all along the South American coastline, and a large searchlight positioned at the mouth of Trinidad harbor constantly scanned the seas. The presence of coastal radar was accepted as a given. Even a sub in perfect condition would be tempting the fates with such boldness, but in our crippled condition, we considered it tantamount to suicide.

Nevertheless, we followed the skipper's orders without hesitation and steered a course directly up the shipping channel towards Trinidad's harbor mouth. Before long, the boys with the big binoculars on the bridge spotted a smoke plume zig-zagging towards us at high speed.

Several men and I were still on the upper deck making last-minute repairs when we heard Zschech's command, *"Einsteigen! Auf Gefechtsstationen!"* (Everyone inside! Battle stations!). We scurried about, frantically collecting tools before jumping down the hatch to our duty stations.

The target was a big freighter. Would the goddess of war really reward Zschech's audacity? We lined up for the attack and fired two torpedoes at medium range. Both missed by wide margins because, once again, the skipper had misjudged the target's speed. Zschech's face turned red with frustration and anger. Naturally, he blamed someone else for a mistake that could only have been his. The Exec comforted his friend with his usual degree of tenderness and intimacy. We turned our heads away in embarrassment and distaste.

We crewmen were in no mood to share in the Exec's pity for our commander. Zschech's blood fever had put us at great risk in return for a very small chance of success. We grumbled to each other that instead of sticking our head in the tiger's mouth, we should be putting as much distance between Trinidad and us as possible. We wanted a bold skipper, but one who also had some common sense. After all, we had wounded to tend and repairs to make. Why risk everything on a crazy move like that? Resentment continued to simmer inside us.

The enemy immediately detected our presence and sent the full force of their air power against us. We had no choice now but to reverse course and made a run for it. We had narrow escapes from five separate air attacks before we finally shook free of the Trinidad hornet's nest. It was a miracle we made it out of those shallow waters alive. Luckily for us, the weather started getting rough once the sun set, grounding the enemy planes.

Once we were safely out in open sea, we attempted a quick sprint using our diesel. But as luck would have it, the big rolling waves were crashing against our damaged port side. One particularly large wave knocked one of the remaining torpedo storage tubes loose. With every swell, it would swing back and forth, smashing against the diesel exhaust pipe. The storage tube was still loaded with a live torpedo, and if it detonated, we would be finished in an instant. All off-duty personnel were assigned the task of lashing down the loose canister. Unfortunately, the loading rails beneath the torpedo were crushed and we had no tools to properly deal with the situation. Meanwhile, the weather worsened. The waves, now towering, cresting breakers, kept snapping the tie-downs we were using to secure the canister. Every time the ties broke, the canister swung out a bit more, causing even more damage when it swung back inboard.

Everyone was mad as hell at Zschech. We wouldn't have been caught in that storm if we hadn't wasted all that time in the harbor. Fortunately for us, the sound of the crashing waves and pounding metal prevented the Exec from hearing our curses. In the end, we had to lift the 3,400-pound torpedo out by hand and drop it overboard. It took us twelve hours to finally get rid of the damned thing. We thanked God that no one was crushed or thrown overboard during the storm.

We stumbled like sleepwalkers toward our bunks. Our voices were hoarse from shouting over the roar of the surf, and our hair was as stiff as straw with wind-blown salt. Most of us also had deep lacerations on our hands from the sharp edges of torn metal. But as every sailor knows, the sea gives in equal measure to what she takes. The salt water acted as a sort of natural first aid, helping to stop the bleeding and close the wounds. The cuts itched like crazy, but they healed quickly.

A bit after midnight, we received a message from Headquarters directing us to rendezvous in Sea Square EH6555 with two other U-boats. Zschech radioed back with a detailed description of our boat's condition. It was staggering to hear the complete catalog of damage we had sustained.

A few hours later, we got the official order to end our operational patrol and return to base after the rendezvous. We crew members were enormously relieved to hear the news. This for sure, we thought, would put an end to Zschech's reckless attempts to sink another enemy ship.

The consensus of our feelings: get *U-505* back to Lorient, put her back into shape, then have another go at the enemy.

As day broke on the 17th, we were told another damaged torpedo had to be thrown overboard. Like zombies, we clambered up the ladder to the upper deck to once again hand-wrestle one of the giant "eels" out of its storage tube. This one's warhead was heavily damaged, adding an additional worry to the exercise.

"Watch out, boys, that beast is as dangerous as a big shark!" yelled the crew chief over the thunder of the pounding waves.

It took every single ounce of our physical and spiritual strength, but by timing our efforts with the heave of the waves, we were finally able to slide the torpedo off the stern of the boat.

That night we crawled into our bunks thinking that for the first time in three days, the off-watch crew would get some sleep. For a few hours we reposed in the sleep of the dead. Then, suddenly, someone began shouting in our ears to get up. I remember blindly following the sailor in front of me towards the ladder to the bridge, more asleep than awake. Then Neptune gave us a wet welcome, showering us with the water from a giant wave that crested over the top of the conning tower. Fully awake now, we lashed ourselves to the railings and once again began to work on the topside damage. From the corners of our eyes we could see Zschech appearing on the bridge every twenty minutes or so, nervously scanning the horizon. Most of the crew assumed he was on the lookout for enemy aircraft, helping to keep us safe on our return journey. But we control room mates suspected a darker truth: he was looking for a target, still desperate to sink another ship before returning to Lorient.

We worked on the upper deck until it was time for us to start our regular duty in the control room. As we staggered down the ladder to our duty stations below, we were treated to another example of our Executive Officer's sadistic sense of humor. There before us was Thilo Bode, chasing a young seaman through the main passageway of the boat.

"I'll teach you to walk faster!" he screamed, as the frightened boy struggled to drag a heavy sea bag behind him.

Earlier, the Exec had told some torpedo room mates to fill a bag with about three hundred pounds of heavy metal items, then ordered the boy to carry it to the control room. When the boy couldn't lift the bag, Bode began screaming in his ear and chasing him throughout the length of the boat.

Zschech and a couple of his sycophant officers thought this was uproariously funny, but none of us crewmen laughed. Don't get me wrong, we all thought there was a proper time and place for the playful hazing of new recruits. After all, a little harmless harassment has always been part of the traditional ritual of becoming accepted as a member of an elite unit. That has been true in virtually every army in the world throughout history. But there was no sense in what this officer was doing. It was plain cruelty, made all the more senseless by our exhaustion and precarious situation. Besides, the bag would have blocked the passageway in an emergency. We felt as if our boat had become an insane asylum.

*   *   *

The work and abuse continued unabated as our one good engine slowly propelled us back to Lorient. I don't know what secret reserve of spiritual energy enabled us to persist day after day without rebelling, but we did. Long after the emergency repairs were completed, Zschech kept running us to the point of collapse, with no regard to our health. It was as if he were exorcizing his own frustrations and disappointments by making us suffer.

Zschech seemed to be equally unconcerned about the wounded men. I don't recall ever seeing him expressing any interest in their welfare. The injured enlisted man had received some ugly-looking head wounds that bled profusely for several hours after the attack. He went into a deep coma, but when he awoke a few days later, he seemed much better. We reckoned that he had suffered a severe concussion and some bad scalp lacerations, but nothing life threatening. Nevertheless, he was bedridden for weeks to come.

The other two men were in much more serious condition. Both had metal splinters penetrating their skulls and we suspected they also had crushed ribs. *Leutnant* Stolzenburg's plight was especially worrisome to us. He was coughing up blood, and when we submerged, his breathing became very labored. Our medic guessed that his lungs had been punctured, but he had no way of properly diagnosing or treating internal injuries. During the *Leutnant*'s brief periods of consciousness, he hallucinated and often lapsed into violent seizures.

We all pondered the irony of why, of all the officers, it had been Stolzenburg who had been wounded. After all, it was he who had warned Zschech about throwing away the unlucky flowers and about doubling the bridge watch the day of Sillcock's attack. Superstitious scuttlebutt making its rounds through the boat maintained that Zschech was cursed, and that righteous innocents like poor Stolzenburg were the ones who would pay for the skipper's sins.

I also felt very bad for the third wounded man, a Petty Officer. He was the one who, after being wounded, had fallen down through the conning tower hatches and landed unconscious at my feet in the control room. He was in very bad shape: deaf, with burns and splinter wounds all over his body.

He was quite old for a U-boat crewman, easily in his late twenties or early thirties. He originally had a comfortable job in the Flotilla Staff, but his insatiable desire to earn a golden U-boat badge led him to volunteer for duty aboard a frontline boat. As luck would have it, Zschech had already made it impossible for him to achieve his dream. A couple of weeks before Sillcock's attack, Zschech was storming through the front hatch into the control room when he collided with the Petty Officer, knocking the man off his feet. The fellow instinctively grabbed the only thing in reach that would break his fall: the skipper's shirt. Zschech angrily pushed him aside, whereupon the poor man fell onto the navigator's table, breaking an exposed light bulb.

With the hissing sound of a snake, Zschech turned around and summarily gave the petty officer his punishment for clumsiness . . . five days under close arrest. That stain on his record effectively ended the man's naval career, not to mention making it impossible for him to earn one of the U-boat badges he coveted so much. And now he had suffered these terrible injuries, also (arguably) because of Zschech.

The fact that Zschech was so unconcerned about the condition of these men made us shake our heads in disbelief. Even the oldest salts in the crew had never seen a skipper such as this! As the days passed, exhaustion, desperation, and hatred began to fuse into a single white-hot flame of indistinguishable emotion that burned at the cores of our souls. We were German sailors and there was never any question of disobedience, much less mutiny. But, my God, how we loathed that man Peter Zschech!

*   *   *

On the morning of the 22nd we rendezvoused with *U-68* and the Milk Cow supply submarine *U-462*. *U-332* was also in the vicinity, but she loitered in the distance, providing anti-aircraft protection while waiting her turn to get a drink of diesel fuel.

We got a few spare parts from *U-68*, but most of our assistance came from the fat-bellied *U-462*. We took on all sorts of needed parts, tools, food, and fuel from her. While we stowed the equipment and took on diesel fuel, a doctor came aboard and checked the condition of the wounded men. Stolzenburg, who was in the worst condition, was transferred to *U-462* for emergency surgery. As a replacement for Stolzenburg, *Leutnant* Knocke joined our crew as our new Second Watch Officer.

My job was helping to load fresh provisions into the food lockers. We took the opportunity to divert several rings of hard salami and

Gottfried Stolzenburg, *U-505's II.W.O.*, was nearly killed standing on the conning tower when Sillcock's Hudson shot down and dropped its depth-charges. Stolzenburg's head, rib and lung injuries required a transfer to another U-boat, where he underwent life-saving surgery. He is shown above smiling his thanks to a comrade as he is hauled aboard *U-462*, a Type XIV under the command of Bruno Vowe. Author's Collection knockwurst into various hiding places in the control room, right under the noses of the officers. Toni the cook, who was supervising the stowage of food, saw what was happening and gave us the go-ahead with a discrete wink of his eye. Toni not only let us get away with the theft, he himself contributed some food to our secret larder. When we checked on what he had squirreled away, we were surprised to find several cans of goose liver paté with whole truffles, expensive delicacies obviously meant for the officers' mess. Good old Toni! He knew whose hard work had earned those gourmet treats.

From then on, whenever someone from the control room or diesel engine room wanted a snack, we communicated through secret eye gestures to signal when the coast was clear to grab a bite. The officers never suspected a thing. It all went to prove the wisdom of the old folk saying, "*Redn ist Silber, Schweigen ist Gold*" (Talk is silver, but silence is gold).

I suppose we should have been ashamed for stealing that food, but we weren't. After all, once we had been re-supplied by *U-462*, we all had plenty to eat. We weren't taking anything out of anyone's mouth, just rewarding ourselves for a job well done. If Zschech had half the common sense and humanity of *Kapitänleutnant* Löwe, we would have never dreamed of doing such a thing in the first place. As it was, eating the officers' liver pate became more than just a supplement to our diet; it was a tiny act of rebellion. To sneak up to the fresh open air of the bridge and enjoy one of those forbidden little snacks became an almost spiritual experience. It was, if only for a moment, like we were escaping from a universe ruled by a mad god.

After we finished taking on supplies from the Milk Cow, we sent a *FT* to Dönitz's Headquarters advising them that we were on our way home. We all breathed a sigh of relief that in less than three weeks, we would be back, safe and sound in Lorient.

The fates, however, were not content to let us return quietly to base. The very next day, Zschech spotted the mast tops of a freighter off the starboard bow. He immediately ordered that we give chase. Unfortunately, our one working diesel engine couldn't propel us fast enough to catch the ship hovering so tantalizingly just over the horizon.

Just before midnight, though, a lucky course change by the freighter allowed us to move within firing range. Zschech ordered us down to periscope depth to make an attack, but our leaking diving tanks wouldn't allow us to maintain a steady depth. Characteristically, Zschech turned beet-red with anger and blamed the Engineering Officer for everything. Almost everyone in the control room shook their heads over the skipper's pathetic behavior.

We continued to chase the ship underwater until our battery power ran dangerously low. At long last, Zschech ordered us to stand down from battle stations. There was no rest for us, however, and we continued working 18-hour days. Because of my training as a diesel mechanic, I spent most of my time working on the port Jumbo.

The very next night, we stumbled across another freighter of 6,000 tons. We fired two torpedoes at long range, both of which missed. The speed of the target had been triple-checked, so we knew it wasn't Zschech's fault this time. It was the opinion of the torpedo mechanics that our torpedoes missed because the delicate steering gyros within the weapons had been damaged by the shock from Sillcock's depth charges. The mechanics considered any further firing of the torpedoes to be a waste, not to mention very dangerous.

Their opinion didn't dampen Zschech's fixation with scoring another kill. He ordered the diesel to be run at its highest speed in order to line-up another shot. The old engine was hissing and pounding, giving every indication of being ready to blow a piston. Now it was the engine room boys' turn to think Zschech had gone insane. They pleaded with him to reduce RPMs. After all, if our remaining diesel broke-down, we would be stranded in the middle of the Atlantic with zero chance of survival.

Zschech ignored them until we had pulled close enough to fire another torpedo at long range. There was no excitement surrounding the firing of the weapon, for we crewmen had no expectation that it would hit. As anticipated, it was a miss. I'm not sure we could have reacted even if the torpedo hit, since most of us had been working without sleep for more than 72 hours, and some of us were literally sleeping on our feet.

About 45 minutes later, Zschech ordered yet another torpedo to be fired. The distance to the quickly-vanishing target was approximately 4,000 meters—the very limit of the weapon's theoretical range. When Löwe was our skipper, he seldom fired a torpedo at a target further than 1,000 meters away, and never more than 1,500 meters distant. With each torpedo fired, more and more of us became convinced that Zschech was quite literally insane.

As for me, I was lost in a sleep-deprived reverie about our predicament. With a chill, I remembered the captain in *Moby Dick*, and how his obsessive pursuit of the whale eventually destroyed himself and his ship. My mind was a million miles away when, suddenly, we heard a loud metallic clang on the side of our hull. The torpedo we had just fired had circled around and struck the side of our boat! A few minutes later, we heard the faint rumbling sound of a torpedo exploding at great depth.

Evidently, the torpedo had a damaged steering or guidance mechanism that caused it to circle instead of running straight and true. After hitting our hull, the eel must have kept circling until its batteries ran dry. Once its motor stopped running, it sank, finally detonating on the ocean floor far below us.

Zschech ordered us deeper in case other torpedoes were circling around us. As our boat slowly submerged, one of the damaged exhaust valves stuck in the open position, causing water to flood into one of the buoyancy tanks. The sudden increase in weight made our boat plummet downward in a rapid, uncontrolled dive. We sank to a dangerous depth before we were finally able to pull our boat's bow up and power our way back to the surface with electric motors. Our double brush with death finally shook Zschech out of his blood lust. We gave up the fruitless chase of the freighter and resumed a course for home. Zschech went to sulk in his cabin, the wind completely taken out of his sails.

We surfaced the next morning to examine the spot where our errant torpedo had hit the hull. We couldn't see any damage, but once we were back in port and in dry dock, we found a gouging dent in our boat's side. It was apparent from the damage that the torpedo had struck us at a very narrow angle from behind. Evidently, the angle was too small to detonate the contact pistol fuse in the firing mechanism, so the torpedo merely bounced away. If the torpedo had been armed with a magnetic detonator, or if there had been a few more degrees on the angle at which it struck us, we would have all been food for the fishes.

During the war, several submarines were struck by their own malfunctioning torpedoes. *U-505* may be the only one to have ever survived the actual experience. Incidents like this make me wonder how anyone in his right mind could call *U-505* an unlucky boat, as several writers and commentators had done since the war ended.

* * *

We continued to plod eastward back to Lorient. At that point in the war, the Allies still hadn't plugged the mid-Atlantic "air gap" with their aircraft carriers, so we were able to make fairly good progress on the surface, even with only one good engine. While our morale was soaring with anticipation stepping onto dry land, Zschech isolated himself in his little cabin, wallowing in gloom and self-pity.

On the afternoon of November 30, we rendezvoused with yet another Milk Cow, Stiebler's *U-461*. This boat gave us a replacement antenna cross for our *Metox* radar detector in preparation for our passing through the Biscay "Suicide Stretch." Stiebler also sent over a sick sailor for us to transport back to base. The unlucky lad had contracted a venereal disease back in Lorient and was in deep trouble for his indiscretion. To make matters worse, the doctor who had transferred over to us from *U-462* ordered the infected sailor to be quarantined. The poor guy spent the next eleven days in isolation, confined to the small forward bathroom that in normal times functioned as our spare food locker.

On December 3, we passed through a cold front that caused a dramatic drop in temperature inside the boat. We were still accustomed to the Caribbean heat, so we wrapped towels around our midsections to protect our kidneys from the chill. The condensation water dripping down on us seemed ice cold. The boys who slept in the uppermost bunks were especially miserable.

A couple days later, someone noticed that one of the big dents in the pressure hull caused by Sillcock's bombing was starting to cave inwards. Every time we dived, the hull would bend in noticeably closer. We prayed that we wouldn't have to dive deeper than 40 or 50 meters before we got back to base. We did have a bit of good news, though. The wounded sailor with the scalp wounds took his first unassisted stroll through the boat. He walked like an old man, but everyone was glad to see him about. The Petty Officer, however, remained bedridden and not fully in command of any of his five senses.

On December 7, for the first time in weeks, we received several *Metox* alarms warning us of enemy radar beams. This was a sure sign we were nearing the entrance to the Bay of Biscay. From that point on, we stayed on full alert for the approach of any hostile ships or aircraft. We were especially wary when we passed through the flight path of the British planes flying shuttle patrols between Gibraltar in the south and Landsend, England, in the north—the infamous "Suicide Stretch."

The next day, we radioed Lorient to arrange our escort into port. They expected us to be there in 36 hours, but we had to delay our arrival because of numerous emergency dives and heavy winter storms. Planning what to do in Lorient's entertainment district dominated every conversation. Except for the poor lad with venereal disease, of course. He remained silent and depressed about his inevitable arrest and the frightening medical treatments awaiting him back in port.

We had a bit of trouble navigating the last leg to Lorient because our radio directional finder was out of commission. Chief Navigator Reinig tried to fix our position with the sextant, but thick gray clouds obscured all the stars. Zschech made one of his rare appearances in the control room to angrily berate the navigator for all our troubles. By now, of course, Zschech's irrational outbursts hardly raised an eyebrow. Anyway, we were far too close to Lorient for anything to spoil our mood. Our spirits were so high, some of us even softened our attitude a bit toward our skipper. Perhaps, we hoped, his foul temper and fits of madness would fade after a few weeks of rest.

The weather worsened as we neared the Brittany coast. Giant waves sent icy torrents of seawater crashing over the top of the conning tower and down the hatches into the control room. We control room mates were miserable, forced to sit for hours at a time being periodically soaked by the frigid brine. When we were wet, the seawater burned our eyes with salt. When we were dry, the salt residue made us itch all over. We cursed the wretched winter weather. Our discomfort was made all the more intolerable by the knowledge that we were so close to home. We were literally counting down every hour until that first, luxuriously hot shower in our barracks.

We spent our off-duty hours getting our personal possessions packed for the move to the barracks. In view of the weather, the uniform chosen for our arrival was gray leather jacket and pants. We had to beat and rub the leather to get out the mold that had grown during their storage.

I could hardly sleep that final night before our arrival home. Mostly it was excitement that kept me up, but I was also worried. After all the close brushes with death during this patrol, I didn't want to die now, just a few miles from comfort and safety. Lying in my bunk, I listened to every little sound that was made by man or machinery. Exhaustion finally won out and I drifted off to a dreamless sleep.

Chapter 8

Terror From Above

We rendezvoused with our escort exactly as planned at 0800 hours, December 12. We were surprised by the size and strength of the escort force; anti-aircraft weapons were especially abundant on the ships that met us.

Two and one-half hours later, we arrived at the pier. There was a military band in attendance, along with hundreds of sailors, army soldiers, female nurses, and shipyard workers. We could plainly hear their cries of astonishment when they spotted the massive damage we had sustained in Sillcock's attack. As word of our damage spread throughout the dock area, the crowd grew even larger with hundreds of additional curiosity seekers. In front of the crowd was the Flotilla Staff, waving their caps and leading everyone in three cheers for *U-505*.

Once our boat was securely tied to the dock, we assembled in formation on the narrow pier. I remember how amusing it was to once again experience the funny feeling of the land seeming to pitch and roll under my feet for the first few hours after a long sea voyage.

Zschech stepped out in front of our formation and saluted the commander of our Flotilla, *Korvettenkapitän* Victor Schütze. "*U-505* reporting back from war patrol."

Schütze smiled broadly. "Glad you made it home! Hail to the crew of *U-505*!"

We all shouted back in unison, "Hail, *Herr Korvettenkapitän*!"

Zschech twirled around back toward us, clearly annoyed that the Flotilla Commander had acknowledged us crewmen. Eyes glaring with anger, he dismissed us, hissing the words like an angry snake.

We didn't give a damn about Zschech's hurt feelings. Once dismissed, we gave a big cheer and scrambled back aboard *U-505* to get our sea bags. There were a few unfortunate souls on watch who had to stay onboard a bit longer to secure important valves and other devices, but they would soon be relieved by the Flotilla Reserve, so we didn't feel too bad about them. There was really only one thing on our minds: a long hot shower. In our eagerness, most of us ran nonstop to the barracks. I loitered about the crowd for a while looking for Jeanette, but did not see her.

On the way to the barracks, I discovered why our naval escort into Lorient harbor had been so thick with anti-aircraft weapons: everywhere I looked were large bomb craters and burned buildings. Despite all the damage, however, we didn't experience any equipment shortages or delays during our stay in port.

Later that afternoon, our crew assembled in a big dining room for the traditional post-patrol banquet with the Flotilla Staff. As usual, the sparkling white tablecloths were littered with dozens of bottles of beer, Cognac, and liqueurs. Everything smelled so clean! The only disappointment was that food shortages had compelled the *Kriegsmarine* to curtail the elaborate feast we had come to expect.

We drank for an hour, then mail was passed out. A great number of the men received news of brothers and uncles killed or missing in action. There were also many tragic tales of the bombing raids our cities were suffering.

The bitter news from home caused many of us to abandon all restraint with the alcohol. After a while, someone began singing old sailor songs. They weren't sentimental or melodious songs, but ones with a sharp edge to them. It was clear that we were a crew who needed to blow-off some steam. Our self-restraint weakened by drink, the frustrations and tensions of the past several weeks started flooding back, ever more boisterously.

The Flotilla Staff picked up on the mood of the crew and discretely left early. Some of our officers left soon after as well. For the rest of us, though, it was to be a long night of drinking. By the time midnight came around, several of the boys had passed out, snoring like steam engines. Their heads were flat on the table, face down in whatever happened to be in front of them. Others were awake enough to sing along, but only managed to make babbling sounds.

It was at this point we decided, in our very intoxicated judgment, that it was time to execute our long-planned revenge against the two Petty Officers who had tried to make us do infantry barracks drills and exercises aboard *U-505*. During the course of the evening's festivities, we noticed some big barrels of water and several large jute sacks filled with sand stacked next to the second floor bathrooms. The sand and water had been stockpiled there as fire-fighting materials in case the building was hit by incendiaries during a bombing raid. We emptied the sand out of a couple of the bags and then hid in ambush positions around the corner from the bathrooms. Then it was just a matter of waiting for the two Petty Officers to answer the call of nature.

We only had to wait a few minutes before we heard one of the Petty Officers coming up the stairs. We had arranged a secret system of whistles with our mates downstairs to alert us of the Petty Officers' approach, but we ended up not needing any warning because those two were the loudest talkers in the entire crew.

The first Petty Officer walked around the corner and we jumped him. With a few of us holding his arms and legs, we placed the sack over his body and tied the bottom closed with a rope around his knees. He kicked like a wild animal, but the rope kept him securely imprisoned within the sack. Between the hand over his mouth and all the other noise in the dining hall, no one heard his half-angry, half-frightened cries for help.

A few minutes later, the second Petty Officer stumbled into our trap and was given the same treatment. We lifted our captives and placed them, feet first, into the barrels of water. God in Heaven, the way they cursed when they landed in that cold fetid water! We left them there and ran like schoolchildren, laughing all the way back to our barracks.

The Petty Officers stood in the water for about thirty minutes before the Barracks Watch Officer came along and freed them. By the time we heard the two Petty Officers and the Barracks Watch Officer coming down the hall toward our room, we were safely in our bunks pretending to be asleep. The Petty Officers seemed to have sobered up a bit, but they were still angry as hell. The Watch Officer, for his part, seemed rather amused by the entire incident.

A moment later, our barracks room door flew open and a flashlight beam stabbed out through the darkness toward our beds. The light lingered on each of our bunks, one by one. All that could be seen was a room full of perfect angels enjoying the sleep of the innocent.

The Barracks Watch Officer gave a little chuckle of appreciation for our performance, then angrily turned back toward the two protesting Petty Officers. "Listen, you two. Get back to your rooms right now, and don't make any noise that will wake these sleeping men! Understand?"

The Petty Officers clicked to attention. "*Jawohl, Herr Ober-leutnant!*" they said in unison. As the three walked back down the hallway, they had to have heard our laughter and cheers of approval for the understanding Watch Officer.

Far too early the next morning, we heard a man with a shrill whistle slowly making his way down the length of our barracks hallway. It was some young Boatswains Mate from the Flotilla garrison going from room to room, trying to wake our crew up. When he opened our door, he was met with a hail of shoes, pillows, helmets, and curses. He ran like lightning to get some reinforcements.

Of course, we knew exactly what we could get away with, so despite our throbbing heads and queasy stomachs, we stumbled out of our bunks and tried to sober up with an ice-cold shower. By the time the Boatswains Mate returned with his Chief, we were dressed and ready for morning formation.

After breakfast, we assembled to receive our orders. Zschech notified us that, as usual, half of us would go on furlough. The other half would undergo infantry training "so that moss won't grow on your back," as he put it. Today, however, we were to report to *U-505* to help the shipyard repair crews. Nothing was mentioned about the previous night's high jinks with the Petty Officers. Interestingly, our little prank must have worked because from then on, those two were very comradely toward us ordinary crewmen.

Before we left for *U-505*, we saw the Petty Officer who had been wounded in Sillcock's attack being sent off to the hospital. The poor man was still deaf and mentally confused. We never saw him again. Zschech didn't even say a word of thanks or farewell to him, despite his sacrifice. To a man, we wished we had our old Skipper in command again, but we knew that was just a dream.

After we were dismissed, some control room mates and I took a longboat to the submarine bunkers. Our boat was still in the wet dock, surrounded by several small barks unloading supplies. The Flotilla Chief

Engineer was aboard, shaking his head in disbelief at the damage old *U-505* had suffered. Other shipyard officials were swarming over the decks, making a detailed inventory of the wreckage. The report they wrote confirmed that *U-505* was the most heavily-damaged U-boat to ever make it back to base under its own power. That record held up for the entire course of the war. When the damage report reached Dönitz's headquarters, the Great Lion wrote a personal letter of commendation to our boat's crew.

Later, we learned that a special note had also been entered into our ship's log praising Zschech's actions during the patrol. Didn't Headquarters know about his readiness to abandon ship? Or his abusive, self-defeating behavior towards the crew? Or the reckless endangerment to which he exposed his crippled boat—all because of his manic desire to sink another ship before returning to base? We reckoned that Headquarters either didn't know the whole story, or just wrote that in the log to boost Zschech's morale. Either way, we shook our heads when we heard about the entry.

Meanwhile, back on *U-505*, we just stood there on the upper deck of our boat, dumbfounded by the buzz of activity taking place around us. In the background, there was a gramophone playing military songs and marches. The noisy crowd, combined with the echoing background music, created a sort of nightmarish carnival atmosphere that seemed very surreal to us.

We were still suffering from the previous night's festivities and were in no particular hurry to get back to duty, so we decided to get a bit of rest while the damage survey was being completed. My buddies and I took some tools and disappeared beneath the floor plates of the bilge. We laid down some rags we had brought with us and created cozy little nesting places among the jumble of ducts and valves. Every few minutes or so, one of us would bang on a pipe and shout a curse to create the impression topside that we were hard at work. Our dark little hiding place didn't smell very good, but the nap we enjoyed was just what we needed.

After a couple of hours, someone shouted down an order for us to assemble on the upper deck for assignment to another work detail. But when we appeared topside, the filth and stench of the bilge on our coveralls made the Petty Officer turn his head in disgust. He ordered us to get cleaned up, so we happily ran back to the barracks before anyone found something else for us to do. When the rest of the crew returned from their duty assignments, they were surprised to see us control room mates already showered and dressed for the much-anticipated awards ceremony later that afternoon.

*   *   *

After everyone had cleaned up and put on their blue dress uniforms, we gathered in the big square in front of our barracks for the ceremony. Zschech began by calling the names of several men. They lined up in front of our ranks and were awarded the Iron Cross. Selfish aristocratic bastard that he was, Zschech refused to award enlisted men anything higher than the Iron Cross, Second Class. He had been awarded the Iron Cross, First Class, for being Jochen Mohr's Exec, and he hated seeing any enlisted man with a medal as high as his.

During our first war patrol to the Caribbean, *Kapitänleutnant* Löwe had recommended several other men, including me, be awarded the Iron Cross, Second Class. Zschech ignored Löwe's recommendations when he became our Skipper, and we never got our medals. From then on, Iron Crosses were primarily reserved for Zschech's favorites in the crew. We really didn't care; the respect of our fellow crewmen meant a lot more to us than another ribbon on the chest.

Anyway, after the Iron Crosses were handed out, a larger number, myself included, were called-up to receive the coveted *U-Boot-kampfabzeichen* (Submarine Combat Badge). This handsome golden badge signified extended combat experience in our submarine service. Accompanying the medal was the highly-prized *Urkunde* award document, graced by Dönitz's signature. We submariners were much prouder of the U-boat badge than the Iron Cross. Later in the war, they were handing out Iron Crosses to everyone, but the golden *U-Bootkampfabzeichen* remained until the very end a badge of elite status and unquestionable bravery. (NOTE: The boys who kept their medals and documents with them during our war patrols ended up having them snatched by the souvenir-hungry American sailors who captured us a year and a half later. Luckily for me, I sent my original badge and *Urkunde* back to my parents for safekeeping. Even during the years of the Allied Occupation, while I was incarcerated as a prisoner of war, my parents kept all my war mementos safely hidden in their home. I still have both my U-boat badge and the award document, and today they are among my most prized possessions.)

But wouldn't you know it, even this proud moment was almost ruined by the contemptible actions of Zschech's second-in-command. Not two minutes after he had received his submarine badge, an Electric Engine Mate was called forward by the Exec and berated for his appearance.

"You look like a vagabond!" Bode shouted. "You don't deserve to be on a submarine. I should tear that badge off your chest!"

Luckily, this veteran sailor—who knew more about our boat's electrical system than anyone else in the crew—just stood there at attention, not saying a word nor moving an eyelash. Bode grew tired of trying to goad him into reacting, and allowed him to rejoin the rest of us. We couldn't believe how the Exec had violated the solemnity of the occasion by this senseless outburst. Our feelings of pride were swept away and replaced with the rancid taste of disgust and hatred for him. From then on, everyone in the crew made a point of giving the Exec the cold shoulder.

Of course, we also felt an equal level of contempt for Zschech, who just stood there watching with smiling approval as his lap dog meted-out this abuse. It also brought back to mind the poor wounded Petty Officer who, by all rights, should have been here to receive his submarine badge, too. My God, how we missed our old skipper Löwe, who was so generous with praise and rewards for those who had earned them!

In all fairness to the Exec, however, he eventually did mature as an officer. Some thought it was the unity of our reaction to the awards ceremony incident that finally made him change. Others thought he finally realized that Zschech's method of command-by-fear didn't work as well as leading by example. Whatever it was, in the following months Thilo Bode gradually transformed from a martinet into an officer men could have confidence in. Certainly his attitude toward discipline made a 180-degree turn! By the time he transferred off our boat, he recognized us for the tough and able crew we knew we were. He even wrote us a letter to that effect. "If I ever become the skipper of a boat," he explained, "I hope I have a crew that demonstrates the same pluck and courage that you have."

We were gratified Bode finally came around to our way of thinking—that it was sweat and blood that win wars, not spit and polish.

Unfortunately, unlike the Exec, Zschech was unable to overcome his personal demons before it was too late.

Soon after the war, an amateur historian took the side of Zschech in all of this. He expressed the opinion that Sillcock's bombing attack had cracked our morale and that we had lost the ability to fight or obey orders. He suggested that Zschech and his Exec were only trying to restore discipline and that it would have been better to split up our crew and distribute us to other boats. This so-called historian would have been better off using his common sense instead of using his fingers to hammer out such groundless nonsense! Sure, we were disappointed we had not returned to Lorient with more victory pennants flying from our conning tower. Of course we would bend the rules to have a bit of fun when in port. But none of that mattered when we went into combat. To suggest we had lost the will to fight or were anything less than a first rate crew is absolutely absurd. Such fairy tales are based on ignorance and pity for what happened to Zschech, rather than the facts as I personally know them to be.

*   *   *

After the awards ceremony, we were given permission to go into town on liberty until 2200 hours that night. Of course, we had no intention of returning by the appointed hour because we had discovered secret routes that would allow us to sneak back into base undetected any time we wanted. Before we left, however, we had to leave our bunks looking like someone was sleeping in them. By using a steel helmet, a few bundles of rolled-up clothing, and a pair of shoes, it was easy. Our bunks thus prepared, we stuffed some money into our pockets and strode out the gate, eager to shower our girlfriends with our accumulated pay and pent-up passion.

Once outside the base, we were shocked to see the utter devastation the British bombers had visited upon the city center of Lorient. Whole sections of the town were nothing but dusty piles of rubble. We walked wide-eyed through the desolate streets, surrounded by absolute silence save for the crunching of stone and broken glass beneath our shoes.

A few blocks from our favorite district, however, we were surprised and heartened to hear the familiar strains of saxophone music echoing faintly in the distance. Sure enough, it was still there: our favorite entertainment district had miraculously escaped damage! All around were hundreds of beautiful girls in colorful dresses. The air was filled with the sweet scents of perfume and exotic cocktails, making the street seem like a magical kind of garden. The girls, of course, were the lovely, fragrant flowers of this garden, waiting to be plucked by us lonely sailors.

The military police, as usual, were also out in force. They walked in pairs, wearily eyeing us as we passed. They knew, as well as we did, that we would be brawling with them before the night was through. A crew on its first night of leave needs to blow-off a lot of steam, and there was no better way to do that than to get into a good fight with the Chained Dogs.

First, though, we needed some drinks and a little taste of female companionship. We couldn't wait to show our favorite girls our shiny new medals, so we split-up into small groups, promising to rendezvous later that afternoon. The ladies were certainly happy to see us, especially since we had plenty of money and more than enough will to spend it.

Inside my favorite house, the Madam at the reception desk greeted me by name. With a wide smile on her face, she helped me off with my heavy, gray leather coat and bade me enter. I tossed my fur cap through the air and scored a perfect hit on the hook on the wall . . . surely a sign of good luck! In the blink of an eye, I had a drink in my hand and a pretty girl on my lap.

When I asked about Jeanette, however, the Madam told me that she had quit without notice and left town. I was stunned by the news. I pushed the girl off my lap and began drinking. The more drinks I had, the more angry I got about her leaving without saying goodbye. How could I have been so wrong about her feelings? How could I have been so foolish?

After a while, with much encouragement from my buddies, I found consolation in the arms of another young woman who said she had always liked me. I didn't believe that for a minute, but it was a nice gesture designed to get me over my hurt and disappointment.

A couple of hours later, we stumbled out of the house into the painfully bright light of the afternoon sun. Our faces were covered with lipstick, rouge . . . and very broad smiles. Despite my clown's face, however, I still felt a deep, lingering ache inside because of Jeanette.

As a group of us ambled toward another favored haunt, air raid warning sirens began to wail. Combat-seasoned (not to mention, very drunk) warriors such as we felt total contempt for the enemy bombers.

After all, if Sillcock's bombs couldn't hurt us, what could a few dozen high-flying bombers do?

Even when the naval base's anti-aircraft batteries commenced to fire, we refused to seek shelter. Indeed, we didn't even quicken our pace when bombs began hitting the vicinity of our barracks. In our tipsy state, the action intrigued us, but it somehow seemed distant and unreal . . . like the combat newsreels we watched in the cinemas.

As we entered the town's central square, however, we were slapped out of our complacency by the sharp crack of a 37mm Flak gun opening fire from the roof of the adjacent six-story building. For such a small gun to be firing meant that the enemy bombers were very close indeed. Suddenly, we realized that a rolling carpet of exploding bombs was heading directly towards us.

Windows began to rattle and break as the literally earth-shaking wave of explosions came closer and closer. All thoughts of nonchalance were forgotten as we sprinted for the main air raid shelter in the central square. It was a large underground bunker, built to accommodate three or four hundred people. We ran down the flight of 20 stairs to the shelter entrance, only to have the big iron door slam shut and lock in our faces. We were too late! There was nothing for us to do except crouch in the corners of the stairwell and await our fate.

The shaking of the ground became more violent. The concussion from each deafening blast felt like a punch to the chest. I curled up as tightly as I could into a fetal position in a desperate attempt to make as small a target as possible. The tension was excruciating as the line of thundering blasts approached the shelter entrance.

Then came four or five blasts that were virtually on top of us. We were stunned to the very edge of unconsciousness by the violence of the concussions. Miraculously, we were not struck by any bomb splinters, though for several minutes we could see nothing because of the dust and smoke. When we finally recovered our senses, we realized that the curtain of explosions was past us and heading away.

We were determined to get some cover over our heads, but no amount of pleading or pounding would convince the occupants of the shelter to open the door for us. Animal fear finally took over and we decided to make a run for it. Someone suggested we take cover in the building with the flak gun; perhaps the presence of the gun would make the bombers veer around us. We reckoned that we had a minute or so before the next group of bombers arrived, so on the count of three, we ran up the shelter stairs to the ruined streets above.

Debris was everywhere. Scattered here and there, dazed survivors wandered senselessly about. Blood streamed from their noses and ears, their mouths frozen wide open in silent screams.

We quickly made our way through the nightmarish scenery back to the tall building with the rooftop flak gun. The pressure from a bomb blast had smashed the entrance door inwards, so we entered without hesitation. We were familiar with 37mm guns, so rather than quiver like frightened children on the ground floor, we decided to climb the stairs to the roof and assist the gunners.

We were about half way up when we heard the unmistakable sound of heavy bombers droning overhead, interspersed with frantic bursts of fire from the flak gun on the roof. Before we could say a word, the entire building shook with a deafening roar. A bomb had hit the top of the building, collapsing one entire exterior wall and sending a landslide of smoke, dust, and debris thundering down our stairwell.

The gunners were surely in need of help, so we clamored over the piles of wood and plaster clogging the stairwell up to the top of the building. When we got to the roof, we could see that a bomb had scored an almost direct hit on the little anti-aircraft position. We heard a soft groan and found one man still alive, covered from head to foot in blood. The other gunners were nowhere to be found; they must have been blown to pieces or thrown off the top of the building by the force of the explosion.

As gently as we could, my buddy Willi and I carried the injured man down the stairs. When we reached the ground floor, Willi suddenly dropped the man's legs. When I turned around to see what the trouble was, I saw Willi frozen in terror, staring saucer-eyed at the biggest bomb I had ever seen in my life. It was a giant monster, its bent tail fins sticking straight out of a pile of rubble. The memory of that sight still chills my blood to this day.

We knew that the British often dropped bombs that appeared to be duds, but were actually time bombs with the detonation times on the fuses purposely calculated to kill firemen and rescue workers sifting through the rubble for survivors. Willi and I didn't want to wait around to find out if it was one of those. We carried the wounded man as quickly as possible out of the building and into the relative safety of the main square. We knew that the big air raid shelter had a medic assigned to it, so we headed back there.

On the way, we passed an old Catholic church. Twenty minutes ago it had been a beautiful landmark, one of my favorites in all of Lorient. Now it was nothing but a smoking shell of a building. It angered me that nothing was to be left sacred in this war. I cursed the unholy alliance between the British capitalists and the Russian communists, whose brutal determination to conquer Germany and incorporate it into their empires was bringing such destruction to Europe.

We handed the wounded gunner over to the shelter medic and headed back to our barracks. The streets of Lorient looked like one of those medieval paintings of the underworld. Deep craters pockmarked the roads and there were burning houses all around. The air was filled with a hellish symphony of ambulance sirens and the frightened cries of women and children.

With the sounding of the "All Clear" siren, the streets suddenly filled with thousands of panicky civilians. Military policemen shouted and gestured angrily at the crowds, helpless to restore order or prevent looting. Soon, dozens of horse-drawn carts appeared on the streets, piled high with family members and their worldly possessions. Weeks ago, the RAF had dropped leaflets on the city, warning the civilians to evacuate. It appeared now that these civilians were finally ready to heed the advice.

We arrived back at our barracks compound a little while later, covered from head to foot with dust and soot. The sour-faced guards at the gate scrutinized our identity papers more carefully than usual. We were surprised to find the harbor area totally undamaged. Apparently, the bombing attack had not been targeted at our U-boat base at all. Rather, the British seemed to be deliberately taking aim at the civilian population of Lorient, presumably to deprive us of our shipyard workforce.

Once we got back to our barracks, we were relieved to find that everyone in our crew had survived the bombing raid more or less intact. We spent the next few hours drinking Cognac and telling each other of our experiences during the attack. Our drunken conclusion: we had met old friends, fraternized with the *Mademoiselles*, had a bit of excitement, and none of us got seriously hurt. In sum, a very good first day in port!

The tension of the day finally caught up with me and I slept very soundly that night. The next morning, half the crew was allowed to go on furlough. For the rest of us, it was more infantry training. Luckily, the bombers did not visit us again. When we returned to the barracks that afternoon, construction was well underway on two large air raid bunkers next to our billets.

Naturally, we again spent the evening in downtown Lorient. Amazingly, the entertainment district was once again carrying on as if there had never been an air raid. Music, girls, brawling with the military police—nothing had changed! The same was true for us; the horrors we had witnessed the previous day seemed like distant, ancient history.

Security was tighter than usual, so we all got back to the barracks on time that night. Sometime after midnight, I was awakened from a deep slumber by the ear-splitting scream of air raid sirens. Almost immediately, our base anti-aircraft batteries began a furious barrage at the unseen intruders. We didn't move an inch out of our warm bunks except to try to drown out the sirens with our pillows.

A moment later, the boy on barracks watch came down the hallway yelling, "Everyone go down to Bunker Number One! Hurry, *U-505* crew, out! OUT!"

Still, we would not budge. The five minutes of silence that followed the first flurry of fire seemed to vindicate our feeling that we were not in any danger. Then, suddenly, three or four extremely large bombs exploded right next to our barracks. The whole building shook crazily with the force of the blasts. We didn't need the barracks watch to get us out of bed now! We grabbed our stuff and ran toward the stairs.

As we approached the stairwell, a bomb hit the corner of our building. The lights went out and the air was filled with choking dust and the sounds of heavy falling rubble. The stairs that we had intended to use to evacuate the building were no longer there. Nevertheless, bombs were still falling and we were desperate to get out of the building, fast! We dropped our sea bags down the shaft of the stairwell to form a sort of cushion, then jumped.

It was bright as day outside of our barracks because of all of the burning buildings around us. We ran like greyhounds to the entrance of Bunker Number One. A man was holding the door of the bunker open, screaming at the top of his lungs at us.

"You assholes! Hurry up, because we're closing the doors right now!"

We emerged from the bunker the next morning to find that the entire barracks complex had been reduced to a pile of smoking rubble. Buses brought us and the other U-boat crews to our new barracks at *Lager Lemp*, a former physical rehabilitation camp about eight kilometers east of Lorient. We spent the rest of the morning moving into our new billets. In the afternoon, we were ordered to return to *U-505* for maintenance duties.

* * *

While we were all having so much fun, boat was moved. She was now tied-up at the *Keroman* repair docks on the other side of the city. Since the regular longboat service only went to the submarine pens, my buddy Willi and I decided to walk to the boat. Our route took us through Lorient, or rather, what was left of it. About a half-kilometer from the pens, with no warning from the air raid sirens, the anti-aircraft guns began to fire. Sure enough, there were the bombers again, dropping their deadly eggs and heading straight for us.

Close to us, perhaps 25 meters away, was an old French cemetery surrounded by a tall stone wall. Yesterday's air raid had blown a large hole in the wall fairly close to us, which instantaneously gave Willi and me the same idea. Without a word needing to be said, we sprinted through the breach and into the graveyard. We gave the place a quick looking-over, then jumped into a large crater for extra cover.

Bombs began hitting all around us, so Willi and I instinctively huddled for protection on either side of a stone coffin that had been partially unearthed by one of the previous day's bombs. After a few moments, we noticed that the coffin's marble cover had been dislodged. Peeking inside, we found ourselves staring into the hollow eye sockets of the coffin occupant's skull. The man had apparently been a naval officer, judging from the dark tattered uniform he wore. Confirmation came from a brass plaque on the casket's cover which identified him as a French *Capitain de Fregatte* [sic: Fregate Joigniere].

We crouched next to our silent host, the good Capitain, for what seemed to us like an eternity. Sailors are naturally a superstitious lot. To us the situation was a clear premonition of death. As soon as the bomb blasts began moving away from us, Willi and I looked at each other and nodded. *"Raus hier!"*

With that, we ran nonstop to the U-boat bunkers. With a seven-meter thick concrete roof over our heads, we finally felt safe. Other members of our crew were quite relieved to see us, for they assumed we had been killed in the raid because of the rain of bombs that had fallen along our planned route.

All of the excitement was over within an hour. It was good to be close to the U-boat bunkers, where we felt so secure from the enemy bombs. When our comrades began returning from leave, however, we began to hear firsthand of the terrible agony being inflicted by the bombers on our families back home. Our reaction? A greater determination than ever to send the enemy's ships to the bottom of the sea, where their cargoes of airplanes and bombs could do no harm.

*   *   *

We slept aboard *U-505* that night, but for the next month, *Lager Lemp* was to be our home. Crews from both the Second and Tenth U-boat Flotillas were to be housed there. We weren't very happy about the situation, but the army soldiers stationed in the area liked it even less. For one thing, there was only one small town in the vicinity, Pont Scorf. Soon all of the Army's favorite pubs and bistros were overflowing with sailors. Adding insult to injury, the few mademoiselles in Pont Scorf clearly preferred us U-boat men over ordinary infantry. Nonetheless, I began to spend more time in the *U-bootsheim* recreation center because, unlike Lorient, there wasn't much entertainment to be found in the little town.

At the beginning, there were plenty of fights between Army soldiers and U-boat sailors, but over time we became very friendly toward each other. We knew the soldiers had a tough life, with none of the special comforts the *Kriegsmarine* provided to us. They, in turn, respected us because of the high casualties we were suffering. Eventually, we began to invite the soldiers to come eat and drink with us in the *U-bootsheim*. The recreation center was like a heaven on earth for those poor soldiers. Most of them had never enjoyed luxury like that, even in civilian life. It was certainly unequaled in all of the German armed forces. We spent many an enjoyable evening there eating gourmet food, drinking fine wines and liqueurs, watching movies, listening to concerts, and dancing with the local girls.

As for the exotic entertainment of Lorient, if Mohammed would not go to the mountain, then the mountain would come to Mohammed! Before long, the area outside *Lager Lemp* was filled with French vendors from Lorient hawking colorful scarves, silk stockings, champagne, *Hennessee* liqueur, and the naughty little booklets that featured pictures of young *Mademoiselles* in shameless poses. Of course, why buy pictures of women when you can have the real thing? Soon the gates to *Lager Lemp* were swarming with attractive French women, all eager to help a German sailor spend his time and money.

"The more things change, the more they stay the same," as the French were fond of saying.

Chapter 9

Furlough at Last

Our first night in *Lager Lemp* was not an enjoyable one. All of our woolen blankets had burned in the bombing attack on our barracks, so we shivered all night long. In the morning we returned to our boat for emergency drills, mostly practicing to slide down ladders using only the handrails. We didn't mind this because we knew that saving just a few seconds in getting to one's battle station could mean the difference between life and death on a submarine.

When we returned to *Lager Lemp* for lunch, we found the entire place had been draped in camouflage. They even went so far as to completely hide a nearby pond from aerial view in order to deny the enemy its use as a navigational aid. These measures didn't inspire much confidence in us because we knew it was only a matter of time before the French Resistance provided our location to Bomber Command. Worse yet, we had no underground bomb shelters. Our sole protection against bombs were a few shallow slit trenches. We began to wonder what was more dangerous: facing combat at sea or "relaxing" here at base.

The trenches did, however, provide us with an unexpected advantage besides protection. While standing in the trenches, we noticed a clump of small trees and bushes growing next to one part of the perimeter fence. Obscured from view by the greenery, we secretly dug a short tunnel under the fence that would allow us to slip in and out at night unnoticed.

From then on, we were free to make unauthorized forays into town whenever we wished.

Some of our crew mates, for some strange reason, never liked to leave the barracks. While we were out on one of our late night expeditions, they would arrange our bed sheets to create the impression we were asleep in our bunks. The payment demanded for such consideration? Make a complete report to them of all our experiences, including the tiniest, most sordid detail. I could never understand why they didn't just go out and experience these things firsthand for themselves.

Being housed in *Lager Lemp* with our comrades from the *Tenth U-boat Flotilla* had other advantages, too. They told us of a nearby French farmer who distilled a rather potent and fairly tolerable tasting *Calvados*, a local version of apple schnapps. Sure enough, we found him outside his farmhouse with a large basket filled to overflowing with bottles of the stuff. We were in luck because the old man was happy to accept *Renten Marks* (our German occupation money) on the condition that we not allow his wife to find out about his little side business. We were happy to comply.

Forty years after the war, during a visit to the area with my wife Erika, I visited the same old farmer. He and his wife graciously asked us into his house for coffee and to chat about the old days. After a while, my wife asked me (in German, so they would not understand) if the old farmer had a nerve affliction that made him keep winking at us. I knew what the winking meant: he wanted to tell me something that he didn't want his wife to hear. I told Erika to start a conversation with the farmer's wife so he could have a chance to talk with me in private. He asked if I would show him my Mercedes-Benz, and I replied, "Of course."

Once out of sight, he told me to wait. He disappeared around a corner and returned a minute later with something clenched tightly to his belly. We hurried to my car, where he produced two large bottles of *Calvados* from under his sweater. After forty years, not only was the old man still trying to keep his moonshining activities secret from his wife, but he still preferred to be paid in Deutsch Marks! We left on the friendliest of terms, the ancient farmer still proclaiming in broken French-German his admiration for the U-boat men who were once his neighbors.

* * *

As the year 1942 came to a close, our boat began undergoing major repairs. Once the shipyard workers removed all the damaged sections of the hull and conning tower, our poor *U-505* began to look like one of those cut-away display models used for training. Nevertheless, we crewmen were pleased. The repairs and modifications would make our boat better than ever, not to mention giving us a few extra weeks of furlough and light duty before our next war patrol.

Those days and nights in port passed very quickly for us. I was free on many days to wander about the harbor area. A favorite pastime of mine was to scrounge for small pieces of scrap aluminum that my mates and I could use for handcrafting souvenirs during our next voyage. We used to call this sort of scavenging activity "organizing." Thanks to my skill at organizing scrap metal, our crew always had plenty of little *U-505* ax symbols to attach to our caps or give away as mementos to family and friends. (NOTE: Almost all of our uniform insignia and medals were made of aluminum or brass because they would not rust at sea and were poor conductors of electricity. It wouldn't do to cause an electrical short with one's cap insignia!)

I also began visiting a nearby town called Hennebont. It was a beautiful little place that had all the charms of Lorient, but without so many sailors. I remember a castle there with very high spires that particularly impressed me. One had to be careful, however, since the French Resistance would sometimes ambush our boys walking on the road between *Lager Lemp* and Hennebont. In order to avoid these attacks, we were eventually forced to travel cross country over the fields instead of on the roads. A few times, groups of our sailors hiking through the fields surprised would-be ambushers from behind. Those Resistance fighters learned the hard way that it was very costly to incur the wrath of U-boat men.

*   *   *

One noteworthy day around Christmas, our boat was visited by two of the greatest German military heroes of the war: *Generalfeldmarschall* Erwin Rommel and *Luftwaffe General* Adolf Galland. Popularly known as "the Desert Fox," Rommel was the deeply beloved commander of our *Afrika Korps.* Galland was famous for his exploits as an ace fighter pilot during the Battle of Britain and was the leader of our nation's fighter defenses. They, along with a large delegation of other officers, were making an inspection tour of our Atlantic fortifications. The inspection group included representatives from virtually every branch of our armed forces: *Fallschirmjägers* (paratroopers), *Panzers* (tanks), and even the *Waffen SS* (military SS). Almost all of them wore the coveted Knights Cross medal about their necks. I could not hear exactly what Rommel was saying, but several times I saw him shake his head in disbelief at the damage our *U-505* had suffered. He wished us more luck next time, then led the delegation away. We were all honored that such a famous national hero would pay us a personal visit.

After the inspection was over, the real work on *U-505* began. Big compressors cranked up, making a deafening racket that echoed throughout the entire submarine pen complex. Rivets were extracted from the hull and huge pieces of the pressure hull were lifted out by cranes. Our boat began looking like a giant whale undergoing major surgery. No one had ever seen such extensive repairs being performed on a sub, and the operations attracted quite a crowd of onlookers. Always eager to obtain souvenirs, I retrieved a small piece of *U-505*'s hull that had been torn by Sillcock's depth charges. I still have it to this day.

*   *   *

A few days after our visit by Rommel, I had a memorable experience while on guard duty. Late one night, I was standing watch on the upper deck when I heard footsteps approaching from the direction of the pier. It was a lone *Kriegsmarine* officer, wearing the uniform of a *Kapitänleutnant*. He entered the gangway and nonchalantly attempted to board the boat. I knew that he wasn't one of our boat's officers, nor was he the Officer of the Guard for that night, so I followed standard procedure and shouted, "Halt! What is the password?"

He ignored my challenge, and with a haughty look of mild annoyance, attempted to walk past me. I had no alternative other than to unlock the safety of my *Schmeisser MP-40* machine pistol and aim the barrel directly at his chest. "Remain where you are or I will shoot! Hands up!"

He evidently believed I would carry out my threat, because the intruder immediately stopped in his tracks and raised his hands. Although he didn't dare move a muscle, he was absolutely furious at me. "Are you crazy? Can't you see I'm an officer?"

I ignored his tantrum and called the Petty Officer in charge of the watch. The Petty Officer arrived and requested to see the officer's identity papers. When the man refused, we immediately arrested him. Twenty minutes later, the Officer of the Guard himself came to investigate the situation. A quick search of the so-called *Kapitänleutnant* revealed a miniature camera hidden in his uniform. The spy was led away to what, I presume, was a very unpleasant fate.

The next day, during our noontime formation, I was singled out for a commendation by our Exec. Unfortunately, that was not to be my last encounter with spies and saboteurs in Lorient.

*   *   *

Allied bombing raids on Lorient steadily increased, both in terms of frequency and intensity, during this period. By January 1943, most of the civilian inhabitants had packed their possessions and left the city. That, of course, was the major objective of these "terror raids." Since the enemy knew they couldn't knock out our submarine bunkers, they tried to do the next best thing by either driving away our civilian work force or killing those who chose to remain.

As far as our base was concerned, virtually everything not hidden in the concrete submarine bunkers was dispersed to the surrounding countryside. *Lager Lemp* was even more heavily camouflaged. This effort was aided by our *Luftwaffe*, which flew photo reconnaissance missions over the base to discover any weakness.

The British bombers were paying us a visit almost every night. Our slit trenches became ringside seats as we watched the nightly dramas taking place over our heads. And exciting dramas they were, with our searchlights crisscrossing the sky like giant fingers feeling for targets in the darkness. Quite a few times we witnessed them spot one of the big bombers in their light. The beams from several lamps would then converge on the helpless target, capturing it in an inescapable spider web of light. Then, it would be just a matter of time before one of the heavy anti-aircraft cannons scored a hit, sending the plane into a flaming plunge toward the earth. Sometimes we were even able to see the yellow-orange fireball when plane hit the ground.

During the rare daytime raids, our comrades in the *Luftwaffe* sometimes managed to send a few fighter aircraft against the bombers and we would be treated to the spectacle of a dogfight. Despite our pilots' best attempts, however, the enemy bombers always managed to get through to drop their deadly loads on us. Of course, our boats were still perfectly safe from air attack under cover of the armored submarine bunkers, so the enemy shifted their tactics and began to try to kill us crewmen instead. In order to give us a measure of protection, some of our air defense units started generating gigantic smoke screens on the ground in order to hide the buses driving us between the barracks and the submarine bunkers.

Air attacks also got heavier on our U-boats entering and leaving the harbor. Our escorts, which at the beginning of the campaign were composed of one or two small minesweepers, now included a sizable number of larger, more heavily armed ships. How different things had become from just six months ago! In the end, however, our will to fight never flagged in the face of these determined attacks against us. Indeed, the heavy air assault against us seemed to be proof of the threat our U-boats posed to the survival of the Allied war effort. My crew mates and I were more determined than ever to make the enemy pay for the pain and destruction they were raining down upon us.

*   *   *

With the return of the first half of our crew from furlough, it now became my turn to take three weeks leave. I felt proud as a peacock to be wearing the smart-looking Navy dress uniform in public. The dark blue color of the uniform instantly set me apart from the oceans of gray-attired Army boys, and the glittering golden submarine badge on my left breast caught the admiring glances of many young ladies.

The train trip back home was uneventful, though I noticed severe bomb damage in some of the cities along the route. I spent the first two weeks with my parents in Bottendorf. Needless to say, they were very happy to see me. I was especially gratified to see the look of pride on my father's face as he gazed misty-eyed at me in my uniform. Father never was one for saying much, but his eyes were barometers to his emotions.

Several neighbors came to visit me. They brought all manner of sausages, smoked meats, and even some baked goods for me to enjoy or take back to share with my crew mates. These foodstuffs were precious commodities, even in a farming community. Only someone who has lived through wartime food rationing can appreciate how much of a sacrifice these modest-sounding gifts really were.

It was wonderful to be back home again, but after a few days I began to itch for a little more adventure. Instead of staying home every night, I began to frequent the taverns in the nearby town of Frankenburg. My mother, a very religious woman, was concerned about the long hours I spent drinking with my old and new friends. But my father intervened on my behalf. As a combat veteran, he knew what it was like to be a young soldier on leave.

One night, I ran into a young lady I had met a couple of years previously. She was the daughter of a farmer who lived not far from my parent's house. She was an attractive young woman, with light blonde hair and a figure that had blossomed enchantingly in the two years since I had seen her last.

We found that we had much in common. I ended up spending the third and final week of my furlough sightseeing in Vienna with her. We had a lovely time in the beautiful old city.

Back in Frankenburg, we had a long talk about the future. I liked her very much, but given the dismal chances of survival for us U-boat crewmen, I didn't feel it was fair for me to promise anything permanent. In the end, we parted as friends.

Far too soon, it seemed, it was time to return to Lorient. I spent my last two days of freedom with my parents, trying to soak in every detail of the warm little cocoon that was my childhood home. The thought that this might be the last time we would be together weighed heavily on our hearts. As usual, my mother was very emotional, while my father kept a pose of quiet stoicism. Our farewells said, I headed to the train station.

I had foolishly waited until the last minute to make my departure from Frankenburg station, only to discover the train to Frankfurt had been unexpectedly canceled. This meant I would miss my connection to Paris. The *Kriegsmarine* did not take kindly to men returning late to their units in time of war; indeed, the penalty for being even one minute late was three days in the brig. I became desperate.

My father, luckily for me, was still a railway official. By pulling some strings he arranged for me to ride an old steam engine to Marburg. There, a train waited three minutes beyond its scheduled departure time for me to arrive. I had to run and jump on the moving train to make my connection to Frankfurt. I made it safely to Lorient, but right after I left the train station for my barracks, a heavy bombing attack devastated the railroad yards. I quite literally made it through the gates at the last minute. The train ride back to my barracks had turned out to be one of the most exciting parts of my leave!

*   *   *

On the 7th of February, our entire crew traveled by train to Bad Wiessee, a ski resort area south of Munich. There, we were set to spend ten days at *Hotel Wolf*, a *U-boot-Sportheim* recreational facility renowned for its luxurious accommodations. Unfortunately, six men and I were traveling separate from the rest of the crew. We had been detailed to transport our baggage and four large trunks filled with administrative paperwork.

Because of delays, we ended up missing our connecting train in Paris. The only other train going in our direction was a special train reserved for staff personnel and couriers. I felt confident about my ability to "improvise" rail travel, so we decided to board the special train. We waited until two minutes before its departure, then two of us barged onto the train. We opened some windows and the others passed the baggage to us. A few of the compartments had only a couple of occupants, so we kicked them out and loaded the baggage inside.

There was quite a bit of shouting as some of the little desk monkeys complained about being moved. One of them returned with the train's Railroad Police detachment: a captain and three unarmed soldiers. Chief Navigator Reinig, who was in charge of our detachment, tried to explain to them that we were carrying secret documents that had to arrive in 36 hours at our destination. The grim-faced captain, however, would not listen. He ordered us to leave the train at the next stop.

At the next station, the captain returned to our compartment and reiterated his order for us to leave. We ignored him. When one of the soldiers tried to grab our baggage, a terrific brawl broke out. Suffice it to say we managed to beat some sense into those soldiers and they decided to leave us alone.

At Metz, we unloaded our baggage and changed trains to Munich. Unfortunately, there was a reception waiting to greet us there: a Railway

Police detachment with orders to arrest us—and this time they were armed! But to arrest us, they first had to catch us! A comical chase ensued, with us pushing a cart piled high with our baggage, being pursued by several railway policemen. Luckily for us, there were several hundred Army soldiers waiting on the platform. Soldiers, sailors, and airmen often have their disagreements, and sometimes violent ones. But when confronted with the police, we were all brothers-in-arms. The soldiers made way for our cart, but "accidentally" got in the way of the police, allowing us to make good our escape.

Alas, *Kapitänleutnant* Zschech had also been notified by telephone of our little adventure and was waiting for us when we arrived in Bad Wiessee. He cursed us in the very strongest of language. The next morning we received our punishment. The Navigator and the Chief Torpedo Mechanic got ten days of close arrest in the brig. The Boatswain got six, and the rest of us received three. Fortunately, the punishment wouldn't take effect until our return to Lorient, so we all managed to have a great time skiing at the beautiful Alpine resort.

*   *   *

We were shocked to see the condition of *U-505* upon our return to Lorient. The entire conning tower had been removed and was being replaced with a completely new and improved style unit. The 105mm deck gun had also been removed. Because of increased Allied defenses, surface attacks with a deck gun were no longer considered practical. In lieu of the single large cannon, we would now be armed with a four-barreled 20mm anti-aircraft weapon. Two twin-barreled 20mm guns were also installed. In order to accommodate the mounts for the new weapons, the rear of the new conning tower featured a large extended platform nicknamed the *"Wintergarten"* (Winter Garden). The replacement of our deck gun with a flak gun was eloquent testimony to the increasing effectiveness of Allied air attacks on our boats.

There were also internal changes. More than 36 square meters of new pressure hull plating had been riveted and welded into place. One of our electric motors had been exchanged for a quieter, more powerful one. Weeks dragged by as the shipyard workers labored over our boat.

The RAF was equally busy during this period, making bombing raids several nights each week. The Brits were desperate to destroy anything that was even slightly associated with our U-boats, even if they couldn't damage the vessels themselves. Whole neighborhoods of Lorient, including outlying residential districts, had been reduced to dusty rubble.

Despite the damage to the city, we sailors still managed to find what we were looking for in the way of amusement. Actually, our lack of money was putting a bigger crimp into our entertainment than the bombing raids. As our *Reich Marks* and *Renten Marks* dwindled to a precious few, other crews began taking up the slack, inviting us along for dinner and drinks.

Of course, many times it happened that these men perished on their next war patrol. I have heard from veterans of other nations' military services that it was traditional for them to avoid making friends because of the emotional pain involved if they were killed. That idea was never found in the U-boat crews I knew. Fighting alone against a dangerous enemy and the ruthless sea bred a feeling of intimate brotherhood between us. We treasured our friendships with each other, and when the war turned against us and more and more of our comrades failed to return after a mission, the memory of those friends was all we had left.

Of course, these philosophical thoughts come more than a half-century after the end of the war. At the time, despite the heavy losses we were suffering, we remained confident about our future. We were the chosen 10% of the navy; an elite specifically chosen for our physical and mental toughness. The possibility of defeat was never considered. If we should die, we considered it a worthwhile sacrifice in the name of victory. In the meantime, we lived life one day at a time, determined to enjoy every sunrise God granted us.

*   *   *

Work on *U-505* continued through the spring of 1943. We spent most of our time on practice drills and physical training. In early March, however, I was sent with a few other crewmen to an anti-aircraft gunnery school in Mimizan, close to the Spanish border. By coincidence, my cohort included the same group of guys who had gotten in so much trouble delivering the baggage to Bad Wiessee. Somehow, whenever we got together, there was trouble.

We had a five-hour stopover in Bordeaux before we could board our connecting train to Mimizan. Naturally, we went to the Sailor's Quarter for a little amusement while we waited for our train. It was gratifying to know the U-boat men in the Flotillas stationed at Bordeaux had the same tastes in entertainment that we did—probably the same tastes all sailors have had from the beginning of time.

By coincidence, we met some U-boat men who had once been stationed in Lorient. They had returned from patrol the previous week and still had plenty of money to spend. Needless to say, we were happy to accept their generous invitation to join them for a few drinks. The five free hours we had to spend sped by like five minutes as we joked, laughed, and sang with our new friends. We were singing a particularly raunchy sailor ditty when we suddenly realized we had an audience: some military policemen.

The chained dogs not so cordially escorted us to the station and bodily threw us onto the train. On board, we drank a couple more bottles of wine our comrades had given to us as souvenirs of Bordeaux. Luckily, someone woke us up when we reached our destination. Trying to stand at attention in front of the gunnery school barracks turned out to be quite a challenge. One particularly nasty Petty Officer gave us a long speech about life there at the school. There was only one thing we had to do, he said, and that was to obey every order they gave us, and nothing more.

For one full week they chased us like dogs. At one point, we did have target practice against airbags being pulled along the beach by airplanes, but most of the so-called gunnery school was needless harassment. We especially resented the arrogant attitude of the trainers, most of whom had never faced real combat. In the early morning hours of the last day, we cornered the worst offenders and gave them a thorough thrashing. It was a none-too-gentle reminder to them to be more respectful of U-boat men in the future.

By the time we returned to Lorient in mid-March, we were fed-up with being treated like Army soldiers. Some mysterious, timeless power of the sea was calling us, beckoning us to return. I often found myself staring out into the harbor, thinking of the blue-green vastness of the Atlantic.

Most of us were also very eager to get a crack at the enemy again. The past several months had not been a good time for Germany's fortunes in war. Our poor boys in the Stalingrad pocket had finally succumbed to the cruel Russian winter and the endless communist hoards. The Brits and Americans, with their overwhelming material superiority, were doing the same to our valiant *Afrika Korps*. At sea and in the skies over Germany, a bloody war of attrition was being waged, the outcome of which would determine the future course of the war. We were vastly outnumbered and were being squeezed from all directions, just as our fathers had been in the First World War. We were eager to show our families, and the world, that we were prepared to make any sacrifice in order to bring about a victorious end to the war.

That being said, I'm sad to report there was one crewman on board *U-505* who did not share our eagerness to return into combat: my friend Willi. He and I had gotten to be fairly close friends, especially after our experience together in the French graveyard during the bombing raid. A week or so before our scheduled departure date, Willi approached me in confidence and showed me a counterfeit passport he had gotten from his French girlfriend. He told me he planned to run off with her to Switzerland a few days before we sailed on the next war patrol. If I wanted, he said, he could get a false passport for me, too.

Willi's plan struck me like a bolt of lightening. Of course, I had always known he was somewhat of a scoundrel. At the age of 14, he ran away from home to live on the streets of Hamburg's rough port district. Growing up in that environment had given him the morals of a dockyard rat. Still, I never expected Willi to ever do anything like this! If the chained dogs caught him trying to run, he would be executed for desertion in time of war. Besides, I suspected his girlfriend was working for the French Resistance, and that this was a plot to capture a U-boat crewman.

After a long and sometimes heated discussion, I finally promised not to report him, but I warned him if he ever made the slightest move to desert our boat, I would tell the authorities everything I knew. Willi came to his senses and served honorably aboard *U-505* until the day of our capture. Our friendship, however, was never quite the same. Trust is the foundation of any true friendship, and I just couldn't bring myself to be chummy with someone who had considered deserting his crew mates and his country in our hour of crisis.

*   *   *

By late May of 1943, the modifications and repairs on our boat were almost complete. Gone were the large gangs of shipyard workers in their thick brown welder's suits. Only a few technicians were to be still found aboard finishing some small details.

U-505 sported a totally new silhouette. We were especially excited to stand on the spacious *Wintergarten*, with its deadly looking quad-barreled flak gun. Combined with the two twin-barreled 20mm guns on either side of the conning tower, our boat now boasted a total of eight guns for anti-aircraft defense. At least now, we thought, we would have a fighting chance against any enemy birds trying to drop an egg on us.

We also took on an improved type of torpedo that could be programmed to run in predetermined patterns. There were several new radio and sound detection devices installed, too. Parts of the crew were sent to special courses to learn the maintenance and operational details of these mysterious new devices. Everything was very hush-hush because of the danger of espionage. Indeed, many of us did not find out about the new equipment until we were out at sea. Meanwhile, we control room crew mates practiced our tactical maneuvers over and over again until our response times could be reduced no further.

A few new men were also posted to our boat. Most notable was *Oberleutnant* Paul Meyer, the replacement for our wounded Second Watch Officer Stolzenburg. We liked Meyer from the start. He had originally served as Navigation Chief Petty Officer on an auxiliary cruiser, where he had been promoted to officer rank for his bravery in action. His experience as an enlisted man made him relate to us more as a comrade than as a superior. He even came into the enlisted barracks a few times to celebrate with us. This angered Zschech and the Exec, which pleased us even more. Meyer, on his own initiative, discarded the infantry drills in favor of team sports. This was a much more enjoyable way for us to get our physical conditioning. Before long, Paul Meyer was the most popular officer on board.

These final preparations made us all the more impatient to get out of Lorient and back to blue water. The pounding roar of the diesels as they were being tested brought back a flood of nostalgic memories to me: the fresh briny smell of the sea, the pendulum-like swinging of the stars as the boat gently rocked, the choreographed ballet leaps of the dolphins, the thrill of chasing an enemy ship. The restless sea was calling us back to her, and we were eager to answer.

Chapter 10

Sabotage

W hile it was true the sirens of the sea were calling us, at the same time I also felt sentimental about leaving Lorient. After all, the city had been very good to us. To see it so devastated left a hollow feeling in my heart. I took to wandering the shattered streets, desiring to soak in as much as I could in those few remaining days before our departure.

I was strolling through the ruins of a once-beautiful neighborhood one afternoon pondering such thoughts, when I spied an attractively dressed French girl walking my way. There was something familiar about this young lady. When she turned her head toward me, I recognized her at once: Jeanette.

When she saw me, she threw her arms around my neck and started weeping. She was in trouble, she said, because she had been friendly to us U-boat men. She felt her life was in danger from the *Maquis* and that she had no alternative than to leave Lorient for her own safety.

When Jeanette saw that I was still wearing the St. Christopher medal she gave me, she began to cry again. I tried to comfort her the best I could, but since I was leaving on patrol soon, there was very little I could really do for her. I think she appreciated just having someone to talk to since her friends and neighbors had all turned against her.

We spent the night together. The next day she gave me a few packs of cigarettes to enjoy while at sea, then left to start a new life somewhere to the east. I never heard from her again, though I have never forgotten her. I wore her St. Christopher medal until the day we were captured in 1944, when an American sailor snatched it from my neck as a souvenir.

*   *   *

As our departure date neared, we began loading personal equipment aboard *U-505*. The most definite sign of our impending sailing was our own move from *Lager Lemp* back to our old bunks aboard the boat.

One night, one of the torpedo mechanics on upper deck watch was climbing down from the bridge to the control room to wake up his replacement, when the cocking handle of his *Schmeisser MP-40* machine pistol caught one of the rungs of the ladder. The bolt slammed forward, firing a short burst of three rounds down toward the men in the control room. One of the crew received a slight flesh wound in the arm from a 9mm bullet.

When we heard the gunfire, my mates and I flew out of our bunks and ran to the control room, ready to repel boarders with any pipe or wrench we could lay our hands on. When we saw what happened, we broke into laughter. A couple of men had gone to the first aid locker for antiseptic and bandages, and in their excitement had wrapped so many bandages around the poor wounded man he looked like an Egyptian mummy.

We somehow convinced the Watch Petty Officer not to report the little accident, and three rounds of ammunition were found to replace the missing ones in the *Schmeisser*'s magazine. The officers never found out about the incident, though they were always curious how the man on watch got "*Scharfschütze*" (sniper) for a nickname.

On July 1, *U-505* was moved to a wet dock in the bunkers. With her new and much larger conning tower and fresh coat of dark gray paint, she was unrecognizable as the same boat we had limped into harbor more than six months earlier.

Final preparations began for sailing. As usual, the most difficult task was loading the torpedoes. Flat boats came along side *U-505* with the long black eels. These were hoisted up and manhandled by block and tackle down the small fore and aft loading hatches into their respective torpedo rooms. As each was lowered into the bowels of our boat, I often visualized these monsters slamming into the sides of enemy ships.

Next came truckloads of provisions. These were craned up and deposited in huge piles on the upper deck, then loaded in strict order according to a list. I hated seeing the potatoes being loaded because of my disgusting experience with them on the last patrol. The mere smell of potatoes brought forth a queasy feeling in my stomach, even though they were fresh.

Next came the ammunition loading. Our boat's new armament made this a simple task compared to the old days, because the boxes of 20mm ammo were much easier to handle than the massive 105mm artillery rounds we used to store. That big quad-barreled flak gun inspired a lot of confidence that we would be able to fend off attacks by aircraft. Indeed, we were already picking out areas on its broad gun shield where we would paint the silhouettes of planes signifying our kills. But for all the bravado engendered by those 20mm stingers, we still knew all it took was one attacker to get through our defensive fire to put an end to our lives.

The last chore after loading was testing the integrity of the hull. Once the hatches and valves were closed, a big compressor was run to create a partial vacuum inside the boat. The internal barometer was monitored to ensure there were no air leaks. Everything checked out normal and we were given the go-ahead for our operational patrol.

The next day, we backed out of the bunker into the wet slip and completed the lengthy demagnetization process that, hopefully, would help protect our boat from any magnetic mines laid in the harbor by Allied aircraft. A nervous excitement began stirring in our stomachs as we moved, step-by-step, closer to the departure hour.

In the evening we attended the traditional farewell banquet. As usual, there was much drinking and toasting as we consumed the last of our private stocks of beer and liqueurs. With our money gone and our goodbyes said, we were finally ready to leave.

We were allowed to sleep a bit late the next morning to get over the effects of the banquet. Then, at 1030 hours, we took a bus back to the boat and loaded our personal articles onboard. I brought along a cache of several dozen lemons with me as a prophylactic against loosening of the teeth, a common affliction resulting from our poor diet at sea.

Our departure ceremony was a rather muted affair. For one thing, there was no naval band. In its place were a few accordion players who played and sang several traditional sailor songs. Some officers from the Flotilla Staff, along with about 50 well-wishers, came to say goodbye.

Many in the audience had tears in their eyes, and there were a few shed aboard our boat, too.

How different in tone this was from earlier departures! Gone was the wild optimism and swaggering patriotism. In their place was a steely determination to do one's duty, no matter the cost. And we were well aware of the mounting cost of the Battle of the Atlantic. In the past three months, no less than 90 boats had failed to return! Since our entire U-boat fleet consisted of only a few hundred frontline boats, these were staggering losses. But we were professionals, part of a proud naval tradition. Our country was in danger, and we had a job to do. To us, it was as simple as that.

The last lines were cast-off and we got underway. We bade a bittersweet farewell to Lorient and our well-wishers, then got down to business. Once we were clear of the pier, we increased speed to one-half and headed for the mouth of the harbor. Our transit through the harbor out to the Bay of Biscay illustrated the increasing hazards facing us. In an ironic imitation of the enemy's own convoy tactics, we traveled out to sea in the company of four other boats: *U-168*, *U-183*, *U-514*, and *U-533*. By traveling in one group and combining our anti-aircraft defenses, it was believed our chances of being sunk by intruding bombers would be lessened. A surprisingly large force of seven minesweepers formed our escort, making a last minute check for mines and providing an additional anti-aircraft umbrella. Only six of us remained in the boat to handle controls as we left the anchorage. The rest of the crew was kneeling on the upper deck in case we struck a mine.

A curtain of thick drizzly fog greeted us as we departed the harbor. The moonlit mist gave a gray, ghostly appearance to the other ships as we made our way towards deep water. As for the sea itself, the water was as smooth as a dance floor. The overall effect as we left Lorient was quite unearthly.

Around midnight, our diesels began to stutter and cough, finally sputtering to a stop. The rest of our little flotilla rumbled on, leaving us behind in the darkness. One minesweeper stayed behind to give us air cover while we effected repairs. After an hour and a half of feverish work, the diesels roared back to life. We all breathed a sigh of relief; being immobilized in daylight would have meant certain death for us.

Several hours later we arrived at our departure point, code-named *Punkt Kern*. The escorts had already scurried back to harbor to avoid any early morning air attacks, leaving us alone for our deep diving test. This was the moment of truth for our newly-repaired pressure hull. Because the hull was untested, we dove to a depth of only 40 meters. Everything went well with the dive at first, but within thirty minutes our starboard propeller shaft developed a leak. Concerned by the faulty shaft seal, 40 meters became our new maximum depth. Some skippers might have decided to turn back toward port at this point, but we continued on with the mission, hoping against hope that we could somehow fix the leak. Our streak of bad luck continued when a few minutes later, the reflector on our new *FuMB Metox* search radar detection device short-circuited. Less than half a day out of port, and we had already developed severe mechanical and electrical problems!

We were not alone in our mechanical difficulties. Around noon the next day, we received a *FT* from *U-533* reporting that one of her exhaust valves was not functioning. Their problem could not be repaired at sea, so that evening *U-533* was recalled to Lorient. We immediately suspected sabotage from the dock workers. In an effort to reduce the chances of sabotage, virtually all of the men working on U-boats were *Volksdeutsch*, ethnically-German residents of Poland and other Eastern European countries. It was disconcerting to imagine that, if it was sabotage, our own ethnic brethren were the ones plotting our demise.

We made the transit across the Bay of Biscay primarily underwater in order to avoid detection by the ever-increasing numbers of Allied ships and aircraft. Overhead, a virtually constant flow of RAF bombers shuttled back and forth between England and Gibraltar, creating a cordon of death between our U-boat sally ports and the Atlantic we called the "Suicide Stretch." If a boat was spotted but escaped destruction from the air, groups of destroyers were dispatched to the spot. Once the destroyers arrived, the cat and mouse game began. And it literally was like a cat and mouse game. A cat toys with a mouse, waiting until its prey is exhausted before delivering the final blow. In much the same way, the destroyers chased U-boats until their air or electrical power was exhausted. Once forced to surface, a submarine was easy prey for the waiting warships. As the mouse, our only chance was to spot the cats before they spotted us. The officers didn't need to remind us how crucial it was to keep our eyes open and alert when on bridge watch!

On the morning of July 7, we passed a cluster of Portuguese fishing vessels. The Portuguese were neutrals, but it was widely assumed there were some British spies with radios among them. We gave the boats a wide berth to avoid detection.

That evening, our *GHG* underwater listening device went out of commission. This left our boat virtually deaf, robbing us of one of our most crucial survival tools. Our string of bad luck, especially at such an early stage of the mission, was too much for even the skeptics among us to dismiss as mere coincidence. Grumbling that we were the victims of a well-coordinated program of sabotage began to dominate our off-duty conversations. Our skipper seemed to be especially troubled by our situation. With each malfunction, Zschech's behavior became more erratic, alternating between morose introversion and sadistic outbursts of aggression.

Despite the mechanical difficulties that hobbled us, we stubbornly continued our patrol. The newcomers to our crew soon got accustomed to the rhythm of this leg of our voyage. There were long stretches of underwater travel, with nothing but the monotonous hum of the electric motors to remind us we were moving. Then, interrupting the tedium, short exhilarating sprints on the surface with the diesels hammering away as we replenished our air and recharged the batteries. The sea was getting rough, so our time spent on the surface was a real roller coaster ride compared to the quiet calm of underwater travel.

Bridge watch duty was especially tension-filled because we were absolutely determined not to get surprised by an airplane again. Meanwhile, the new sailors in the crew were still gaining their sea legs and had to be taught a hard lesson: getting seasick is not an excuse for failing to perform one's bridge watch duties.

"You hold the binoculars to the eyes, not to the mouth," they were told. "If you turn green, just spit-up on the deck; the sea will clean it up with the next wave." We could only smile in knowing sympathy as the newcomers slowly became accustomed to the motions of the boat.

The next morning, we lost contact with Auffermann's *U-514*, our partner for the voyage across the Atlantic. We had been traveling with her along the 200-meter line when we discovered our radio was out of commission. As a consequence, we missed our scheduled transmission time, and in the heavy seas, could not establish visual contact with her. Around noon, we found we were unable to deploy our radio direction finder antenna from its stowed, diving position. That simple, circular device was one of the most necessary pieces of equipment on board.

Later, we managed to repair the radio and our *FuMB Metox* device. Two steps forward, two steps back!

As we cruised underwater near Cape Finisterre on the Spanish coast, we were unexpectedly shaken by a rapid series of six explosions, very loud and very close. An airplane had somehow spotted us, despite our 40-meter depth. We had dived from 18 meters to the lower depth just a few minutes before, and that small additional bit of depth probably saved our lives. A little while later, four large depth charges exploded even closer, severely rattling our boat. We hoped the plane was out of depth charges, but just to be on the safe side, we released a *Bold*, a canister of chemicals designed to create a large mass of bubbles. We hoped our attackers would deduce we had been sunk. The ruse apparently worked because there were no further attacks.

With an inoperative direction finder and *GHG*, not to mention an inability to dive deep, our boat was clearly in no condition to fight. We also suspected we had a fuel leak that was allowing the enemy to detect our position underwater by means of a trailing oil slick. In light of our nearly crippled condition, Zschech decided to return to Lorient for repairs. We all concurred with his decision. At 2000 hours, we dove back down to 40 meters and headed back for base.

Just a few minutes after we turned for home, however, we heard the sound that all submariners fear: the whir of high-speed propellers, the unmistakable signature of approaching destroyers. The aircraft had obviously radioed our position so the warships could finish the job they had started. We secured all of the hatches with clamps and braced ourselves for the inevitable.

The destroyers homed right in on us. In the deathly quiet inside our sub, we could clearly hear the splash of nine depth charges being dropped directly over our heads. Seconds later, our world dissolved into a thundering nightmare of flying objects and breaking glass. Anything and anyone who was not tied down was tossed to the deck by the blasts.

Men were shouting, but no one lost their nerve. Despite the horrendous battering we took, there were only a few small leaks. In the momentary calm before the next storm, everyone grabbed something to hold on to, unconsciously gazing upward at the unseen enemy. (NOTE: For some reason, men in submarines always look up during a depth charge attack, despite the well-known fact that the most dangerous ones explode underneath the hull. I could never understand this phenomenon, nor explain why I, too, would stare upward during the attacks.)

Ten minutes later, we heard the propellers rev up for another pass. Nine more gigantic blasts rocked our boat, then . . . nothing. Gradually, the propeller noises faded into the distance. We stared at each other for a moment, not fully comprehending that we were still alive.

Afterward, everyone chattered about the attack. We imagined the enemy sailors up there petting the sides of the depth charges and praying for the worst to happen to us, expecting any moment to see the boiling swell of air, oil, and bodies that signal the death of a U-boat. Then, in soft, furtive whispers, men who had watched Zschech during the depth charge attack told the others what they had seen: how his facial expressions had absolutely convinced them our skipper's wishes were no different than those of the enemy sailors above us. A strong suspicion spread through our crew, repeated only in the most hushed of tones, that Zschech had a death wish. Several of his close friends from the naval academy had recently been killed, and we surmised he had an unconscious desire to join them.

I was lying in my bunk trying to conserve oxygen and relax from the previous attack when we heard the humming propellers of destroyers returning. As Heaven is my witness, they sounded for all the world like a chorus of funeral chants. Again came the salvo of nine barrels of death. Our boat became a giant kettledrum resonating with the beat of the devil's own tattoo. This time the explosions straddled us; it was a miracle we were not blasted in two by the hammer-like blows from both sides.

We released two more canisters of *Bold* and tried to sneak out of the area through slow, silent running. After an hour of relative silence, Zschech took *U-505* up to periscope depth and ventured to take a peek at our assailants. Sure enough, laying 3,000 meters off to port were three destroyers. One was unusually large and resembled a cruiser of the *Birmingham* class. Believing an attack against the destroyers would be futile because of the mirror-smooth sea, Zschech ordered us to leave the area as quickly as our electric motors could propel us.

The damage control parties started reporting back with their inventories of needed repairs. We discovered our underwater telegraph device was now also out of commission. We clearly had no alternative but to return to base as quickly and directly as possible.

*   *   *

Running silently underwater, we arrived off the coast of La Coruna late that evening. We surfaced and used our diesels for a high-speed dash. To provide some protection against radar detection, we hugged the Spanish coastline, cruising about three nautical miles off shore. It was quite thrilling to sail at full speed through the shallow waters. Bonfires lining the beaches as fishing boat beacons bathed our boat in an eerie yellow light.

We submerged just before dawn. After a couple of hours, Zschech brought us up to periscope depth to take a look around. We all heard him shout from the conning tower attack room, *"Verdammte Scheiße!"* (Dammed Shit!). He told us that a huge wedge of shimmering, rainbow-colored diesel oil was trailing our boat as far as the eye could see. Our suspicions about a fuel leak were correct. Zschech stormed back to his cabin without saying a word.

For the next few days we repeated our tactics: high speed runs close to shore at night, slow speed underwater runs during the day. We sometimes stopped and rested on the bottom very close to shore in the hope the beach waves would conceal our oil trail. We would sit there for hours, gently rocking in time with the waves, until we reckoned the oil had marked our position. Then we would rise off the bottom and make a short run out of the vicinity.

For our transit across the Bay of Biscay, we often risked surface travel. Rough weather made us less worried about being spotted by airborne radar. We also found we left less of an oil slick when traveling on the surface. The final leg to Lorient, however, was completed almost entirely underwater due to the threat of air attack.

On the afternoon of the 11th, we received an underwater telegraph message which we suspected was for us, but which we could not decipher because of our defective equipment. While cruising on the surface that night, we received a *FT* from Western U-boat Command advising us of our rendezvous time and location. We had 24 hours to get back to *Punkt Kern* to meet our escort.

By the grace of God, we arrived at our rendezvous point on time. Just as our two escort ships came into view, however, the eagle eyes on the bridge spotted a couple of enemy aircraft approaching fast and low from the east, altitude 300 meters. Our brand new *Metox* gave us absolutely no warning of their approach, despite the fact that they must have been using radar to find us. A prompt crash dive allowed us to elude attack, but as the sounds of explosions echoed through the boat, we wondered whether our escorts would still be there when we surfaced. We rose to periscope depth 20 minutes later. Sure enough, there were our escorts; the tiny mine sweepers had stood firm in the face of the Allied bombers. We sailed back toward Lorient harbor flanked by our gallant little escort.

Around 0130 hours, a mine-laying bomber suddenly swept out of the darkness and began strafing us with heavy machine guns. The bullets kicked up long lines of florescent splashes all around us. We replied with our 20mm cannons, spraying the sky with streams of brightly colored tracers. The welcome we provided for our visitor was apparently a little too hot for his taste and he quickly flew away. Once again, *Metox* had given us no warning of the plane which, in the darkness of the night, absolutely must have been using radar to find us.

A German blockade-runner ship that was hiding in the nearby darkness was attracted by all the fireworks and joined us for an escort back into the harbor. The sweepers took the lead in case the Brits had laid mines in our path. We proceeded unmolested the rest of the way into port.

Just before dawn, we rumbled into the armored *Skorff Bunker* in the Lorient submarine pens. There were no bands or fanfare this time, just a few skeptical-looking officials standing on the pier. We got the distinct impression they were displeased to see us back in port so soon. Once they learned the extent of our equipment failures, however, their attitude became more apologetic.

The morning after our arrival, the Flotilla Engineer and a large contingent of high-ranking shipyard officials conducted a careful inspection of our boat. They found that nearly all the seals for our air relief valves, emergency valves, diving tanks, battery cells, and fuel bunkers were totally corroded. This explained the fuel leak that nearly cost us our lives. At first, the shipyard staff insisted that the materials sent to them by the manufacturers were defective, but they were later forced to admit this was not true. Their final, reluctant conclusion was that someone had poured battery acid on the seals.

Several other boats had complained about mysterious failures of equipment, too. Some of them, undoubtedly, were just cases of bad luck. But there were many irrefutable instances of sabotage. One boat found sugar in the lube oils. Another found a dead dog poisoning its drinking water tank. Many of the boats had cans of foodstuffs explode from botulism or improperly sealed lids. Of course, these were mere annoyances compared to some of the more serious instances of sabotage, such as magnetic bombs attached to hulls. As scattered rumors of sabotage segued into ironclad certainty, stern security measures began to be taken.

For the next two weeks, our boat underwent repairs. They also replaced our huge four-barreled 20mm anti-aircraft gun with a newly designed single-barreled *Oerlikon* 37mm automatic cannon. The trim little flak weapon worked flawlessly for us until the very end. Meanwhile, a few of the crew were sent to special technical courses, but the majority of us stayed on board and assisted with the repairs. Needless to say, we kept a very close eye on all work being done by the shipyard workers.

*   *   *

As I mentioned before, one author came to the conclusion, and others have repeated the story, that the Sillcock bombing incident had crushed our morale during this period. He implied that our fighting spirit had been shattered by the experience and that the technical failures we experienced were a flimsy excuse to return to Lorient and avoid combat. I can tell you categorically that is total nonsense!

No submarine would have continued on a patrol with the equipment failures we experienced. Furthermore, our morale was excellent. We U-boat men were handpicked and specially trained for this profession. We were proud, even eager, to do our duty, despite the mounting odds against us. When our boat was hit by Sillcock's bombing attack, we never stopped fighting to keep her afloat. *U-505*'s record as having been the most heavily damaged U-boat to get back to port is eloquent testimony to our determination not to give up. We were equally determined to get back into the fight as soon as possible. Given what later happened to Zschech, I can understand how some authors got a mistaken impression about our boat, but the rest of the crew's morale never faltered.

During the course of the war, I came to know many of the 32,000 U-boat comrades who did not return from a patrol and are forever resting in their "iron coffins" at the bottom of the sea. I also know many of them who survive today. To a man, they were, and still are, a tough breed. The

U-boat arm of the German Navy in World War II suffered a higher percentage of casualties than any combat arm in history. And yet, despite those horrible losses, we continued to sail forth against the enemy until the very last day of the war. Although history has judged harshly Germany's political leadership during the war, no one can deny the valor and devotion to duty demonstrated by the U-boat service.

Today, there are lots of people who read books and look at pictures, and call themselves experts about what life was like aboard the U-boats. But no one knows what it was really like except those who were there. The purpose of this book is to set the record straight, at least for the small bit of the war I witnessed. And I tell you now, sincerely and without reservation, the crew of *U-505* never failed to live up to the high standards set for our service by Admiral Dönitz.

*   *   *

On August 1, 1943, we once again departed Lorient harbor for the bountiful hunting grounds of the Western Atlantic. This time we left in the company of *U-68, U-523*, and *U-123*. I joined the majority of the crew, kneeling on the upper deck with a life preserver around my neck as a precaution against injury from mines. The religious symbolism of departing the harbor on bended knee was not lost on us.

The Bay of Biscay gave us an unfriendly welcome. Rough green waves crashed over our bow and soaked the bridge watch. By dawn, we had managed to punch our way through heavy swells to *Punkt Kern* and were ready to make our final test dive before heading west. We still had not had an opportunity to make a dive deeper than 40 meters since the general repairs on our pressure hull, including during our previous, abbreviated patrol. Although these dives were a part of the routine ritual before leaving for patrol, this one made us nervous.

In light of our untested pressure hull, the descent was made a bit slower than usual. We sank to 40 meters with no problem. Then, with every additional meter of depth, we watched and listened with greater intensity.

At 50 meters, we heard a loud metallic crack, followed by a succession of more cracking sounds. We held at that depth for a few minutes to check for damage, but none could be found. It was decided that, one way or another, we would have to discover the source of the sounds and determine whether it was some harmless settling of the plates or something more serious. We resumed our descent.

At 60 meters, we heard a distinct hissing sound that got progressively louder the deeper we sank. Then suddenly, a loud gurgling noise, apparently coming from outside the pressure hull. We stayed at that depth for more than an hour checking every conceivable problem. Nothing could be found.

We surfaced and inspected the upper deck and the pressurized tubes containing the spare torpedoes, but found nothing. We dove again. At 60 meters an enormous bang was heard, emanating astern of the control room on the starboard side. A whispered conference between the Engineering Officer and Zschech resulted in the order to abort the patrol and return to base. *U-523*, which was to accompany us on the patrol, was notified of our situation. By midnight, we were back in *Skorff Bunker*.

The shipyard engineers could find no obvious evidence of leaking in our boat. Nevertheless, they decided to keep us in port for a week while the *FuG Naxos* device, an improvement on our *Metox* search radar detection gear, was installed on board.

It was aggravating to watch the slow progress of the *Naxos* installation, but what really galled us was the skepticism that greeted our reports of the diving noises—as if we had merely imagined such things!

Vindication was sweet when the shipyard engineers sheepishly reported that they had indeed found evidence of sabotage: hollow sweat seams in the newly repaired areas of the pressure hull. Instead of solidly welded seams, they found that strips of oakum (a sort of oil-soaked rope used for caulking) had been placed in between the plate joints. The oakum was then covered with a thin cover of solder to hide the sabotage. With the joints in our pressure hull thus weakened, a deep dive would have meant instant death. Over the next two weeks, the damage was repaired. Every inch of every welding seam was given a minute inspection before we were given the go-ahead for another patrol.

Just after sunset on August 14, we once again cast off the lines from the pier and made our way out of Lorient harbor. This time, *U-68* would be our hunting partner.

At the 200-meter line offshore, we started our test dive. When our boat successfully reached 50 meters of depth without incident, we became optimistic that all our technical troubles were behind us. Our hopes were dashed when, at 60 meters, another thunderous crashing noise was heard, followed by the now familiar gurgling. The air intake foot valve began vibrating madly as the gurgling sound became much louder.

Zschech turned beet red in the face, then ghostly white. Pressing his lips together tightly, he motioned for the Engineering Officer to join him in his cabin. A few moments later, the Engineering Officer returned to the control room, grim faced and silent.

Zschech emerged from his cabin and angrily shouted the order to surface. Once again, we would be heading back to port. Everyone in the crew was livid with frustration. Once on the surface, we discovered that the air intake duct was crushed flat and torn. We received an *FT* from our partner *U-68*, reporting that she was also experiencing serious technical problems.

With word that *U-68*, too, was crippled with mechanical failures, our anger reached white-hot intensity. How could anyone expect us to win the war when our best weapons were suffering from a deliberate and pervasive program of sabotage by shipyard personnel?

We turned back towards Lorient, running on the surface in order to make it back as quickly as possible. Just before sundown, a twin-engined aircraft swooped at very low level toward us. The boys manning the anti-aircraft guns, with the memory of Sillcock still fresh in their minds, didn't hesitate to fire. Luckily, they recognized it as a German aircraft before it was hit.

By the time we arrived back in Lorient that evening, the mood of the crew was one of seething rage against the saboteurs. Quite a few of our boats had gone down with all hands without apparent reason, and sabotage was becoming the most likely explanation. It was bad enough to face a powerful and sophisticated enemy on the high seas; now we had to worry about enemies in port, too!

Some writers have suggested we crewmen believed we were being haunted by Sillcock's ghost, or Löwe's sailing ship, or even the flowers. Again, these speculations are without basis. True, sailors are generally a superstitious lot, but in the end one is forced to be realist—a romantic dreamer or a superstitious fool wouldn't last long at sea, especially during wartime. No, we had no doubt as to the source of these particular troubles.

Another untruth writers have spread about *U-505*'s crew during this period is that we were the objects of laughter and ridicule by other boats' crews. This is also false. Almost every boat in the Flotilla was experiencing sabotage of some sort or another; no one blamed us for these technical failures. There was always an undercurrent of good-natured competition between crews, but I never heard anyone ever question our bravery or ridicule us.

It was during this stay in port, on August 16 to be exact, that Zschech's good friend the Executive Officer was transferred to another boat to take over as skipper. Bode's attitude toward us crewmen had changed quite a bit during the last several weeks. During his farewell ceremony, he took the unusual step of walking down the ranks of our formation, saluting each man as he passed. In his parting speech, he said, "I've learned a lot since I joined you. Now that I'm leaving, I wish all of you success and a happy return from all of your patrols. I wish for myself a crew on my future boat with your spirit and pluck!"

We were gratified Bode had matured as an officer and as a man during his tenure as our Exec. Happily, he became one of the few U-boat skippers to survive the Battle of the Atlantic. Today, he lives a quiet, prosperous life in Germany.

The next day, Second Watch Officer *Oberleutnant* Paul Meyer was promoted to Executive Officer. The Flotilla Staff had originally ordered him to attend Commanding Officers School, but he appealed the decision to the Flotilla Personnel Office, preferring instead to stay aboard our boat. This is in itself strong evidence that we were a first-rate crew. Meyer said he wanted to stay with a crew with such guts and cohesion that they had gotten the most heavily damaged U-boat in the war safely back to base from across the Atlantic. He was immensely well liked by the crew, and we were ecstatic that he was now our Exec. We felt that if we could just get *U-505* in shape, we would really cause some damage to the enemy. Today, with the advantage of hindsight, the replacement of our skipper's buddy with this popular officer probably left Zschech more emotionally isolated than ever.

*   *   *

That same evening I had my closest encounter ever with espionage. In some ways, it was the most frightening experience in my life.

I had gone with a comrade of mine to Hennebont, a small town located about six kilometers away from our barracks. At the end of Pont

Skorff was a small restaurant renowned for its *Pommes de Terre* (fried potatoes). They usually added small bits of meat that they claimed was rabbit, but which were widely regarded as cat by us sailors. In any event, I thought the dish was very tasty, especially when washed down with a few glasses of strong red wine.

My friend had a bit of luck with another kind of tasty dish, so to speak, and left with a French girl. I decided to linger a bit longer and have some more wine. As soon as I was alone, however, a guy sitting with several other men at a nearby table began talking very loudly, obviously for my benefit. He was staring straight at me as he spoke, commenting to his friends that the hatchet emblem on my cap denoted that I was from *U-505*. I was sure I recognized him as one of the dockworkers who had attended to our boat.

"Well, *U-505* is back again. She didn't make it out!" he said in German, in case I could not understand. "We'll make sure that they don't get very far in the future, too!"

Everyone in the small room turned around to see my reaction to this obvious provocation. As for me, that was all the hint I needed to conclude that this fellow was one of the bastards who had been sabotaging our boat. All of the frustration and anger that had been building in my gut for the past few months exploded into an uncontrollable rage. I stormed over to his table and slapped him hard across the face, the traditional challenge to a fight. His rat-like eyes stared at me, filled with fear and hate, but he made no move to answer my challenge. I was disgusted by the cowardice of this back-stabbing saboteur. After a moment of hesitation, I grabbed him by the scruff of his collar and hauled him outside. Not one of his companions lifted a finger to stop me. As soon as we were out of sight in the rear of the restaurant, I began to hit him.

I don't remember much of the actual beating I gave him. I only remember suddenly being surrounded by German Army police, being arrested, and being brought to the engineer barracks for questioning. The captain on duty told me I could have killed the man and that they had arrested me for my own safety, lest I get lynched by the French civilians. As far as the dockyard worker was concerned, he had refused medical attention and vanished. After three hours of detention, they returned my *Soldbuch* identity papers and released me.

When I arrived at the main gate of *Lager Lemp*, I was told to go immediately to the officers quarters and report to Zschech. Up I went, knocking three times on his door. Someone inside yelled, "Come in!"

As prescribed by regulations, I opened the door, took three long steps inside, took my cap in my left hand and saluted with my right. "*Maschinengefreiter* Göbeler reporting as ordered, Sir!"

"As if we didn't have enough trouble already! Now this new mess. Well, what happened? Why did you get arrested?"

I explained what I had heard and what I had done. Zschech asked where this so-called saboteur was, and I told him the *Wehrmacht* police had allowed him to go free.

"O.K.," he said, calming down some. "But I have to do something, perhaps even court martial you. But I'll give you one chance. You have exactly 48 hours to get that bastard into custody, and I don't care how you do it. You're excused from duty for the next couple of days. Now get out of here!"

I saluted and quickly left the room, eager not to waste a single minute of my 48 hours. I heard Zschech shout, "You'd better find him!" through the closed door as I ran down the hall.

When I arrived back at the barracks, I found that everyone was already aware of my plight. Everyone had a different suggestion regarding how to find the saboteur, but since I was the only one who could identify the guy, I knew this was something I had to do on my own.

Early the next morning, I accompanied the crew to the bunkers, but did not board the boat. Instead, I walked to the section of the shipyard where I thought the saboteur might work and stood next to the punch clock. I had a good chance to look over everyone in line, one by one, as they punched-in for work. After a while, everyone began looking the same. I was beginning to doubt whether I could recognize my nemesis, even if I saw him face to face.

Five minutes later, the night shift began lining up to punch-out. I quickly realized that I could never find the man this way, so I went to the personnel office to look through the files. The personnel clerks were very suspicious of me, but after some vigorous argument, they finally allowed me to search through the photograph file of employees. I pored over the files for hours. After a while the photos, too, began to all look the same. This was worse than standing next to the punch clock.

I was getting desperate. Although my memory of the saboteur was getting fuzzier, the one image that was becoming clearer in my head was one of me in my dress blue uniform, standing in front of my court martial committee. But what else could I do?

That evening and the next morning, I loitered around our boat to see if the culprit would show up for work at the docks. Again, no luck. I only had a few hours left, and I was going crazy with desperation.

In what I felt was surely a futile, last-ditch attempt to find him, I decided to go back to Hennebont, the site of the original incident. A *Wehrmacht* soldier on a motorbike saw me walking along the side of the road and gave me a lift. I spent the entire afternoon walking up and down the streets of that little town, like a condemned man pacing in his jail cell, waiting for the hour of his execution.

Literally minutes before I was going to return to my barracks to turn myself in to the authorities, I saw a group of men and young French girls walking toward me. They were laughing and singing together in French, but I could tell from their accents that the men were not French. Most of the men wore civilian dress, but a few were in the uniform of the *Organization Todt* labor force. As they passed me, I couldn't believe my eyes: the man in the center of the group, the jolliest of the lot, was the saboteur! A few black and blue marks on his face confirmed he was the one.

I quickly explained my situation to a couple of German Army soldiers who were standing nearby and asked them to give me a hand in case there was any trouble from the man's friends.

Broad grins spread across their faces. "Sure, go ahead! We're in the right mood to fight a bit."

With the Army soldiers watching from a short distance away, I crept up behind the group. I grabbed the bastard's arm with my right hand and twisted it behind his back. He struggled to get free, but by jerking his arm high up his back, I soon convinced him to stop resisting.

My comrades from the Army were there in the blink of an eye, telling the rest of the group to just keep on walking and singing or else there would be trouble. Once again, the man's friends didn't lift a hand to help him.

I walked the saboteur, locked tightly in the arm hold, all the way back to the barracks. Every time I sensed he was tempted to try something, a quick jerk on his arm reminded him who was in control. I walked straight through the gate of the barracks towards the military police office, shouting to the guard to get the Officer of the Watch as I walked by. Less than five minutes later, the saboteur was behind bars.

An officer interviewed me and wrote a lengthy report. Then a Staff Sergeant with a motorbike drove me back to *Lager Lemp*. When I reported my success to Zschech, he seemed very relieved.

"You did a good job, Göbeler. Tomorrow, you will have another day off." He even smiled and slapped me on the back. It was one of the few times I ever heard him say something kind to anyone. I got out of there quickly, before his mood changed.

Later, I learned the saboteur was pardoned because he had five children and had received a good recommendation from his supervisor. To be on the safe side, however, he was prohibited from working on U-boats. I was quite angry he got off with such light punishment, but at least I had avoided a court martial, not to mention having enjoyed the satisfaction of teaching him a personal lesson with my fists.

In the meantime, the sabotage on our boat was repaired. The engineers also discovered the source of the cracking and gurgling sounds: the casing on one of the pressure-proof storage tubes for the spare torpedoes had failed. They also mounted a new air intake and connecting piece to replace the damaged ones. For the next four days, everything on board the boat was given a scrupulous inspection. On August 20, everything was declared in order. Surely, we thought, we would be able to sail this time with no problems.

*   *   *

On the evening of August 21, 1943, we once again cast off lines and rumbled out of the bunker towards the harbor mouth. By 0547 hours, we were in position at *Punkt Liebe*, ready for our test dive.

We passed the test dive with flying colors; there was no trace of unusual noises at all. We were ecstatic! Nothing but smiles and back slaps for the crew of a boat which had finally shaken the off the saboteurs' cold, cowardly grip!

We rose to periscope depth so Zschech could take a look around before the sun rose. In the control room, passing the test dive had put us in an almost giddy mood. Soon we would hear the marvelous sound of the Jumbos roar with life and smell the fresh aroma of the sea. We were tired of being land-locked mechanics and longed to be submarine warriors once again.

Suddenly, from the direction of the conning tower hatch, we heard Zschech's unmistakable voice begin to curse. His voice had the hissing sound that we had long ago learned to associate with deep trouble. Sure enough, trailing behind our boat was another broad wedge of shimmering, multi-colored water: we were leaking oil again!

It was as if someone had poured ice-cold water on our good spirits. For several moments we were in shock, then the anger took over. How could this happen again? *Kapitänleutnant* Henke, commander of the boat accompanying us on our voyage, was notified of our condition. The two skippers agreed the mission should be aborted, and both boats turned back for Lorient.

Never had I seen a crew returning to port in such miserable spirits. There was none of the usual happy chatter while the lines were secured to the dock. Instead, we assembled on the upper deck for instructions, picked up our sea bags, and trudged aboard buses for *Lager Lemp*, all without a single word being spoken.

After dropping off our possessions in the barracks, we proceeded *en masse* to the canteen for some drinks. We wanted to get drunk and we didn't waste any time. After several hours, we had more than achieved our goal. But it was an angry, bitter drunk instead of the usual jovial mood. Around midnight, the manager ordered us to leave the premises, but we refused until he agreed to sell us a few more bottles of rum.

We staggered our way up to the barracks, complaining about our rotten luck the whole way. When we opened the door, there was Executive Officer Meyer, standing there waiting for us. "Oh shit," we thought, "we are in trouble now."

We braced ourselves for a good yelling from him, but instead, we quickly discovered that he was drunk, too. Indeed, he even brought some liqueur with him to share with us. This man Paul Meyer is our kind of Exec, we proclaimed, and settled down for some serious drinking. The bacchanal lasted 'till dawn.

Zschech must have somehow heard about our behavior, because the next day he ordered the entire crew to scrape paint and clean the bilge. I didn't mind going down into the dark, cool bilge to recover from the previous night's activities. The fact is, a bilge looks the same whether its been cleaned or not. So, as we had so often done before, we found a cozy little spot amongst the pipes and valves, laid down some rags for comfort, and took a nap for a few hours. The only important thing to remember was to remove all the rags when one was done resting in order to prevent any chance of them plugging a valve. As usual, some of the men periodically clanged on the pipes to give the impression of industriousness. Our nap was especially delicious because, supposedly, we were being punished at the time.

*   *   *

The shipyard engineers once again tried to blame our oil leak on faulty seals. It took three weeks to change them out. Once that job was completed, they tested the tanks to see if they leaked. To their apparent surprise, the test indicated that the seals were not the problem: our boat was still leaking diesel oil. A closer inspection revealed someone had drilled a small pencil-sized hole in one of the fuel bunkers. The hole was too small to notice, but large enough to let out a tell-tale oil slick once we sailed. The shipyard officials sheepishly admitted they were wrong and repaired the sabotage. They also installed yet another newly-developed radar detection apparatus, which was nicknamed the "*Wanze*" (bedbug).

On September 18, just after sundown, we slipped out of the bunker for another stab at the enemy. This time, we all, officers and men alike, decided that we were going to go into action against the enemy, no matter what technical difficulties arose. We even "knocked on wood" as we boarded the boat to give us an additional boost of luck.

We left Lorient in the company of *U-103, U-155, U-228,* and several escort craft. Our little flotilla bristled with a virtual forest of skyward-pointing anti-aircraft guns. I found myself almost wishing the damned British bombers would try something with us.

Passing the ancient Fort Louis at the edge of the harbor was our signal to start up the diesel engines. Our Jumbos roared to life and out into the bay we sped. Once again, we arrived at *Punkt Liebe* just before dawn for our test dive. The Engineering officer, wracked by anxiety, had the grimmest face imaginable as he listened to the diving tanks slowly filling with water. Our spirits were momentarily buoyed by a quiet and successful test dive, but then the engine room gloomily reported that the starboard diesel exhaust valve was loose and leaking water. Within 30 minutes, the diesel room bilge had taken on more than one ton of water.

Faulty exhaust valves would surely abort our patrol. A chorus of groans erupted. Not again! But our clever Diesel Chief Otto Fricke suggested that if we surfaced and ran the diesels for a while, the heat might expand the metal and close the leak. We were willing to try anything rather than return to base again, so we carried out his suggestion. Sure enough, the leak slowed to a manageable rate. The valve still leaked in about three tons of water a day, but our bilge pump could handle that.

We cruised underwater all day, surfacing under the cloak of darkness to charge our batteries and make some faster time with the diesels. The bridge watch was on the very highest of alerts during these periods on the surface. By now the Bay of Biscay had well-earned its nickname of *Selbstmord Biskaya* ("the Biscay Suicide Stretch") because of the frequent and often deadly Allied attacks.

The next night, our direction finder once again got stuck in the stowed position. At the same time, either our radio failed or the Tommies were jamming it in some new diabolical manner. A different failure in our electrical equipment made it impossible for us to clear the interference, so we could only receive messages on the very longest frequency end of the bands. Nevertheless, there was no talk of returning to base. We were determined to continue the mission.

*   *   *

In the predawn hours of September 22, we were running at high speed on the surface when the machine telegraph signaled to us in the control room the order to dive. The Raccoon, our inexperienced Engineering Officer, immediately opened the bow diving tanks, but was too slow in opening the rear ones. The imbalance of weight caused our nose to dive violently into the water. Within seconds we were pointing downward at a 42-degree angle and plummeting toward the bottom at an extremely dangerous rate.

My duty position on that day was manning the big knock valve control wheel, located just above the chart table. To the right of the wheel was the Navigator's stopwatch, hanging on a big fishhook suspended by a chain. Usually the chain hung straight down, but at the extreme angle we were at, the watch had moved next to the edge of the wheel I was operating.

All my attention was fixed on the depth meter because we had to blow the tanks at 35 meters or risk sinking for good. When we reached 38 meters, I shouted a warning to the Engineering Officer that we needed to blow the tanks. When he finally gave the order "*Ausblassen!*" I turned the wheel as fast as I could. Unfortunately, the stopwatch had moved next to my hand and before I knew it, the fishhook had pierced my left forefinger completely through the joint.

My left hand was now hanging from the hook and chain like a bloody pink fish, useless to operate the wheel. But turning the wheel was vital to our survival. I had to stretch as far as I could to operate the valve with my right hand, causing intense pain as my left hand pulled at the hook.

The valve was wide open, yet we continued to plunge downward because of our momentum. We sank like a stone to a depth of 100 meters before our descent finally slowed to a stop. A dozen men had to climb their way to the stern of the boat to help offset the imbalance in weight. Only after several minutes did we manage to get the boat on an even keel again.

This was not the first time the Engineering Officer had done this. The previous occasion, our old Engineering Officer Fritz Förster cussed him out roundly. The only thing that diverted me from my pain was seeing that, this time, the Raccoon's face was even more pale than mine.

A few minutes later, two of my crewmates came up to me with broad grins on their faces. They carried a set of large tweezers and a first aid kit. "Now we'll get you off the hook, Hans!" they laughed.

Someone handed me a bottle of Schnapps as an anesthetic. "Have a drink—but not too much!"

After a couple of good gulps, the mate with the tweezers gave a hard pull and the hook tore its way back out of my flesh.

While recuperating in my bunk, I remembered the old folk saying, "After the child fell into the well, it got covered up." Heeding that bit of wisdom, I returned to the control room and filed the tip of the hook until it was blunt and round. No one would ever have an accident like that again if I could help it. My finger hurt for quite some time after that, but at least I was alive to complain about it.

Chapter 11

Goodbye to Zschech

*T*he sea became very rough as we entered the center of the Bay of Biscay. The entire boat shook as we smashed our way through the rolling crests and troughs. Waves were so high, sometimes more than 10 meters in height, that they crashed over the top of the bridge, flooding the control room deck with brine. Indeed, our intake of water was so severe the trim pump was kept constantly running in order to prevent the boat from becoming too heavy. None of us minded the bobsled ride, though. The cool stiff breeze that ran through the boat to the diesels was a welcome change from the clammy staleness of prolonged underwater travel.

We heard countless bomb and depth charge detonations as we made our way across the Bay. Zschech decided to change course in light of the heavy enemy activity and worsening weather. Just when we thought we had outrun the danger area, we had a catastrophic electrical failure. The starboard electric motor and the main pump failed after our newly installed Siemens electrical switchboard erupted in a smoky short circuit. Despite these critical equipment failures, we continued on our mission. Our reports to Flotilla Headquarters were purposely incomplete because if they knew the extent of our damage, they would have probably ordered us to turn about. By keeping our mouths shut, we were gambling we could somehow repair the equipment before we engaged in battle.

We eventually managed to get the electric motor working again, but not the main pump. The main pump failure was especially worrisome as it was the only pump capable of removing water from the boat at depths deeper than 30 meters. The mechanics discovered the switchboard short had caused the pump to activate while the valves were closed. The resulting back pressure had damaged the pump—probably beyond our capacity to repair it at sea. Under normal conditions, this would have meant the premature end of yet another patrol because the main pump is one of the most fundamental pieces of equipment aboard a submarine. Because of our anxiousness to get at the enemy, however, we proceeded with our mission. Anything, maybe even death in battle, was preferable to once again limping back into Lorient without having fired a shot.

*   *   *

We continued to cruise, primarily submerged, toward our destination. The mileage we traveled on the surface was approximately equal to the distance we traveled underwater. But since surface travel was so much faster, the vast bulk of our time was actually spent submerged. What a change from the early days of the war when we felt secure enough on the surface to sunbathe and dine on the upper deck! Underwater travel in those days was reserved almost exclusively for conducting attacks and quick escapes from danger. Now we were forced to spend most of our time underwater, something submarines in those days were never designed to do.

These long underwater stretches were quite boring. As long as we weren't surfacing and diving, only a handful of men were required to be on duty at any one time. The off-duty crew spent most of their time playing cards, throwing dice, gossiping, or sleeping. I spent much of my time reading my English books.

On the bright side, we hardly saw Zschech anymore. He would go through long periods of silence, emerging pale and nervous-looking from his cabin only when duty absolutely required his presence. He even shunned the company of his fellow officers. When he gave one of his infrequent orders to us, his eyes scanned back and forth over our faces as if to ask, "Am I doing the right thing?"

In addition to his loss of confidence, there were also unmistakable signs of deep depression. Many of his classmates from the Naval

Academy were dead, including almost all of the members of his "Olympic Ring" boat symbol clique. Zschech seemed convinced his turn would come sooner rather than later. Also, nasty rumors concerning his bravery and competence were making their rounds back in Lorient, and he had undoubtedly gotten wind of them. Of course, when we heard someone spreading rumors about him back at base, we quickly shut them up. We might complain bitterly about our Skipper, but no one outside our crew had that right.

Our feelings toward him gradually turned from hatred to pity, and I think he knew it. Who knows, that may have made it even worse. He obviously had high expectations for himself at one time, and we certainly thought (at least initially) he would bring our boat great success, but that was not how it turned out to be.

We reserved our anger those days for the treacherous shipyard workers who were inventing ever more ingenious ways to kill us. While we faced the hazards of the sea and enemy guns, those malicious, murderous cowards sat fat and happy in the relative safety of Lorient. We decided that anyone not in our crew who came aboard our boat while in port was to be regarded as the enemy. In the meantime, we tried to get along without a fully capable skipper at the helm.

*   *   *

In the early morning hours of September 28, Zschech finally threw in the towel and radioed Second U-boat Flotilla Headquarters that we were returning to base. All attempts to repair the main pump had failed, and without it we would be helpless in any deep-water situation. We were expecting some sort of morale-building speech from Zschech, but he was the one who looked like he needed a morale boost. It was as if all the spirit had drained out of him. Without his buddy Bode as Exec to keep him company, Zschech became a sort of reclusive ghost haunting our boat.

With Zschech pretty much staying out of the way, our new Executive Officer, Paul Meyer, moved boldly to get us back to base as quickly as possible. Rather than continue to crawl along underwater at a snail's pace, Meyer brought us to the surface for a sustained high-speed run. He reasoned that since the winter squalls were beginning to kick-up, we had a fair chance to race back to Lorient without detection. The Exec's gamble worked. Heavy storms made for a rough ride, but we were able to make excellent time back across the Bay. Meyer surprised us with his boldness and keen judgment. We were very relieved when we realized we had such a competent Executive Officer filling the vacuum created by the skipper's despondency.

On the morning of September 30, we pulled into the safety of the bunkers. Zschech immediately disembarked to report to Ernst Kals, our new Flotilla Commander and holder of Knight's Cross. The shame and anguish of once again having to return to base without having contacted the enemy was plain on his face as he disembarked.

As far as our morale went, we were still in fairly good spirits, at least superficially. We still honestly believed in the final victory, but I don't think there were many of us who thought we would still be alive to see it.

The British bomber offensive against Lorient had intensified during our absence. Air activity over our submarine installations was especially heavy during the hours of darkness. Virtually every night we were awakened from our slumber by the screaming air raid sirens. We had only a minute or two to scamper to the slit trenches outside our barracks before the bomb splinters began flying in every direction.

Once safely in the trenches, we would break out bottles of *Calvados* and get drunk while watching the drama taking place in the skies above us. It was great entertainment, almost like a sporting event. A direct hit on a bomber by our Flak artillery still brought wild hoots of joy. Our own *Luftwaffe*, however, was seldom seen any more. When the "all clear" sounded, we ambled back to the barracks, singing sailor songs. This ritual was repeated almost every night, and sometimes twice a night.

Lorient itself was now a totally shattered, burned-out ruin. The only activity in town was a few forlorn residents sifting through the ashes of their former residences looking for belongings. There were a few cases of looting, but we Germans were under strict orders not to touch anything. Signs were posted everywhere with this warning: "Those who are caught robbing or stealing will be shot, without trial." We knew the police weren't bluffing.

After a solid week of feverish repair work, our boat cleared *Skorff Bunker* on the afternoon of October 10. Once again, we were bound for the Caribbean, this time in the company of *U-129* and *U-510*. Gone were the elaborate departure ceremonies of previous voyages, though a small group of friends did manage to show up. In lieu of a military band, there was one lone guy sitting on the pier playing the harmonica. I can still remember the melody of the popular little ditty he played: something about an old white horse and how we are both happy when we ride downhill.

The weather was rather chilly as we made our way across Lorient harbor. To escape the cold sea spray, most of the men clustered on the bridge and the *Wintergarten* weapons platform aft of the bridge. The large number of anti-aircraft guns in our mixed convoy was very reassuring to a group of men kneeling on a deck with nothing but the shirts on their backs to protect them from enemy guns.

The boat was far more cramped than usual because the *Kriegsmarine* had decided to add ten additional men to the crew compliment of all Type IXc subs. Some of the extra men were technicians needed for the new electronic devices the subs were being equipped with. Most of them, however, were extra gunners for the flak guns. The new tactical doctrine for air defense dictated that we should shoot it out on the surface with attacking Allied aircraft rather than crash-diving to escape. Our anti-aircraft gun crews, very vulnerable in their exposed gun mounts, were suffering heavy casualties as a result. Additional men were therefore assigned to each boat to replace the expected losses.

Despite the crowded conditions and devastating losses, morale was good. We were determined to perform our duties as professionally as possible. This attitude was not based on some naive notion of glory or of our own invincibility. Indeed, quite the opposite. The watchword for this patrol was some advice Löwe had given us long ago: "Have no illusions!" We believed that only through expertise and clear-eyed realism could we maximize our chances of success and survival.

At first, Zschech acted very calmly and seemed to have regained some of his old ability to concentrate. Despite his demeanor, we were still worried about him. It seemed like a lifetime ago that he, so full of promise, had transferred to our boat from the famous *U-124*. But now that boat was gone forever, its heroic crew entombed in their steel coffin at the bottom of the sea. Sometimes it seemed as if the spiritual part of Peter Zschech had died along with his old crew, and that the soulless body that was acting as our skipper was impatiently waiting to join them.

This may seem strange or cold, but frankly, we young sailors didn't often brood over our lost comrades. There were already too many of them to remember. If we had dwelled on our fallen friends, our performance would have suffered. Sometimes it even drove men mad. Most of us were fatalistic about our chances: live for today, and if we should die—*C'est la Vie*! That was the only way we could cope with so many of our mates disappearing for the last time. But as I said, we were young and really didn't think deeply about such things. What I say here are the thoughts of an old man, not what filled our minds back then.

For Zschech, though, I think it was different. For all of his outward hardness and cruelty, I think on the inside he must have been very sensitive. Too sensitive, we were soon to realize, to command a U-boat. How opposite he was from our first skipper! Löwe was a natural leader and wise in the ways of human nature. He somehow could sense the inner strengths and weakness of his crew, and like a chess player, used that knowledge to organize a team that could accomplish the mission. He also had an iron will and self-control that set a constant example for us. Löwe was a great asset to our boat, and one that brought out the best in us.

Zschech, on the other hand, clearly lacked the qualities needed to be a commander. An excellent staff officer, perhaps, but not a commander. His loneliness and self-doubts were causing him to crumble under the stresses of a wartime command. These days, of course, it's fashionable to feel sorry for the weakling and root for the underdog. But facing the odds that we did as we sailed out to meet the enemy, we could not afford the luxury of a second-rate skipper. All of these thoughts, too, are the musings of an old man, combined with the advantage of hindsight. At the time, we prayed that by doing the best job we could, we could make up for whatever failings Zschech had as our skipper. We clung to a shred of a hope that, just as his former Exec Thilo Bode had matured as an officer and leader of men, so too would Zschech . We just hoped that we lived long enough for that to happen.

*   *   *

Our first few days out of Lorient passed without much incident. Zschech actually seemed to appreciate our professionalism for once. A few times, he even smiled at the quickness and proficiency with which we performed our duties. Once again, however, he was playing it extremely timidly on this outbound stretch. The old reckless and abusive Zschech we used to know was gone. In his place was a weak, frightened rabbit. We couldn't decide which was worse.

We almost never ran surfaced, and when we did, Zschech overcompensated for his earlier over-reliance on the radar warning gear. Don't get me wrong, we were also worried about the Suicide Stretch. We felt like cats who, even when sleeping keep one ear open to listen for trouble. But Zschech was taking vigilance and caution much too far.

Our voyage through the Bay of Biscay began to take on a surreal quality. Traveling underwater for so long removed all sensation of being at sea. Instead of the wild surf and pounding diesel noise, we experienced day after day of the monotonous, mechanical hum of the electric motors. The weather was quite cold, too. We shivered in our bunks as ice cold drops of condensed moisture soaked our clothing. The long periods under water also influenced the smell of the boat. We were steeped in the stench of rotting potatoes, the reek of the "shit" bucket in the engine room, and the stench of own bodies as far too many unwashed men tried to sleep in far too few unlaundered bunks. The fetid stink of rot and decay made our boat seem like a cold, clammy coffin in which we were already decomposing.

On the morning of October 12, we were taking a quick pre-dawn run on the surface to recharge our air and batteries when the whole boat began vibrating in time with the RPMs of the diesels. A great hissing and roar suddenly emanated from the engine room. A moment later, the port diesel engine stopped dead. Our Diesel Chief Otto Fricke appeared in the control room, his brilliant white teeth in stark contrast to his grease and soot-smeared face. He reported that piston #2 on the port diesel had frozen up in its cylinder. Fricke saw me there in the control room and, knowing I had a master's certificate in diesel repair, asked permission for me to assist him in the repairs.

"Great," I muttered to myself, "there goes my sleep time!" I wasn't eager to get assigned to the engine room, no matter how temporarily. I enjoyed my work in the control room. It was complex, demanding work, and I was good at it. Besides, it was clean work, and when your watch time was over, you could usually get some uninterrupted rest.

Those poor guys in the engine room, on the other hand, looked like chimney sweeps caught in a rain shower. The deafening noise, the heat, the oily soot, the constant exposure to diesel fumes and monoxide gas, combined to make it the most unpleasant place to work on a sub. The *piece d' resistance* was that the shit bucket we used while submerged was kept in the narrow aisle between the diesels. To relieve oneself, you had to squat over the bucket in full view of the engine room crew. Not that they were interested in watching you. Usually they were too busy toiling over some stubborn piece of machinery, shouting every oath in the lexicon of sailors' curses. But its sight and smell did add a bit of insult to injury.

No, I wasn't happy to be working in the diesel room. To make matters worse, changing a piston in one of those big diesel engines was the single most arduous task a submarine mechanic can undertake. We had to detach the connecting rod, lift the monstrous piston out of the cylinder, replace the rings, and gently lower it back into its place. All of this had to be done by hand, without assistance from pulleys or crowbars.

At one point, Zschech poked his head into the engine room and asked Fricke how long it would be. The Chief's face turned red, obviously straining not to lose his temper.

"We will be completely done in one-half hour, Sir. I will report when it is!" Zschech backed out of the Chief's domain without another word.

True to his word, the port diesel was reassembled and ready for a test a half-hour later. To everyone's immense relief, the engine cranked-up just fine. We ran it at slow RPMs for ten minutes to break-in the rings before testing it at high speed. The job had taken us a total of almost eight hours to finish, but the engine was back to its normal, thundering self. Zschech gave us four hours of off-duty time as reward for our efforts.

It took us an inordinately long time to travel across the Bay of Biscay. On the one hand, traveling underwater gave us less exposure to prowling Allied aircraft. But on the other hand, our slower speed increased the chances we would be detected by one of the many enemy destroyers lurking in the Bay. The greater expenditure of our provisions also meant we would have less patrol time at our destination. We understood Zschech's reluctance to be caught on the surface by an aircraft again, but we were eager to get at the enemy. Frustrations mounted because of the slow progress we were making.

I spent a lot of time during this period reading my English books, and I took plenty of teasing from my crewmates because of it.

"What the hell do Shakespeare and Robert Lewis Stevenson have to say about U-boats?" they would ask.

I ignored them and kept my nose poked between the pages. To be honest, the books meant more to me than just English practice. They offered a dream world where I could go to escape the freezing, stinking reality of the boat. But then the alarm would ring, the books would drop, and I would be back in the war.

* * *

As we neared the outer edge of the Bay, the weather calmed down a bit. After a long underwater run, Zschech took quick peeks with the *Spargel* ("asparagus," our nickname for the periscope) and then, like some great whale rising to take a breath of fresh air, we would break through to the surface. The green waves were long and tall, and the cold, stiff breeze kicked up a spray that stung the faces of the men on watch. Crisp, fragrant air rushed through our boat, acting like a tonic on us oxygen-deprived crewmen. An hour or so later (sooner if we had a radar alarm), the hatches slammed shut and we would descend once again into the nether world of the deep.

The replacement of the inner Bay of Biscay map with the Atlantic map on the chart table stirred a great deal of excitement among the crew. Even though we were still thousands of miles from the Caribbean, a sort of hunter's blood fever took hold of us.

Zschech, though, looked more tired and nervous than ever. Despite the fact that we had passed the area of maximum danger in the Bay, he still insisted on cruising almost exclusively underwater. Even when the ocean whipped up into Sea State 6, far too rough for any aircraft or ship to attack us, he kept us in the basement, crawling across the Atlantic at a couple of knots. It was whispered that our skipper was beginning to lose his nerve to perform even the most routine operations.

* * *

I was lying in my bunk during the pre-dawn hours of October 23, when I realized I was breathing fresh air. The gentle rocking of the boat, followed moments later by the throaty throb of the diesels, confirmed we were indeed on the surface. The air was cold and I was reluctant to leave my bunk. But I had duty to perform, so leave it I did. It surely made no difference to the bunk, for another man would be lying in it before the sheets cooled.

A few minutes later, I was dressed and at my station in the control room. Zschech seemed more agitated than usual, climbing up and down between the bridge and the control room like a nervous cat.

I didn't pay much attention to him. My concern was with the ship's doctor who, as usual, was trying to steal my breakfast bowl of *Kujamble Eis*. This mixture of crushed ice and raspberry syrup was much treasured by us crewmen. It was also strictly rationed by Toni, our cook. Toni was of the opinion the doctor was too fat and therefore never gave him anything beyond the normal ration of food.

"That man eats too much. He is putting more in the diesel room pail than any two of us!" Toni was fond of saying.

Naturally, this made the doctor all the more obsessed with obtaining some of the frozen confection. Several times a day he would peek his head into the control room to see if there was an unattended bowl of the stuff. I'm proud to say he never got any of mine.

The day passed quietly, as if we were on a vacation cruise. We dived as soon as the batteries were recharged and didn't resurface until well after dark. I was back on duty that evening when, a little after midnight, we began hearing faint, distant rumbles. Over the course of several hours, the rumbling became louder and more distinct. They were clearly the explosions of depth charges. A long, steady series of them would go off, followed by a few minutes of silence, then another long series. The drum roll of the depth charges seemed to affect Zschech very deeply.

Around noon on the 24th, we once again heard the steady rumble of depth charges exploding in the distance. We had often heard this noise before, but never for such a prolonged period. We knew that, somewhere, a U-boat was catching hell.

Over the next several hours, the noise gradually grew louder. It would stop for a short while, then resume, closer than before. I'm not being melodramatic when I tell you it began to sound like the slow, steady drumbeat of a military funeral procession, inching ever closer to our position.

After six full hours of this morbid tattoo, Zschech retreated to his cabin, closing the curtain behind him. Occasionally, he would call the radioman and sound man into his cabin for an update, but otherwise nothing was heard from him. Meanwhile, we continued on course through Sea Square CF5424. After sunset, the detonations started getting quite loud. We in the control room began asking ourselves what the hell

Zschech was doing lying in his cabin as the kettledrum beat of depth charges got closer and closer.

At exactly 1948 hours, the sound man ran to Zschech's cabin and reported engine noises. At long last, Zschech pushed aside the curtains of his cabin and emerged. As he walked by me, I could see that his face was ashen gray. Instead of issuing orders, however, Zschech climbed the ladder to the vacant conning tower.

We control room mates looked at each other in total puzzlement, silently asking each other what he was doing up there. On German subs, the only time the conning tower was used was when the skipper wanted to look through the periscope. But we were cruising at a depth of 100 meters, far too deep to use the periscope.

Two minutes later, the radioman shouted a report up to Zschech through the conning tower hatch, informing him of what we all could hear with our bare ears: we were being scanned by *Asdic*. The pause between each *Asdic* "ping" was rapidly getting shorter. They had obviously located us and were headed right toward us.

Soon the enemy ships were almost directly above us. And yet, still no orders, still no skipper. Where the hell was Zschech?

Before we had time to ask, BOOM! We were thrown off our feet by a giant depth charge explosion. The whole boat was rocking crazily as the control room air filled with broken glass and flying objects.

I grabbed for any hold I could grasp because they never dropped just one. BLANG! The lights went out and the pressure hull rang like a church bell with the concussion from the second charge.

Finally, Zschech came down the ladder from the conning tower. His expressionless face, illuminated by the florescent paint on the air ducts, was ghostly white. We all stared at him, anticipating some orders for maneuvers, but still he said nothing. Instead, he walked zombie-like through the forward hatch into the radio room. As he passed me, I could see his wide-open, unblinking eyes shine in the half-light.

Two more charges exploded in quick succession. They were a bit farther off than the others and we dared to hope that the worst was over. Then, W-H-O-O-O-M! The biggest explosion I had ever heard. It nearly turned the boat over. Men were sent sprawling to the deck in heaps.

Amongst all the clamor, I thought I had heard a little bang coming from inside the boat, but didn't think anything of it at the moment. Then I glanced around and spotted Zschech slowly leaning over. I figured he had just bruised his head against a bulkhead, so I turned my attention back to my controls.

Then, BOOOM! An explosion even closer than the last deafened our ears, turning our world into a shattering, nightmarish blur of tumbling men and flying debris. Sprawled on the deck, I listened as well I could with my ringing ears for the telltale sound of in-rushing water that would signal our doom. Instead, there followed a few minutes of utter silence. The destroyers were evidently reloading their depth charge mechanisms as they circled for another run.

During that brief respite, our emergency lighting system came on. Our control room looked as if a hurricane had hit it, but we were still alive. Then, I heard some commotion coming through the open forward control room hatch. From my position I could see a body laying face down, motionless on the deck. A shiny pool of dark blood was quickly spreading around the man's legs.

A moment later, I saw the Radio Petty Officer kneeling down and examining the bleeding man. With some effort, he managed to turn the man over onto his back. After another minute, the lifeless legs were dragged into the *Olymp*, our nickname for the area around the skipper's cabin. It was then we realized something was very, very wrong. A few of us crept quietly up to the skipper's cabin to see what had happened.

There was Zschech, lying in his bed. He had shot himself in the head with his pistol during the depth charge attack!

It seemed like a million years had passed since Peter Zschech first occupied the commander's cabin. Now there he was, lying on his bunk, blood streaming out in little gushes from a small hole in the side of his head.

But even in this last act, Zschech had failed to fully accomplish his purpose. He was still alive, though he was making the loud, unmistakable sounds of a dying man.

The doctor came running to the cabin. "What can we do?" the doctor asked. "What can we do!?" The good doctor was clearly panicked and unable to think clearly.

"Shut up!" someone snarled in a stage whisper, "The destroyers are listening for any sound."

For several minutes Zschech lingered in this vegetative state, making loud death rattles. Finally, one of us placed Zschech's pillow over his face to muffle the noise and, out of mercy, hasten the inevitable. The doctor tried desperately to pull the pillow away, but four strong hands kept it in place. We knew that all of us—poor Zschech included—would be better off if he died as quickly and quietly as possible.

The doctor began shouting hysterically to remove the pillow. Our Exec, Paul Meyer, was now the acting commander. He calmly but sternly ordered the doctor to be quiet. "There's nothing you can do for him now," Meyer explained. "Those ships up there are still trying to send us to hell. Sound travels better through water, and any noise we make down here can be heard up there. So, please, doctor, be quiet."

Now completely in command of the situation, Meyer ordered two *Bold* capsules ejected to decoy the enemy *Asdic*. Once the chemicals had released their cloud of bubbles and metal particles, we crept away at our most silent speed. The next spread of depth charges landed directly on the *Bold* bubbles, close enough to shake us severely, but not enough to cause us damage.

A few minutes later, however, another spread nearly finished us off. We suffered substantial damage, but luck was with us and that was the last close shave. An hour later, we were safely out of range of the destroyers. We busied ourselves with repairing the most serious leaks and broken equipment while the enemy continued to plaster our previous location.

At exactly 2129 hours on October 24, 1943, a terse entry was made in *U-505's* logbook: "*Kommandant tot*" (Commanding Officer dead). No other explanation was made. At this point, most of the crew still didn't know Zschech was no longer among the living, much less how he died. There would be time enough for that later. Meanwhile, those of us who did know believed we were better off with our new skipper.

Before any of this could really sink into our heads, the ssing-ssing-ssing sound of the enemy *Asdic* devices began anew. Soon we were surrounded by propeller noises. A moment later we heard the clearly audible sound of big drums of explosives splashing into the sea over our heads. Once again the devil's drumbeat began, the deafening noise and jarring shock waves getting closer and closer.

I fervently prayed to heaven for a miracle to happen: that one of those drums would explode too soon and blow to pieces the bastards trying to kill us. I hope God forgave my sacrilege, but that is exactly what I prayed.

We endured several more depth charge attacks before we managed to shake the tormentors off our trail. Two and a half hours later, Meyer finally felt it was safe enough for us to risk recharging on the surface. He made a very short speech over the intercom to the crew, explaining that Zschech was dead and that he, as Exec, was assuming command. He also announced we were returning to base. Heads kept poking through the fore and aft control room hatches, asking what happened.

"There's no time to explain." was the only answer.

Luckily, there were no enemy vessels in sight when we surfaced. A bright phosphorous glow followed in our wake as we prepared for a burial at sea. A few mates and I dragged Zschech's inert body back into the control room. When we turned around, we realized a yellow cloth tampon that had been inserted into his head wound had popped out, leaving a long trail of blood behind us.

Seeing pieces of Zschech's brains clinging to the cloth was too much for most of us to bear. Only two guys were able to carry on. They placed his body into a hammock, put a trim weight between his feet, and sewed the hammock closed from bottom to top. I just stood there frozen in shock, watching with horrified fascination as our skipper's body was slowly encased in his canvas coffin.

Just before dawn the body was ready to be hauled up to the conning tower for burial. Meyer ordered, "Control room: Attention!" but none of us moved. Perhaps if he wasn't sealed inside the hammock, we could have saluted the uniform. But none of us could bring ourselves to stand at attention for the man. Meyer understood and did not press the matter.

Zschech's body was lifted up to the bridge and, without any ceremony, dumped over the side . We continued running on the surface at high speed in order to put as much distance as possible between us and the destroyers. In the meantime, the story of how Zschech had met his end made its way throughout the boat.

Today, of course, I feel great sorrow for Peter Zschech. He is, as far as I know, the only German submarine commander to have ever committed suicide while in action. But at the time we felt no sympathy for the man. Rather, we felt a mixture of anger and betrayal. From our perspective, by committing suicide when he did, Zschech had acted as a selfish coward. If he wanted to kill himself, we asked each other, why didn't he do it back in Lorient instead of deserting us at the exact moment we needed a skipper most?

He never brought our boat the success he promised, nor did he ever treat us with the respect that we, as a veteran crew, felt we deserved.

Zschech was a very bright man, and could have served with distinction as a staff officer, but he lacked the sterner stuff required for command. It is uncomfortable to admit now, but at the time, most of us were not especially sorry to see him gone.

*   *   *

The burial of Zschech did not end our danger. Just after sunset on the 25th, we were once again heavily depth charged by the enemy. On and on, the big barrels of TNT rained down upon us. It was as if Death was knocking on our pressure hull, asking permission to enter. We somehow managed to slip away after an hour of pummeling from the destroyers.

Around 2000 hours, after darkness had completely fallen, Meyer decided to risk a high speed sprint on the surface to get us out of the danger area. Just two minutes after we surfaced, however, our eagle eyes on watch spotted the dark shadows of our tormentors close by off our starboard bow. Meyer decided to gamble that we would not be spotted and made a run for it. We began slicing through the waves full speed ahead.

For about ten minutes it looked like we might make it. But the destroyers must have picked us up on radar because suddenly, one of the devils turned and headed straight for us at top speed. We had only seconds to get the boys on watch off the bridge and back inside before diving.

"*Schnell auf tiefe gehen!*" (Go deep, quickly!) shouted Meyer. We plunged beneath the waves just as the big ship started its depth charge run. We crash dove down to 150 meters and began evasive maneuvers.

The Second Watch Officer retrieved a *Bold* capsule from the aft torpedo room and took it to the head where the miniature "Torpedo Tube #7" was located. A moment later he ran to the control room in a very agitated state. He needed help because the tube's outer door was jammed. I ran back to the head with him and together we managed to load the tube.

Depth charges were exploding very close, making the entire boat shake with their concussion. When we attempted to expel the *Bold*, however, it refused to budge. I grabbed a big wooden dowel and pressed with all my might against the expelling rod. Finally, the capsule shot loose and released its mass of bubbles and metal flakes. The crew breathed an audible sigh of relief when they heard the capsule firing. Sure enough, the enemy ships above us were decoyed by the bubbles. The zzing-zzing-zzing of their *Asdic* gradually faded into the distance.

(By the way, I don't mention this incident to in any way portray myself as a hero who saved our boat. Every single man in our crew performed hundreds of similar acts that, taken together, helped us survive. I only allude to it because it was something I remember from this incident.)

By midnight, we had put a safe distance between us and the hunters. After taking a quick peek with the periscope, we popped up to the surface to re-fill our air tanks and recharge our batteries. While on the surface, we received an *FT* ordering Zschech and four other boats to rendezvous with a Milk Cow supply boat at position Blu 2860. Headquarters was still unaware of our change in command.

Soon after, however, an airborne radar alert from our *Naxos* device forced us to dive to the cellar again. All night and for most of the next day, we were subjected to a non-stop barrage of bombs and depth charges dropped by the omnipresent buzzards and their friends the destroyers. It had long been a habit among some of the crew to keep a tally of the number of depth charges dropped on us, but on this occasion, even the most conscientious counter lost track of how many explosions we endured. For sure they were upwards of 300.

Unfortunately, our brief time on the surface had been insufficient to fully charge our tanks with air. As a consequence, after about five hours, our oxygen monitoring device indicated that we were breathing dangerous levels of carbon dioxide. The sound of propeller noises churning above us ruled out any return to the surface. Our boat was equipped with an oxygen recycler, but we didn't have enough juice left in the batteries to run it for long.

We eventually had to break out our emergency personal respirators to avoid asphyxiation. Then, all but the most essential crewmen on duty were ordered to lay motionless in order to conserve oxygen. We hated wearing those damned respirators! A clip was fitted over your nostrils to close your nose while you sucked air through a hose in your mouth. They never worked very well, and after a while, the potassium compounds inside the canister would begin to heat up like a little furnace.

It seemed like an eternity before the propeller sounds moved sufficiently distant for us to risk surfacing. The metallic clang of the top hatch, when it finally opened, sounded as beautiful as Christmas bells to us. The diesel air intake was switched to internal and our Jumbos began pulling a deliciously cool, invigorating breeze into the boat. You can't imagine how marvelous something as simple as fresh air can seem to a man who has had to breathe through those suffocating respirator devices for several hours. Before long, we had recovered from the drowsy symptoms of dioxide poisoning and were ourselves again. We prayed we would never need to breathe through those respirators again.

The mere memory of wearing those things still upsets me to this day.

*　　*　　*

The next few days passed uneventfully. We only surfaced at night, so we hardly ever saw the sun. But the sea was calm, and as the depth charge noises faded into the distance, we thought our chances were getting better that we could make it back to Lorient. Perhaps we were fooling ourselves, but we were young and strong and confident. You had to be an optimist aboard a U-boat because a pessimist would have ended up like Zschech.

We also had lots of confidence in our acting skipper, *Oberleutnant* Paul Meyer. Although he had never attended Commander's School, he really seemed to know his job. He also understood that we knew our job. We handled routine duties without him even having to say a word. Naturally, we would report to him what we had done, but he trusted us to do what needed to be done.

Josef Hauser, our grim-faced Engineering Officer we referred to as "the Raccoon," was another matter. He was obviously still in shock over the death of his guardian angel Zschech. Only gradually did he realize we were a professional crew, and that our chances of survival actually improved once Meyer took over. In time, he too began to have confidence in our survival.

Just before dawn on the 30th, we sent *FT* messages to the Second U-boat Flotilla and Dönitz's U-boat Command Headquarters. We apprised them of Zschech's death and of our intention to return to base. They were very happy to hear from us, for our boat had been officially reported as lost.

Unfortunately, the enemy intercepted our radio transmission. Armed with our secret codes and a superb radio signal triangulation service, the Allies calculated our location to within a radius of one nautical mile. As a result, the next morning we suffered through another heavy beating by destroyers. The drum concert they played on our hull lasted more than eight hours. I personally counted 175 depth charges. Once again though, our lucky old boat *U-505* beat the odds.

As we approached the entrance to the Bay of Biscay, the weather turned very nasty. Our prow had to literally smash its way through huge, breaking waves. Conditions were so rough, the bridge watch was reduced to only 30 minutes in duration, the physical limit of human endurance in the face of such a pounding. Mammoth waves crashed over the top of the bridge, pouring more seawater through the conning tower hatch than I had ever seen before. At times, the conning tower was flooded several feet deep in salty brine.

In our control room, the bilge pump could barely keep up with the influx of water. It was quite a task to perform one's duty when the boat was pitching and rocking so violently. Even when we were technically off duty, we were kept busy drying binoculars and oiling the anti-aircraft weapons. The poor torpedo mechanics were frantically trying to keep their new torpedoes dry because the new programmable models were capable of exploding if they suffered a short circuit. We were all very relieved whenever our batteries had been recharged enough for us to submerge.

It was during one of those dives that I once again got in trouble with an officer. On the night of October 31, we were cruising along at a depth of 120 meters when our boat's doctor appeared in the control room. The other officers were catching up on some much-needed sleep, so this medical quack was at liberty to indulge his fantasies of being a real submariner.

He sat himself down in the Diving Control Officer's motorcycle-like seat and began giving orders to the diving plane operators. The boat began swimming up and down like a dolphin as the doctor amused himself at the controls. We control room crew members gave each other worried looks, but as long as he didn't endanger the boat, we played along with his unauthorized antics.

At one point, however, he ordered me to press out 25 liters of trim ballast with compressed air. Well, I knew quite well that opening a decompression valve against 130 atmospheres of water pressure would result in a loud hammering and squeaking sound that could be heard for miles around. Such a noise would be a dead giveaway of our position to any destroyers lurking in the area. After a moment of thought, I told him that I would not obey his order. He ordered me a second time to blow the ballast, and once again I refused.

The doctor's face flushed with rage. "After your watch is over, you will report to *Oberleutnant* Meyer!"

"*Jawohl, Herr Oberassistenartz!*"

Two and a half hours later, when my watch was over, I reported to the officers' wardroom. The doctor was there, giving Meyer his version of the events. When he was done, I saluted and entered the room. Meyer rose and signaled me to follow him into the galley.

Once we were out of sight, Meyer turned to me and asked, "Are you crazy? Why did you refuse to carry out an order? I want to know exactly what happened!"

I explained what happened and why I did what I did. Meyer lowered his voice so the doctor could not hear. In a sly tone he advised me that the next time a similar situation arose, to merely pretend to carry out the order.

"But *Herr Oberleutnant*, I didn't want to lie to him . . ."

"*Dummkopf*! Don't you realize that, every day, sailors get locked up in the brig for disobeying even the most irresponsible orders? The next time something like this happens, just tell the officer what he wants to hear, then proceed with your duty the best way you see fit. Now, because of our present situation, I'm letting you off with just a warning. But apologize to the doctor, understand?"

"*Jawohl, Herr Oberleutnant!*"

"All right then, get out of here," laughed Meyer, giving me a light kick in the butt as I turned to leave. We exchanged conspiratorial smiles and I returned to my bunk.

Paul Meyer was the right kind of man to be skipper, I thought. He knew his job and he knew how to get along with the crew. As for the doctor, I'm quite sure Meyer was much harsher with him than he was with me. One thing for sure, the quack never again tried playing Diving Officer.

* * *

We entered the Suicide Stretch of the Bay of Biscay on November 1, 1943. Our progress back to base was agonizingly slow. Because of the intense enemy air activity, we were now traveling more than half of our daily mileage totals underwater. During our first war patrol under Löwe, we were traveling an average of less than <u>one-tenth</u> of our daily distances underwater. Our proximity to base made our slow progress all the more frustrating.

The next morning we suffered through another depth-charge attack. This one didn't last long, but the charges exploded extremely close to the hull. Everything that wasn't securely clamped down was thrown about the boat, including we crewmen and the bathroom pail between the diesels.

Speaking of clamping things down, it was quite an art to keep all the waterproof hatches and seals properly clamped as we dived and surfaced during these attacks. You see, whenever a boat dived, the seals between a hatch and its bulkhead got pressed together by the change in air pressure. As a result, as our depth increased, the big wing nuts on the clamps would have to be tightened accordingly. When surfacing, the wing nuts had to be gradually loosened or else the clamp would be too tight to open when we surfaced. At the beginning, I personally was in charge of making sure the seals of the periscope up in the conning tower were adjusted in a similar manner. Having to climb up into the dark, deserted conning tower during a depth charge attack was a daunting task. But all of these procedures were performed almost instinctively, even when enduring the heaviest of depth charging or bad weather. It was just one of the thousand critical little details that had to be taken care of in those old boats that today's submariners never have to be bothered with.

When we surfaced the next morning, we were surprised to find that last night's escape from the depth charges had been closer than we thought. Big pieces of the protective metal sheeting around the conning tower had been blasted off. The explosions had also shattered several of the wooden planks on our upper deck. Seeing with one's own eyes the damage we had suffered reinforced our determination to keep on our toes.

After that close call, we played it very safe. When our wake left a phosphorous wake, Meyer ordered us underwater. That was slower but much safer. Men literally tip-toed across the deck to minimize noise.

During this tense period, my mates became particularly annoyed at my self-taught English lessons. Reading aloud was frowned upon in general, but they were particularly irked with the possibility of being detected by the enemy because of someone speaking English words. As a result, I practiced my pronunciation in silence by merely mouthing the words.

On the morning of the 7th, we celebrated a melancholy anniversary: it had been exactly one year since our last sinking of an enemy vessel. That ship was the first and only kill we had scored under Zschech. We prayed that whatever curse had been hanging over our heads would end, now that Zschech had gotten his wish for everlasting peace.

I was never one to be frightened much by superstitions, but whenever I passed Zschech's cabin, I got goose bumps. We kept the curtain to his cabin closed, and no one had dared to enter it since the day of his suicide. Even *Oberleutnant* Meyer felt more comfortable staying in his junior officer's bunk. Seeing that closed curtain reminded me of the way Zschech would hide in his cabin, alone with his tortured thoughts. It was as if his ghost still haunted the little room. I got over the feeling about the cabin as soon as we got a new skipper, but the memory of poor, tragic Zschech will stay with me forever.

Later that morning, we reached the outer approaches to Lorient harbor. Following orders from *Second U-boat Flotilla* Headquarters, we made the approach on the surface. We were used to running on the surface only in the dark, so it was so strange to see our bow wearing a big, white beard of froth as we sliced through the waves in broad daylight.

We were nearing the entrance to the harbor when, around noon, we received an *FT* ordering us to Sea Square 5530 to render emergency assistance to Von Schröter's *U-123*. Just then, we caught sight of four large aircraft approaching low and fast from the east. Within seconds, our gun crews were at their battle stations and ready to fire. With just seconds to spare, one of the aircraft dropped a recognition flare: they were a flight of German JU-88's on their way to assist *U-123*. A bit later, two of our torpedo boats sped into view, traveling at top speed to augment the rescue force.

For four long hours we searched in vain for our sister boat. We finally received word the *Luftwaffe* boys had spotted *U-123* and taken over the situation. With that mission out of the way, we proceeded back toward Lorient.

As we entered the harbor, everyone busied themselves with emptying their moldy lockers and throwing their possessions into sea bags for the trip to the barracks. When the red buoy came into view, we fell out to assemble on bent knee on the upper deck and the *Wintergarten* anti-aircraft platform. It was quite an experience to rumble into the inner harbor in broad daylight, passing the old fortress on the right and the French cruiser *Strasbourg*, positioned as a permanent barrier on the left.

We made it home, all of us safe and sound. All, that is, except one.

Chapter 12

Rescue at Sea

$\mathcal{T}$here wasn't much of a crowd waiting for us in *Bunker Skorff*, though our Flotilla Commander, *Kapitän zur See* Ernst Kals, was there to personally welcome us home. Kals came aboard and complimented us profusely for getting back safely. We learned that, at the moment, we were the only boat in harbor. He told us the *Second* and *Tenth U-boat Flotillas* had suffered catastrophic losses in the past few weeks and that he was very glad to see the reports of us having been lost were incorrect. Before he departed, Kals warned us not to say anything about Zschech's death. In the interest of security, he said, we would also be sleeping on board.

It therefore struck us like a hammer blow when, later that night, the Allied propaganda radio station *Soldaten-sender-Calais* broadcast the following announcement: "Hello officers in the 'Red Mill' (a small casino near our barracks popular with many Navy officers). It must be quite a surprise to you that your friend Peter Zschech did not return with his *U-505*."

It chilled us to the bone that the enemy knew so many of our military secrets, sometimes even before we knew them. Of course, we assumed the French Underground was reporting details of our local, private activities. That was the obvious explanation for the mention of the "Red Mill." But it perplexed and deeply worried us that they knew of Zschech's death. In hindsight, of course, we now know it was the Allies' ability to decipher our *Enigma* secret code system that allowed them to do it.

*   *   *

On November 9 I celebrated another birthday. It seemed like a thousand lifetimes ago since I had celebrated my last birthday, just before Sillcock bombed us off Trinidad. I must admit though, at the time, my mind was firmly fixed on the present rather than the past. Still a bit in shock over how many of our sister boats had gone down, I wanted to have some fun before the odds finally caught up with us, too.

During the day, we were visited by *Konteradmiral* (Rear Admiral) Hans-Georg von Friedeburg, second-in-command of all U-boat forces. The few crews available in port assembled in formation and were given a pep talk by the Admiral. Later, he addressed our crew personally and told us, "I know that you are a brave crew. Good luck and may there always be a hand's breadth of water under your keel!"

It was comforting to hear von Friedeburg's words, but the news we heard from the war fronts was not good. We were stunned to learn the full scale of the slaughter our boats had suffered. The thought of so many of our friends lying at the bottom of that giant unmarked graveyard (the Atlantic) was just too much to bear. Developments on the ground were equally bad. Reverses on the Eastern Front and the Allied invasion of Italy were especially worrisome. Worst of all, Allied air raids on our cities were becoming heavier and more deadly by the day.

Here in Lorient, the air raids had become less frequent, but only because there was little left to destroy. There was almost nothing left of the city itself, although for some miraculous reason, the entertainment area next to our old barracks was still only slightly damaged. The U-boat bunkers and the other fortress-like military installations in the harbor area were still intact, but when we arrived at the storage barracks to retrieve our belongings, we found that the entire building had been burned to the ground. Allied bombers had attacked the place with phosphorous bombs only a couple of days before. Our dress uniforms and other personal possessions had been stored in the building's basement, and were severely damaged by the fire. We picked through the charred remains for the precious little bits we could salvage. Today, I still have some photographs with burned edges I rescued from the ashes.

Luckily, the Navy was quick to equip us with crisp new uniforms. We were not slow in showing them off to the few remaining ladies of leisure in Lorient. Naturally, they got their fair share of our pay, but for many of us, cavorting with whores had lost much of its charm. This time, I spent my money buying silk scarves, cigarettes, and liqueurs for my furlough home. By the time I was ready to depart for home, I had a large trunk overflowing with precious commodities no longer available in Germany.

The night before I left, we had a proper celebration for my birthday. The party involved quite a bit of drinking since none of us knew if we would be around to celebrate next year. Paul Meyer showed up and drank with us until dawn. As he left our barracks he turned around and told me, "Hans, I was forced to deduct two days from your leave as punishment for your incident with the doctor. But don't worry, you'll get those two days back when you return." I didn't know what he was talking about until I returned from my furlough.

The next morning, I found out part of what the Exec was talking about. Two days had indeed been deducted from my leave because of my run-in with that bastard, our ship's quack doctor. I didn't let it dampen my spirits, though. A group of fifteen of my fellow crewmates and I made our way to the Lorient train station. I was heavily burdened with my trunk and sea bag, but determined to make it home with all my booty. The railway station building didn't exist any more, though most of the tracks were still functioning. We spent the first leg of our trip trying to sleep off the effects of the previous night's celebration.

In Paris, we had a six-hour layover until the departure of our connecting train to Metz. We didn't dare leave our belongings unattended in the Paris train station, so we divided ourselves into impromptu two-hour watches and took turns sightseeing the beautiful and still-undamaged "City of Light."

Our group split up into different directions once we got to Metz. Six hours later, I arrived in Kassel. The town had been devastated by a heavy air raid just the previous night. Smoke and burning houses were everywhere. Nowhere is safe, I thought, from the long reach of the enemy terror-bombers.

Three hours later, the train pulled into my hometown. I was surprised by the bitterly cold weather. It was much warmer in Lorient, where we were bathed in relatively balmy Atlantic breezes. But the warm reception given to me by my family more than made up for the frigid temperature.

Several neighbors came over to my parent's house for the reception. Most of them brought food ration stamps as gifts. A gift of 50 grams of sugar (a person's entire allotment for one month) was an incredibly generous gift indeed, given the terrible shortage of food that had gripped our nation. Such generosity was common among our people during this time. In the same way, we soldiers always tried to bring home some delicacies for our families. In return, they often gave us a cake or liverwurst to share with our comrades when we returned to our units. No one had much to eat, but by sharing what little we had, we made the scarcities a bit more bearable.

While home, I was saddened to learn that my best friend from school had been killed on the Eastern Front. A cousin and another friend of mine had both been killed in Yugoslavia by Tito's guerrillas. What was especially disturbing was that they had been murdered after surrendering to the communists. Yet another cousin of mine had fallen in North Africa, near Mersa Matruk. The war was taking a very high toll; virtually every family in little Bottendorf had similar tragic news to report.

Despite the losses, we still believed in victory and trusted our nation's leadership. This faith lasted right up to the end. (NOTE: After the war I was disgusted at the way many people in my hometown cravenly denied ever being a Party member or aiding the war effort. Even the pastors changed their tunes 180 degrees! It was the same way in France where, suddenly, everyone claimed to be a member of the Resistance. I respect anyone who has the courage to act on their political convictions, even if I believe them to be wrong. But one thing that repels me to this day is a coward's failure to stand up for what he believes (or believed) in. I have never been, nor will I ever be, a chameleon!)

*   *   *

My two weeks of furlough sped by. The farewell with my family and friends was even more emotional than the last time. At the last minute, however, a bombing raid on the rail network west of Frankenburg delayed my departure. Once again, my father used his influence as a railroad official to get me out of trouble. By paying the repairmen at a local facility 100 cigarettes to work overtime, he managed to get an old steam locomotive running. That wheezing old engine got me to my connection just in time.

Unfortunately, my connection was also delayed getting out of the station. By the time I got to Metz, the train for Lorient had already left. I could catch the next train, but I would certainly miss my furlough deadline. I had one chance to avoid a court martial for being late back to base: getting my leave papers stamped by the *Bahnhofs Kommandanteur* (Train Station Commander) in Metz. My heart sank, however, when I saw hundreds of Army soldiers already waiting in line at the Commander's office for exactly the same purpose.

Fortunately, my dark blue Navy uniform stood out from the vast sea of gray-green Army uniforms. Several of the soldiers standing next to me had been admiring my U-boat combat badge, and when I told them I had to be back at base by tomorrow, they made way for me to go to the head of the line. Some of them even helped me carry my luggage. Within a few minutes, I had the Commander's precious signature.

My train arrived an hour and a half later. It was literally overflowing with Army soldiers returning to their units on the Russian Front. A huge mob of soldiers had already gathered on the platform, desperately trying to board the crowded coaches. I tried to elbow my way to the doors of the train, but it was impossible for me to even get close. I couldn't believe I had gotten this far, just to be unable to board the train.

Suddenly, I heard a familiar voice shout, "Hans! Come over here!" It was a friend of mine from the *Second U-boat Flotilla* whom I had known since our days together in Submarine School. He lifted the sea bag off my shoulders and pulled it through the open window of the train car.

An infantry soldier standing next to me saw what was happening and clasped his hands together for me to use as a step up to the window. Once I was safely inside the coach, I handed the soldier a pack of cigarettes as thanks. His tired eyes beamed with gratitude as he gave me a friendly farewell salute. It was only then that I noticed all the medals and decorations on his chest, including the impressive silver badge for hand-to-hand combat. For whatever reason, U-boat sailors and Army soldiers usually got along just fine. It made me feel good inside to provide a bit of pleasure to one of the boys who were sacrificing so much in the bloody fight against communism.

A few minutes later, our train left the station, leaving behind many hundreds of soldiers who were not able to crowd on board. Many of the soldiers in the train with us stuck their heads out the windows, keeping a sharp lookout for enemy fighter-bombers. It was becoming very common for our trains, even plainly marked hospital trains filled with wounded, to be strafed. These attacks almost always resulted in many casualties. I did see some wagons with anti-aircraft guns positioned at the front and rear of our train, but I knew from my experience at sea that these provided but little protection against a determined attacker.

*   *   *

On the 24th of November, I reported back from furlough to our new skipper, *Oberleutnant* Harald Lange. He immediately asked me why my furlough had been shortened by two days. After I told him the story of my encounter with the doctor, our tall and distinguished-looking new skipper just smiled and shook his head.

Lange was completely different than Zschech. At 43 years old he was almost twice the age of most front boat officers. He was like a father figure to us. During peacetime, he had been captain of one of the so-called "Monsoon Boats," merchant steamers that plied the tropical waters of West Africa and the Indian Ocean. Once the war started, he served as Executive Officer aboard the famous *U-180*, one of the few U-boats powered by Mercedes engines. The skipper of *U-180* put Lange's pre-war experience to good use in their long-range patrols in the Indian Ocean.

Lange started his naval career as a regular sailor on a freighter, so he had a good understanding of what life was like for us crewmen. He knew about the drinking, the girls, the brawls with the boys from the *Luftwaffe*, and all of the other activities that pass as entertainment for a young sailor. When we lined up for morning formation, he would go down the line checking on each and every one of us. If he saw a black eye, he would make remarks like, "Close your other eye. Can you still see me? Next time don't let them get so close!" and things of that sort. In many ways, Lange was like our first skipper, Axel Löwe. His main concern was the good of the boat. Everything else was small fish.

Later that day, I found out what *Oberleutnant* Meyer was talking about when he said I would get back my two days of lost furlough. First of all, although the days could not be officially restored to me, he did exempt me from duty. Then I was allowed to join a group of sailors who

Oblt.z.S. der Reserve Harald Lange,
U-505's third and last skipper. NA

were leaving for a resort at Chateau Neuf, located deep in a forest about 40 kilometers southeast of Lorient.

The resort was absolute heaven! It had big double-sized rooms, a huge swimming pool, a fully stocked bar, there was no standing in line for food, and best of all, the delicious meals were served to us individually by a staff of beautiful young *Mademoiselles*. For four wonderful days I lounged about the resort, enjoying uncounted bottles of wine, beer, cognac, and champagne—all paid for by the Navy. I really got spoiled. Too soon, however, I had to return to Lorient and the war.

On November 30, 1943, we had our first official day of duty under our new skipper. Standing there before us, Lange cut a very impressive figure. He was a very tall man, at least a head taller than the tallest man in our crew. In his deep baritone voice, he explained to us that we had no time for anything except getting the boat in shape. Therefore, there would be none of the infantry training that Zschech had deemed so necessary.

Harald Lange and *U-505's* officers just before leaving Lorient on their first war patrol together in late 1943. From left to right: *Leutnant zur See der Reserve* Kurt Brey (Second Watch Officer); *Stabsobermaschinist* Willi Schmidt; *Oberleutnant z.S.* Paul Meyer (First Watch Officer); *Bootsmann* Heinz Möller; *Oblt.z.S.d.R.* Harald Lange (commanding officer); *Obersteuermann* Alfred Reinig; *Marine-oberassistenzarzt* Dr. Friedrich-Wilhelm Rosenmeyer (Ship's Surgeon); *Obermaschinist* Otto Fricke; and *Oblt. (Ing)* Josef Hauser (Chief Engineer). *Author's Collection*

U-505's senior NCOs (left to right in the ascending order of their seniority; Harald Lange is in the middle): *Bootsmann* Heinz Möller; *Obermaschinist* Otto Fricke; *Stabsobermaschinist* Willi Schmidt; and *Obersteuermann* Alfred Reinig. *Author's Collection*

He also warned us to keep a very sharp eye on any shipyard workers doing repairs on our boat.

Lange was usually very soft-spoken and deliberate, but when his voice rose, you'd better watch out! He knew all the tricks of the trade and would not tolerate any slackening of our boat's readiness. At the same time, to us, the new atmosphere of command aboard *U-505* was like a breath of fresh air after a long dive. Lange almost always had a cigarette dangling from his mouth, but he did not smoke out of nervousness. Instead, he exuded an air of calm confidence based on his years of experience. We were sure that, with Lange at the helm, we would be successful.

In no time, we had dubbed our new skipper "the Old Man," a nickname that connoted our respect for his wealth of experience and easy-going attitude toward command. Once in a while, we remembered our previous skipper Peter Zschech, but not with nostalgia. Not many of us missed his hissing voice and sadistic behavior. Nor did we miss his insignia on the conning tower when it was painted over with Lange's emblem, a large sea shell. No, we thought, Lange is definitely the right man for this job.

We worked hard during the day of course, but we were still determined to enjoy our remaining time in Lorient. During the day, farmers would come to the main gate and sell us bottles of home-brewed *Calvados*. At night, we took pleasure in the ruins of Lorient wherever we could find it. Drinks, an occasional girl, and unprovoked fights with the *Luftwaffe* made those days pass very quickly. Slogans frequently made their way through our crew, summing up our attitude toward life. The one that was favored during those days was: "A man only lives once, and then, no more." It was an attitude toward life made logical by the desperate war situation we found ourselves in.

On the 12th, I was handed a bundle of mail from home. A few were flowery missives of love from girls I knew. The rest were letters from my mother. Inevitably, they opened with verses from the Bible, and ended with her asking if I still prayed as she had taught me to. Between the lines, I could tell she was desperately worried about me. I did my best to reassure her that all was well and that we were confident of victory. There was no use in worrying her needlessly.

One bit of news my mother told me was that two days after I passed through Marburg on my way back to base, the town had been savagely bombed by the Allies. The air raid obliterated the rail station and the train I would have been riding. If I had not been punished for my encounter with the doctor, I would have been there when the bombs hit. Another example of the remarkably good luck I experienced during the war!

Other members of the crew, however, did not have such good luck during their furloughs. Many of them, especially those who visited Berlin, Frankfurt, and other large cities, spent most of their leave huddled in air raid shelters. The stories they told of life under the shadow of Allied bombers were not pretty. The purpose of the bombing may have been to break our morale, but I can tell you that seeing the suffering being inflicted on our families and friends only inspired us to fight even harder.

* * *

We worked like crazy during the next two weeks to get *U-505* ready for her scheduled sailing date. Meanwhile, we watched the shipyard workers like hawks for any sign of sabotage. They sensed our obvious mistrust, and they developed a resentful attitude toward us because of it. We didn't mind one bit. Better safe than sorry!

Starting on the 18th, we began loading our boat with torpedoes, provisions, and supplies. Some of the new guys in the crew, fresh out of Submarine School, said that our boat smelled sweet like a whorehouse because of all the *Colibri* perfume we sprinkled on our spare clothes and ourselves.

"Wait until you have to empty the pail in the diesel room a few times," I told them. "You'll wish you still smelled like a *Hure* after that!"

By the afternoon of the 19th, we were ready to sail. We had the obligatory visits by Flotilla officers, as well as a good-sized crowd of civilian well-wishers for our departure. We knew the French Resistance had been using some of the local girls to extract information out of us. To avoid giving any useful intelligence to the enemy, we tried to feed the girls lies and misinformation regarding our boat's technical details and sailing date. Despite our precautions, however, there were a large number of mademoiselles waiting at the dock to see us off. Who knows, perhaps one of us talked in his sleep? For whatever reason, the girls of Lorient always seemed to know as much about our sailing schedule as we did.

*   *   *

Late on the afternoon of December 20, we waved our caps and bade farewell to Lorient. Once our boat was clear of the pier, we increased speed to one-half and headed for the mouth of the harbor. Heavy clouds hung overhead like giant gray cotton balls as we made our way towards open sea.

When we reached the 200-meter depth line, we prepared to make our final test dive. Given our past experience with sabotage, there was a certain amount of anxiety as we slipped underneath the waves. Thirty meters . . . fifty meters . . . eighty meters . . . everything all right so far.

At 120 meters, however, we started to hear a suspicious noise. After another ten meters, a gurgling sound began. A moment later, with a loud hiss, we began taking on water.

We soon located the source of the leak: a faulty welding seam on a cable flange. More sabotage! Lange cursed the shipyard workers with every bad word in the sailor's rich dictionary of curses. There was no alternative but to return to port for more repairs. We dove one last time to see if there was anything else we should know about and, discovering nothing else, headed for home.

Within a couple of hours we were once again tied to our pier in *Bunker Skorff.* Most of the crew boarded buses for our barracks, but the Board Watch, me included, was left behind to tend the boat. Lange must have really raised hell with the shipyard officials, because one-half hour after we docked, a large group of workers came running on board like a bunch of whipped dogs. The repairs, they said, would take a few days to complete.

*   *   *

Although we were frustrated with having yet another mission aborted by shoddy and/or malicious workmanship, we were not displeased with the prospect of spending the Christmas holiday in port. Our Chief Navigator Alfred Reinig, who was also responsible for keeping the crew's pay records, told us that only two of the crewmen had any *Reich Marks* left in their accounts. Luckily, he was able to convince the military bureaucrats in the Finance Department to give us an advance on our next pay. That little cash advance kept us afloat for the next few days while the repairs were completed. "Afloat" is an appropriate word since virtually every *Pfennig* was spent on liqueur to drink.

At noon on December 24, the day we call "Holy Eve," we had a Christmas celebration sponsored by the Flotilla. By order of our skipper, all drinking had to stop at midnight. We knew this meant that we would be sailing the next day—Christmas Day. Twelve hours of feasting and drinking were enough, though, even for us. At midnight, we turned into our bunks and tried to get some sleep.

Sure enough, we departed Lorient the next day. With three minesweepers as escort, we sailed back to the 200-meter depth line. This time, our test dive was performed without incident. But when we surfaced and started the diesels, the starboard engine burst into flame! It took us several harrowing minutes to extinguish the smoky fire. Once the smoke and fumes had been blown out of the compartment, Lange ordered us to submerge to effect repairs.

It wasn't until that evening that Diesel Chief Fricke reported that the repairs were complete. We all walked by the troublesome engine and spat on it for good luck before it was fired-up for a test. The engine functioned just fine and soon the diesels were singing their familiar hissing-hammering song as we knifed through the Bay.

After the batteries were fully recharged, we heard the skipper's unmistakable baritone voice on the intercom ordering the boat to dive. I was laying off-duty in my bunk, listening intently to the sounds of our boat as it step-by-step slipped beneath the waves. When we heard the hiss-hiss-hiss of compressed air opening the relief valves on the diving tanks, we all reflexively braced ourselves so that we would not slip out of our bunks as the boat pitched downward. Within a few minutes, we were cruising at a depth of seventy meters, the soft hum of the electric motors lulling us to sleep.

We were awakened the next morning by the rush of cold air being sucked through the boat to the diesels. We threw on some thick sweaters and woolen caps and reported for duty. It was still a bit strange to enter the control room and see Lange instead of Zschech as skipper. But everything we had seen so far convinced us that Lange was our man. He always smelled like cigarettes and often insisted on "shooting the stars" with the sextant himself. There was no doubt in our hearts and minds that this gruff Old Salt was exactly the kind of skipper we needed.

The first few days of our passage through the Bay of Biscay passed uneventfully. The weather was typical for the winter: choppy waves and low, dark gray overcast clouds. The temperature inside the boat plummeted as we moved further into a very frigid cold front.

Around 1400 hours on the 28th, we started hearing the muffled boom of ship artillery and aircraft bombs exploding in the distance. The barrage continued unabated for more than two hours. After sundown, we cautiously surfaced to recharge the batteries. There was lots of radio traffic in the air, most of it enemy transmissions.

At 1910 hours, we received an *FT* ordering four boats (including *U-505*) to proceed at top speed to Sea Square BE6938. There was no explanation, but we assumed it had something to do with the gunfire we had been hearing. Within minutes we were smashing our way through the breakers at maximum speed, southeast toward our rendezvous point. Ice cold spray drenched the bridge watch as they scanned the horizon for signs of battle.

Tensions ran high among us crew members. We were very excited to get back into action. As we drew closer to our destination, we could plainly see flashes of gunfire. Just as we entered the designated Sea Square, however, the fire slackened and then died away completely.

At 2042 hours, we received a long *FT* from Flotilla Headquarters. It informed us that a group of our destroyers and fast torpedo boats had been battling a superior force of British warships located in Sea Square BE6930. German Destroyer *Z-27* was dead in the water, location BE3938. The four remaining destroyers were trying to fight their way westward. Six of our torpedo boats were attempting to escape toward the east. We were ordered to render immediate assistance to Destroyer *Z-27*, and to attack any enemy naval units we should encounter.

A few minutes later, we received an update through *FT*. We were advised the enemy group consisted of cruisers, destroyers, and aircraft—present location unknown. We were ordered to search for survivors from the *Z-27*, which implied the destroyer had sunk. Given the frigid temperature of the sea, we knew the men in the sea would not last long in the freezing water.

We found ourselves shivering uncontrollably, half from the cold and half from the excitement. It had been a long time since we had gone into action—far too long for our tastes. And now, a chance to tangle with warships! The glory of sinking an enemy cruiser filled our imaginations.

Our first priority, however, was rescuing those boys from the *Z-27*. We entered our destination Sea Square in the early morning hours of the 29th. Sea conditions were becoming rougher, with very poor visibility. Spotting survivors in this kind of weather would be quite a challenge, to say the least. With the size of the waves we were encountering, our only chance of finding them was if we spotted each other as we were both riding the crest of a swell. We were not optimistic. Nevertheless, we began gathering all of our woolen blankets while Toni brewed pot after pot of hot coffee. We prayed that we could save at least some of our sailors from the freezing water.

At 0140 hours, we spotted a red flare almost directly astern of our boat. We wheeled around and began a zig-zag search pattern. A couple of hours later, we located two German sailors floating in "pipe boats"—one-man life rafts designed to help men survive winter sea conditions. The freezing cold swells made their retrieval very difficult, but we finally managed to fish them out of the water. They were slightly injured and very, very cold. They were having shivering fits from hypothermia, so we took them down to the electric engine room and stripped off their wet clothing. After rubbing them dry to help circulation, we gave them some dry clothing and put them into warm bunks.

Meanwhile, the weather continued to deteriorate. A freezing north wind was whipping up, blowing the tops off the waves. Visibility from the bridge was virtually nil. To make matters worse, the motor malfunctioned on our *Wanze* device, our tiny new radar detector, further handicapping us. We were all thinking of the poor boys out there in that ice cold water, and how small our chances were of finding any more of them before it was too late.

Despite dismal odds, Lange was up on the bridge, soaking wet and freezing cold, but he refused to give up on the men. We could see him standing there, smoking cigarette after cigarette, shouting orders over the roar of the wind. He was like the eye of a hurricane: a pillar of utter calm surrounded by the storm. More confirmation that he was a skipper we could be proud of.

Our skipper also had a lot of confidence in us. After the war, Lange told me personally that he was very impressed with our professionalism. He never had a doubt that we were a well-trained and able crew, and was very happy he had us instead of a newly-assembled crew. This is absolute refutation of the opinion of some writers that our spirit had been broken after the Zschech affair, and that we should have been split-up and dispersed as replacements to other boats.

For the next hour, we rumbled back and forth in zig-zag search patterns. With ten-foot swells crashing over our upper deck, visibility was virtually zero. But there was no question of giving up. Up on the bridge, Lange and the rest of the watch crew strained their eyes to spot something through the darkness. Below decks, we continued to ready the boat for more survivors. We couldn't stop thinking of those poor boys out there, exposed to the freezing blasts of wind and sea. We prayed that God would put His thumb between them and the inevitable fate that awaits all sailors exposed to a winter ocean storm.

Just before dawn, one of the bridge watch crew caught a quick glimpse of something being lifted above the whitecaps by the crest of a big wave. As we approached the spot, we could see a group of seven life rafts tied together. Lange maneuvered our boat so that our conning tower sheltered the cluster of rafts in our lee. As we pulled along side, we realized they were German sailors—more than two dozen of them. They were in pitiful condition, hardly able to grab the towline we tossed to them. One by one, we hauled the men on board.

The last one to leave the life rafts was *Korvettenkapitän* Wirich von Gortzen, skipper of torpedo boat *T-25*. Needless to say, he was very grateful to us for rescuing them. He told us his torpedo boat had been sunk by naval gunfire during a savage encounter with British cruisers. On our trip back to base, we learned it was his *T-25* that had rescued the crew of one of our sister boats, *U-106*, when it was attacked by British aircraft in the Bay of Biscay earlier that year. We were happy to return the favor to our comrades in the *Kriegsmarine.*

Everyone not on duty was detailed to helping the newly rescued men. Those fellows were in miserable shape! Several of them were deep in hypothermic shock. One of the biggest problems was finding space for them all. Since we had just left port, our decks were still piled high with provisions. There wasn't enough room on our sub for a dog to lay down. Despite the sardine can conditions, however, we tried to give the sailors the impression they were not in the way.

Meanwhile, the weather continued to worsen. Our guests were not used to the motions of our boat and turned green. Spit pans were brought out, but most of them just threw up into the bilge. They were very apologetic for making such a mess, but we just tried to make a joke of it.

"Don't worry about it!" we assured them. "It just means our cook Toni will have an easy day today. He'll just collect it all up and serve it tonight for stew. It will save us from using our own rations!" Rough sailor talk like that made them laugh and relax a bit.

At 0545 hours, we spotted a red star emergency flare off our port bow. *Korvettenkapitän* von Gartzen thought it might be some of his crew who had been separated from the others by the ferocity of the storm. Unfortunately, whoever fired the flare must have slipped beneath the waves by the time we reached him. Von Gartzen was beside himself with worry about the fate of his missing crewmen.

Conditions were getting too rough on the surface to continue the search, so Lange ordered us down to 40 meters. Our passengers' eyes got wide as soup bowls when the boat tilted down and began slipping beneath the waves. They calmed down a bit when the boat leveled off, but a few of the sailors already delirious from hypothermia began to rant and panic. To keep them from hurting themselves or others, we were forced to carry them to the aft crew quarters and tie them up in hammocks. After an hour or so of warming up, most of them started acting normal again.

Around 0930 Lange brought us up to periscope depth to take another look around. Much to our disbelief, the weather had actually gotten worse since we submerged. The Old Man was looking through the periscope when we heard him growl, *"Verdammte Tommies!"* ("Damned Tommies!"), and lowered the periscope in disgust. He told us we had just passed a large group of empty life preservers. The survivors had probably been chilled to unconsciousness and slipped through the arm straps, or had simply given up and decided to end their freezing misery. After a moment, Lange regained his composure and raised the periscope to once again resume the search. Nothing could be seen but the raging sea.

Around noon, Toni served lunch. Our comrades from the *T-25* got served first. After they had finished, the plates were scraped more or less clean and we were served our food. Their hunger satisfied, the boys from the T-boat tried to find a place to lay down and sleep. Meanwhile, their exhausted skipper was still busy at the second periscope assisting our skipper scan the sea for survivors. Lange finally convinced him to go down and get some rest. Before he laid down, however, von Gartzen inspected the condition of every one of his men. We could tell he was a good, caring skipper of a well-trained and disciplined crew.

Just before sunset, we surfaced to take one last look around. As the skies started to darken, we spotted an emergency signal light off our port bow. The seas had decreased a bit, so we were able to make good speed toward the light. Our prow cut big, white, splashing wedges through the rollers as we raced ahead.

Lange shouted down from the bridge, *"Rettungskommando auf die Brücke!"* ("Rescue crew to the bridge!").

The men scampered up the conning tower ladder like monkeys, salvage equipment in hand. One of our lookouts had spotted two small rafts. As we approached them, we could see they contained five men, obviously delirious and on the verge of death. The men didn't have the strength to catch a line, so we grappled the rafts with hooks and lifted the men on board. They were all stiff as boards from the cold and we weren't sure all of them were still alive. We brought them down below and placed them between the diesels to warm up. After a while, they began to recover. That brought our total number of rescued to 34.

During the night, we turned on our searchlight to help spot survivors. This was an extremely dangerous decision given the large numbers of enemy aircraft and ships operating in the area, but Lange was willing to risk it. Later, we received a radio message reporting more emergency signals scattered throughout three different Sea Squares. A follow-up message reported that a neutral Irish steamer was conducting rescue operations in those areas. We spotted the Irish merchantman at around 2000. She seemed to be doing a conscientious job of searching, so we slipped away, eager not to be noticed.

We continued running to and fro, using the periscopes to look for any sign of survivors. After a few more hours of fruitless searching, our skipper decided to head back to port with the ones we had found. Lange reported to Headquarters by *FT*, took one last look around, and then pointed our nose back toward the French coast.

Chapter 13

Brest

*I*n the early morning hours of December 30, we heard two loud aircraft bombs explode at a moderate distance from our boat. The hollow booms reverberating through the boat frightened our guests from the *T-25*, but they calmed down when they saw our practiced nonchalance.

In general, they were grateful beyond measure for their rescue, but their relief was tempered by a gnawing concern about the fate of their missing crewmates. We tried to assure them the Irish merchantman had probably picked up their comrades, but nothing could console them. These jumbles of mixed feelings, of joy and sadness, guilt and relief, were quite common in those days as more and more of our comrades were lost to enemy action. Only God in Heaven knows why some of us survived, while so many other good men went to their deaths. Who are we to question His wisdom?

Just before dawn, we tried to surface and recharge the batteries. An aircraft alarm quickly put a premature end to that endeavor. We didn't dare try again until after sunset. Because of the large number of extra personnel on board, the carbon dioxide level inside the boat reached dangerous levels by the time we were finally able to surface. Dumping overboard the buckets of human waste was also long overdue. That first gust of clean air that spilled into the boat with the opening of the top hatch smelled sweeter than roses to us. As usual, Lange was up on the bridge in the blink of an eye, chain-smoking one *Jan Maat* cigarette after another.

That evening, we received an *FT* from the Chief of U-boat Western Command. We were ordered to bring our passengers to a position code-named *Eisbär* (Polar Bear). We knew this meant we were being directed to the U-boat base in Brest harbor, rather than our home port of Lorient. We were excited about the prospect of having a few days of liberty in a new city. We knew that with the *First* and *Ninth U-Boat Flotillas* stationed in Brest, we could find everything we wanted.

*   *   *

New Years Eve this year was not an especially festive one for us. We had to put extra toilet pails between the diesels because so many of the crewmen from *T-25* were suffering from acute diarrhea. There were usually two or three of them standing around each pail, urging the poor soul "on the throne" to hurry up. Many of them were also developing agonizing catarrhs, inflammations, and cysts. There was nothing we could do for them since our store of medicines was never intended to serve so many men suffering from such prolonged and severe exposure to the cold.

Although we never complained to them about it, our guests were making even the most routine of operations on the boat very difficult. We knew it would be absolutely impossible to conduct a quick crash dive in the usual manner with so many men crowded about.

Since we would have been sitting ducks on the surface for any attacking aircraft, Lange made the decision to run submerged as much as possible. Typically, after eight or nine hours in the basement, we would rise to periscope depth, take a quick look around, and then pop up to the surface. While the men on watch clamored up the ladder to the bridge, the diesel crew would fire up the big Jumbos. That's when we would feel the delicious, ice cold sea breeze being sucked into the boat, replacing the stale, fetid stenches that had accumulated during the previous hours. The inrush of oxygen had an immediate regenerating effect on our bodies and minds. Broad smiles always creased across the faces of our guests as soon as they smelled the fresh sea air.

We were busy as bees during those brief periods on the surface, emptying the buckets, pumping out the bilges, shooting a "fix" with the sextant, etc. And, of course, there was the Old Man, the inevitable cigarette dangling from his lips, silently overseeing it all like a gargoyle perched on the bridge.

That evening we finally had to confront what we feared the most: an emergency crash dive to avoid an enemy aircraft. There was nothing else to do but elbow our guests out of the way as we grabbed for the various valves and levers needed to submerge. They didn't mind the violent shoving as much as the steep angle of the boat as we dove. They weren't used to such excitement, and their heavy breathing used up our oxygen much faster than usual. Luckily, the plane didn't attack us and everything turned out O.K.

We spent the last few hours of 1943 serenely cruising 60 meters beneath the surface, trading war stories and tall tales with our guests. They couldn't understand why we enjoyed serving on a vessel that sank several times a day. We couldn't understand why they enjoyed serving on a boat that couldn't dive to escape the enemy. The teasing was all good-natured and a close bond developed between our two crews. We laughed and spun yarns until, before we knew it, it was midnight. Lange's deep, resonate voice crackled over the intercom, wishing us a happy New Year. His wish that we all survived to celebrate another New Year in 1945 was met with somber assent.

We surfaced on the first morning of 1944 to find mirror-smooth seas stretching before us. Our course was east toward the big orange rising sun. The diesels were pounding away at high speed, causing our prow to cut a high, clean bow wave. The view from the bridge was gorgeous.

All of the *T-25* crewmen, even the ones who had suffered the worst hypothermia, were up and about. With the fine weather and the full recovery of our guests, spirits were especially high. They had told us where to go in Brest for the best drinks and the prettiest girls, so our minds were filled with anticipation for the charms awaiting us. Everyone was eager to relax and have some fun before getting back in the war.

We reluctantly dove back down to 60 meters to avoid any unpleasant surprises during this last leg of our mission. Around noon, we surfaced for a few minutes in order to get a fix on our position with the sextant. Navigator Reinig calculated we were 30 nautical miles off course. The Old Man, always eager to exercise his seamanship skills, double-checked Reinig's computations. Sure enough, we had drifted significantly off course. As we soon learned, our direction finder device had malfunctioned. Equipment failures on our boat were becoming so common that they barely raised an eyebrow any more. Luckily, we were only 12 hours away from Brest, so no serious problems were anticipated with finding our way to port.

We radioed Brest, informing them of our position and the equipment failure. They radioed back detailed navigation instructions. We would be using a complex system of beacon fires and searchlights to visually find our way to the harbor. *First U-boat Flotilla* would be doing everything they could to ensure our safe return.

We sped away from the area submerged in case the enemy had triangulated our position by monitoring our broadcast. In the small hours of the morning, we surfaced in Sea Square BF5464 to begin our final sprint to base. We all crossed our fingers in the hope we could reach our rendezvous point with the escorts while still under cover of darkness. The diesels, running at maximum speed, left a giant wedge of white foam in our wake. The sea was still calm as a duck pond.

We met our escort a little after dawn. We followed them along the rocky coast towards the entrance of the harbor, all the while keeping an intense lookout for any airborne intruders.

When we arrived in Brest's outer harbor, our sub was met by a barge filled to overflowing with war correspondents. Included among them was a film crew who wanted to take motion pictures of the *T-25* survivors crowded in our boat's interior. The big barge heaved to and the film crew came aboard, carrying with them a large array of photographic equipment.

They were getting some fine footage of the sardine can conditions inside our boat when suddenly, a blinding lightning-like flash erupted from the electric motor room. A huge blue-white bolt of electricity was arcing out from the starboard motor. A great cloud of white smoke, then evil-smelling black smoke, billowed from the motor. Moments later, flames began licking up from the motor housing.

This dramatic electrical display caused an immediate panic among the war correspondents, who stampeded like a herd of frightened cattle toward the control room. The *T-25* survivors joined them when the choking cloud of smoke began to make its way through the boat. We crewmen knew immediately what had happened because it had happened before: it was another short in our electrical control panel. The boys in the

U-505 motors into Brest, France, the 5th T-Flotilla's home port on January 2, 1944, a cold and overcast day. Gathered on deck are the lucky survivors from the sunken destroyer *T-25*. The warship was sunk in the Bay of Biscay five days earlier after a battle with enemy surface ships and aircraft. *NA*

motor room used the CO_2 fire extinguishers to good effect, and within a few minutes the fire was out. The Diesel Chief switched the Jumbos to internal air intake. Before long, the big nine-cylinder engines had inhaled all of the smoke. It took a while before our stoic attitudes had any effect on our guests, though. The lingering odor of burned rubber, and our guests' nervousness, persisted for some time.

Privately, we just had to shake our heads. It just wouldn't have been *U-505* if something like this had not happened. The whole hair-raising episode would have been funny, except we knew the burned-out control panel would probably keep us stranded in Brest for a couple of extra weeks for repairs.

A little later, a couple of small steam-engined tugs met us and guided our boat through the harbor toward the submarine bunker complex. Around noon we finally entered Brest's inner harbor. Our escort vessels veered off to their moorings while we continued on to the big U-boat pens. The massive concrete bunkers were just as large and imposing as the ones back in Lorient. Sailors crowded every inch of *U-505*'s upper deck as we inched up to the pier in front of *Bunker C-1*.

We were happy to see a large reception waiting for us at the pier. The commanders of both the *First U-boat Flotilla* and Brest's *Torpedo Boat Flotilla* were there. An unusually large collection of sailors, soldiers, and staff officers were also in attendance. For the first time in a long time, there was a Navy band to add a bit of old-fashioned pomp to the festivities. It seemed like an eternity since we had enjoyed a reception like this.

As we made our final approach into the slip for *Bunker C-1*, a cluster of crewmen from *T-25*, a little too eager to disembark, simultaneously rushed to climb the ladder from the control room to the bridge. In his excitement, one of the sailors slipped off and landed on the helmsman's rudder control. Our boat immediately swerved starboard, crushing the diving plane fin against the pier. The only thing we felt inside the boat was a momentary shudder and shake, but instinctively we knew the damage was serious. Twelve hundred tons of mass, even when moving slowly, would do terrible damage to a fragile piece like a diving fin.

Later that afternoon, *U-505* was lifted up on rails into dry dock for a close inspection. There, it was discovered that our boat's diving plane shaft had been bent, necessitating at least two weeks for repair. It took two full days of backbreaking labor just to extract the shaft from its housing. Once out, a committee of shipyard engineers decided the shaft was beyond repair and had to be replaced. Unfortunately, there were no spare shafts to be found either in Brest or Lorient. Until another one could be found, *U-505* was stuck in port.

Lange swore like a Turk when he heard the news.

*   *   *

A few days later, word came through to our skipper that a spare shaft had been located in Bordeaux, the southernmost of our U-boat sally ports on the Atlantic. Within a few minutes of hearing that news, I was ordered to report to the Old Man's quarters.

"Göbeler, I understand you have a driver's license. Have you ever driven a truck?"

"*Jawohl, Herr Oberleutnant.*"

"Good! Sign out a pistol from the arsenal this afternoon. Tomorrow morning you will report to the car pool, drive to Bordeaux, and 'organize' a shaft for our diving plane."

Apparently, my reputation for "organizing" supplies had reached our skipper's ears. I was quite annoyed that my leisure time in Brest would be interrupted by this mission. But orders were orders, so I hurried to the arsenal.

As I presented Lange's authorization for a pistol to the arms room duty officer, I found that I was strangely excited by the prospect of carrying a sidearm on this special mission. Would it be a handsome *Luger*? Perhaps one of the sleek *Walther* pistols?

Imagine my shock when the duty officer handed me an enormous, ancient-looking French revolver! The ridiculous antique was well over one foot long and heavy as a small cannon. When I stuck it into my belt, the barrel literally reached down to my knee. The duty officer refused to listen to my pleadings for a replacement weapon and brusquely sent me on my way. I knew I was going to get teased by my crewmates when I arrived back at the barracks. They didn't disappoint me.

"Hey, look! There's Buffalo Bill!"

"Yeah, he's going to kill two buffaloes with one shot from that big gun!"

I got angry at all the laughter and, in disgust, tossed the pistol onto my bunk. Unfortunately, my buddy Willi, who was already quite intoxicated at this hour of the day, picked it up and began waving it around, pretending to be an American cowboy. I was responsible for the weapon, so I tried to wrestle it away from him. Well, the inevitable happened. Willi's finger was on the trigger and before we knew it, the old pistol let loose with a tremendous BANG! No one was hurt, but the bullet went clean through the wall into the bathroom next door, taking a big chip out of a toilet bowl.

We knew we had to act quickly if we were to stay out of the brig. There was an artillery mechanic who was bunking in the same room with us who, through an incredible bit of luck, had a spare bullet that more- or-less fit in the old revolver's cylinder. We replaced the fired cartridge with the new one while others concealed the hole in the wall with a pillow. Someone else blew through the gun barrel to clear the smoke and then gave the pistol a quick wipe with a rag.

Just then, the Raccoon, our Engineering Officer, burst into the room and demanded an explanation for the gunshot noise. He was clearly not convinced by our protestations of innocence, nor even by the pistol's apparently unfired condition.

"If you didn't do it, then who fired the shot?" he demanded.

"There he is!" shouted one of my mates, pointing out the window toward a sailor running across the barracks square.

The Engineering Officer gave a quick glance at the obviously innocent sailor rushing across the square and then turned back to us, annoyance and frustration painted all over his face. He stood there glowering at us for what seemed like an eternity. Finally, he just shook his head and left the room without another word. Willi, sobered by our close brush with a court-martial, spent the rest of the evening "organizing" materials to repair the wall and toilet.

Determined not to get into any further trouble, I was up before dawn and standing in the motor pool by 0600, waiting for them to open. Strapped to my side was "the flak gun," my nickname for the old revolver. I was assigned two drivers for the trip. Together, we loaded several spare gas cans into the back of the truck.

Before we left, we received some quick instructions on what to do in case we encountered any Partisans. There had been several recent ambushes and acts of sabotage by the Resistance along our route, and we were sternly warned not to travel at night. My two companions were also armed, though with more respectable weapons than my embarrassing antique.

Within an hour, we were roaring down the road towards Bordeaux. During daylight hours we drove in shifts, trading places every 150 kilometers. We stopped and spent the night in a small naval anti-aircraft base, but were back on the road by sunrise.

Later that morning, we were passing through a small forest near La Rochelle when some men in civilian clothes suddenly appeared and opened fire on us with rifles. They were obviously in desperate need of some target practice because none of their shots even touched the truck. Nevertheless, we pushed that truck's gas pedal to the floor to get past them as quickly as we could. I must admit, though, we were also trying to get to Bordeaux as early as possible so that we could have some free time out on the town.

We immediately checked into the U-boat base upon our arrival in Bordeaux. The diameter of the diving plane shaft, the authorities told us, was a few hundredths of an inch too thick and would need to be machined down on a giant lathe.

"We are sorry," they said, "but you'll have to wait here in Bordeaux for two or three days until the job is completed."

That's all we needed to hear! We were out the gate and on our way to the entertainment district before they had a chance to change their minds.

Once in town, I decided to have a bite to eat in a little tavern. My naval uniform attracted quite a bit of attention from the other customers. I thought they were just admiring my U-boat badge, as usual. Little did I know the attention being showered upon me was because the establishment was off-limits to German personnel!

Well, I was just sitting there, innocently enjoying a little seafood, when a very attractive woman sat down at my table and struck up a conversation. She insisted on buying me several drinks, and since she was covered in expensive pieces of jewelry, I let her pay without protest. After a few hours of drinking, she invited me to visit her at her house later in the evening. I was happy to accept, especially after she offered to have dinner ready for me, too.

I showed up at the address she had given me at the appointed hour. When she answered the door, she placed a finger to her lips, signaling me to be quiet as I entered the house. As we crept through the parlor, I could see an enormously obese old man sleeping in a chair, his rolls of fat literally dripping over the arms of the chair. I assumed he was the woman's father.

She led me to a bedroom on the third floor. Inside there was a tray covered with bottles of champagne and various delicacies to eat. She told me to make myself comfortable and to start on the food and drink without her. She would be up to join me in an hour or so. I didn't need much encouragement to open a bottle and start to sample the expensive hors d'oeuvres. There was cheese, biscuits, jam, canned sardines, olives, roasted meat, and dried fruit. It was magnificent.

After an hour or so of eating and drinking, curiosity got the better of me and I decided to take a peek outside the room. To my shock, I found that the door had been locked. Panic gripped my heart. Was this a trap set for me by the French Resistance? I pulled the old pistol out and rechecked the cylinder to make sure it was loaded. Just then, I heard a key being inserted into the door lock. I lowered the barrel of the pistol toward the door.

Instead of a band of armed guerillas, however, there was the woman, dressed in fancy red lingerie. The situation still smelled like trouble to me, but the sight of the lady's ample charms soon made me forget all my qualms about the situation.

"Now," she said smilingly, "you've eaten my food and drunk my wine. It's time to repay your debt to me."

Well, that was the kind of debt any sailor would be happy to repay. A little while later, she explained that the fat old man in the parlor was her husband. I didn't have to worry, she said, I was perfectly safe up here on the third floor because he couldn't climb the stairs. I told her I would be happy to continue our arrangement, but that I could only stay for 72 hours. She was more than agreeable, and she spent the next two days and nights serving me rich food and champagne, then making me repay the debt in the fancy canopy bed. Sometimes I heard the giggling of young girls outside the door during our love sessions. I guessed that everyone in the house knew what was going on, except for the foolish old man in the chair.

By the time I left that house, I felt like an orange that has had all the juice squeezed out of it. On the other hand, that mysterious woman had made every single one of my young sailor's wishes come true. I will never forget those days and nights in Bordeaux, when I lived like a king without spending one single *Reich Mark*.

*   *   *

Around noon of the third day, I met my two comrades at the naval base workshop. We loaded the huge shaft and some other spare parts into the truck and headed back to Brest. As we left the base, we noticed some talcum powder the Resistance had sprinkled on the road in order to monitor traffic in and out of the gate. That worried us, so we decided to travel back to our base as quickly as possible. While one of us drove, the other two sat with our fingers on the triggers of our weapons, ready for anything.

The route back to Brest generally followed the coastline of the Bay of Biscay. At this time of year, road conditions were usually quite foggy. To make matters worse, the headlights on the truck had been painted black except for narrow blackout slits. Nevertheless, we made good progress. As night fell, we made the decision to violate orders and keep driving, despite the increased danger of ambush. We soon discovered that the Resistance had turned many of the road signs to the wrong direction. So, by the light of our cigarette lighter, we constantly checked our map to make sure we were traveling the right route.

Finally, very late that night, we came across the encampment of a *Panzer* unit where we could park in security. We slept like mummies for a few hours and then hit the road again at dawn. By that afternoon, we were safely back in Brest.

Lange was happy to see me report back safely with the shaft. My comrades in the barracks were also glad to see me. They were especially curious to hear all the details about the hospitality I been shown by that lovely, mysterious lady of Bordeaux. As for me, I was just relieved to get rid of "the flak gun" and return to the duties of an ordinary sailor.

The boatswain's whistle blew at 0600 the next morning. With a shock, I realized that the sweet dream of Bordeaux was over and that I was back in a bunk instead of a canopy bed. Two hours later, we were lined up in formation, listening to the skipper's orders for the day.

"Today we will be getting that damned shaft in place. I want everybody to do their best to get the job done quickly and correctly. And keep an eye on the shipyard workers! If any of them leave, watch where they go and when they return. Examine everything they bring aboard our boat. Don't hesitate to check what they are carrying in a box or bag. I don't want any sabotage. Dismissed!"

Off we went to work. The task of getting the shaft inserted into the housing was quite problematic. The big steel rod had to be suspended from the ceiling by a crane and slowly, millimeter by millimeter, slid through the hull. Meanwhile, we kept careful watch that no unauthorized personnel approached the boat. With all of our attention focused on the shaft operation, it would have been the perfect time for a sabotage attempt. It ended up taking a day and a half before the shaft was in place.

No sooner was that task finished then we discovered that several of the battery cells needed replacement. Unfortunately, this simple sounding operation entailed removing the mounting hatch and then re-riveting it back in place. This took several more days of arduous work.

Despite our busy days, however, we always seemed to have plenty of energy left over to cruise the streets of Brest in the evenings. The military's *Soldatenheim* (soldiers' recreation center) in Brest was really first class. There were all sorts of activities to be enjoyed there. An all-girl band, for some reason, stands out in my memory.

My favorite place for fun, however, was the *Rue de Pasteur* in downtown Brest. It had all of the attractions that a young sailor in port looks for. To our surprise, we met a number of girls we remembered from Lorient, back in the days before the bombs turned that city into a ghost town. We spent the months of January and February there in Brest, working hard in the daytime, and exerting ourselves even more at night.

It was during this period that someone who would become of my closest, life-long friends was transferred to our crew. It was an interesting story how he came to our boat. Otto Dietz had served on *U-180* during her adventurous war patrols in the Indian Ocean. Our skipper Harald Lange was serving as the Exec on *U-180* at that time. Well, Otto got himself into some trouble and ended up being court-martialed. He was transferred to an Army punishment battalion on the Eastern Front where he was severely wounded in combat. After a long convalescence in a military hospital, he was readmitted to the U-boat service. When Lange discovered his old crewman in Brest, he used his authority as our skipper to have Otto transferred to *U-505*. Otto and I immediately became good friends, and we remained so until his death in May of 1994.

Otto knew all the best places to go in Brest, and he and I spent many a night tasting the charms that city had to offer. Our favorite nightspot was *Le Cheval Blanc*, the last pub before the drawbridge between Brest and the naval base. It was a mysterious place, especially popular among those elements living on the fringes of proper society. While most of Europe was starving, this place was always filled with the most exotic of goods: Jamaican rum, Japanese Sake, pork hams, fresh butter by the hundred-weight, and every imaginable delicacy that most people could only dream about. There was a whiff of danger about the place, and I was always excited and a bit uneasy when we were there.

Unlike me, Otto seemed to be in his natural element in *Le Cheval Blanc*. He was always the adventurous leader and I was always his wary, sometimes reluctant, follower. I remember one night we spent there in particular. We were having some drinks when Otto motioned to the bartender to come over, then whispered something in his ear. The bartender gave me a suspicious looking over, then gestured for us to follow him.

Otto Dietz, Hans Goebeler's good
friend from *U-505*. *Author's Collection*

The bartender pushed aside a few old baskets, revealing a secret trapdoor. We entered the trapdoor and descended a long, dark stairwell to a large cellar. It took a while for my eyes to adjust to the dim light, but when they did I could see an entire oriental bazaar had been set up in the basement. A thick haze of strange, spicy-smelling smoke filled the room, and I could see dozens of people crowded about tables, drinking, gambling, and trading in every conceivable type of goods. A babble of every language I had ever heard, and a few I hadn't, filled the room.

I felt very uncomfortable in this place, which was obviously the nerve center of black market dealing in Brest. For the most part I just stood in a corner, my back against a cold stone wall, taking it all in. After a while, with much encouragement from Otto, I ventured toward the tables and bought a few packs of *Gaulloise* black tobacco cigarettes. I was just starting to get accustomed to the place when, suddenly, we heard a loud banging in the tavern above us. The place was being raided by the German military police!

The room erupted in a pandemonium of shouts and commotion. People grabbed their wares and scurried about like a colony of ants whose nest had been disturbed by the heavy leather boots of the police.

As cool as ever, Otto pulled me over to a large cabinet against a wall. As if by magic, he moved the seemingly heavy cabinet, revealing yet another secret passage. The passageway led to a back alley. After giving a quick glance to the left and right, Otto and I scurried down the alley. Once we got to the main street, we started running as if the devil himself was chasing us. Perhaps by command of the police, or perhaps by pure coincidence, the drawbridge began lifting just as we approached it. We leapt over the quickly widening cleft between the bridge halves and ran without pause back to the barracks.

After that, Otto and I decided *Le Cheval Blanc* was a little too exciting for us. Besides, like everyone else from *U-505*, we were out of money. Luckily, the brother-in-law of our Torpedo Mechanic Chief Hermann Knöss was in charge of refitting boats there in Brest. Being a veteran of the U-boat service in World War I, he understood the sorts of things a submariner in port needs to be happy. Through him, we received cartons of cigarettes, boxes of *Scho-ka-kola* chocolates, and most prized of all, *Colibri* deodorant and cologne. These commodities kept us quite popular with the ladies of *Rue de Pasteur*, despite our lack of money.

Meanwhile, my good luck continued. In February, I met two girls with German-sounding names who gave me everything I desired, free of charge, for six whole weeks. Those girls did everything together—and I mean everything! As final preparations were made on our boat for departure, my time with the two girls seemed like a last ray of warm sunshine before what I expected would be a cold and dark future.

Chapter 14

The Last Patrol

By the Ides of March, our boat was again ready for departure. At precisely 1835 hours on March 16, 1944, the lines were cast off and we unceremoniously backed out of *Bunker C-1*. Once clear of the pier, our diesels revved up and we rumbled toward the harbor mouth. I remember how proud I felt watching our skipper's handsome blue commander's pennant snapping in the breeze. Little did we suspect this would be our last patrol of the war.

Our mood as we headed toward deep water was a bit more somber than usual. Back in port we had heard rumors that during our ten-week stay in Brest, approximately four dozen of our sister U-boats had been sunk. We calculated amongst ourselves and determined there was now only about a 30% chance that a boat would return safely from a war patrol. The statistical probability of us surviving to the war's end was becoming very small indeed. No one had any illusions whatsoever about what we were heading into. At the beginning of the war, our thoughts dwelled on the few comrades who had been lost; now we were struck by how few of our old friends were still alive.

Despite the odds against us, we were absolutely determined to do our duty. With full confidence in our skipper and in ourselves, our attitude was simultaneously hopeful and fatalistic. The slogan that predominated on our boat was: "Let's get going and see what kind of success we can achieve on the open sea. What will be will be."

Personally, I had no qualms about our chances. Perhaps I was merely fooling myself, but at the time, I had absolutely no doubt that we would return safely from this patrol. Not only that, I still had total faith that Germany would win the war. I was far from alone in this belief. We placed most of our hopes on the new generation of weapons our scientists were developing, like rockets, jets, and guided missiles. Of course, my comrades and I spent many hours trading scuttlebutt about the new U-boats, too. It was said they could travel underwater indefinitely and could sail circles around the fastest destroyers. I dreamed of the day when our new boats would sweep the ocean clean of the hated enemy and bring a victorious end to the war.

*   *   *

Our passage through the Bay of Biscay began very well. The weather was excellent and our test dive passed without incident. To be free of the curse of sabotage felt very good indeed. Inside *U-505*, we quickly re-accustomed ourselves to the roar of the diesels, the earthy smell of fresh potatoes, and the complex rituals required for surfacing and diving. All passed as smooth as clockwork. Only the faint rumbling of bomb detonations in the distance reminded us we were not on a peacetime training cruise.

Lange's approach to command was an interesting one. In general, he was fairly cautious, but when the situation demanded, he was more than willing to take a chance based on his intuition. For instance, we had a new, longer-ranged version of the *Naxos* radar detection device on board, but based on our near-fatal experience off Trinidad, the Old Man refused to allow any new-fangled electrical device to relax the alertness of our bridge watch. On the other hand, as we passed through the most dangerous part of the Bay of Biscay, the skipper decided to gamble with a sprint on the surface with the diesels.

"Better to clear the area as quickly as possible," he said, "than to crawl slowly underwater and be stuck in the 'Suicide Stretch' forever."

Unfortunately, unlike most of the new boats now coming out of the shipyards, *U-505* was not equipped with the new *Schnorkel* device that would have allowed us to run the diesels underwater. We had to take our chances on the surface. Lange's intuition was correct, however, and we sailed through the most dangerous part of the Bay without any attacks from the buzzards.

When Lange opened his sealed sailing orders, he learned we would be returning to the old hunting grounds we had prowled in our first war patrol: the West African coast. This news, when it reached our ears, greatly pleased us. We were tired of cold weather, and imagined ourselves returning to Lorient with a suntan and plenty of victory pennants flying from our bridge. We were sure our new skipper had erased Zschech's "Curse of the Flowers" and that we were now sailing under a lucky star. Quite a crowd developed around the chart table when the map of the African coast was spread out.

However, an annoyance immediately arose that complicated our lives: the new *T-5 Zaunkönig* (wren) acoustic-homing torpedoes we had taken on board in Brest. These complex, electrically-propelled eels were nicknamed "Destroyer Killers" because, it was hoped, we could fire them in the general direction of the enemy escorts and they would automatically chase down our tormentors. Unfortunately, they contained delicate instrumentation that required constant attention and maintenance from the torpedo mechanics. Every 24 hours they had to be withdrawn from the tubes, dried, and adjusted. Lamentably, since the fore and aft torpedo rooms doubled as our crew's sleeping quarters, the mechanics had to fold up our bunks out of the way in order to perform their daily maintenance on the torpedoes. We quickly learned to sleep sitting, or even standing upright. Even so, the days and nights began to merge into a sleep-deprived blur.

On the brighter side, the Raccoon, our much-despised Engineering Officer, no longer disciplined us so strictly. Unlike Zschech, Lange did not want his men's leave time arbitrarily deducted for petty infractions. As a result, the Raccoon was robbed of his favorite pastime and our lives became much easier. After a while, he even stopped obsessively trimming his beard. Heavens, how thankful we were to have Harald Lange as our skipper!

There were several youngsters who had transferred into our crew at Brest and they didn't realize how easy they had it, now that the Old Man was running *U-505*. I'm sure many thought we were inventing some of the stories about life under Zschech. Still, they did experience some tough moments when the weather got rough. The water was smooth as a mirror when we left port, but after a week or so the sea started to whip up and those poor fellows had to go through violent bouts of seasickness, just as we all had, until they gained their sea legs. We would just shake our heads and laugh in good-hearted sympathy when the new guys turned green. Occasionally, we gave them "helpful" advice like: "If you vomit so hard that you throw-up your asshole, you'd better swallow, quick!" All new sailors had to go through this rite of passage, and they were not fully accepted as true members of the crew until they had done so.

During the last week in March, as we approached tropical waters, the weather worsened dramatically. Tremendous waves and gale-force winds blowing from the west battered our boat with stunning force. The whole sub shook and shuddered when the breakers crashed against our conning tower. The poor guys on bridge watch really suffered! They would climb down the ladder into the control room looking like drowned cats, cursing the weather with the kind of hair-raising oaths that only sailors at sea can concoct. Naturally, we crewmen on duty in the relative comfort of the control room saw fit to make humorous comments on their soaked condition. In retaliation, they would be intentionally slow to close the bridge hatch, drenching us all with cascades of seawater when the next big wave hit. The real agony started later, when the drying salt water caused us to itch all over.

Eventually, the weather got so rough the Old Man took pity on us and we cruised submerged for a few days. When we surfaced to recharge batteries, however, the torture began all over again for the poor guys on watch. By the time the weather calmed down, most of us had red swollen eyes from staring into the driving salty spray. Through it all, though, none of us begrudged Lange's demand that there be no let up in our vigilance—no matter what the condition of the sea.

As for me, I spent most of my free time reading. I was especially fascinated with Jack London's stories about Alaska. For hours at a time, I lost myself in daydreams about life in the mountains and virgin forests of North America. The quiet open spaces and fresh air of Alaska offered the perfect fantasy escape world. That is, until my next stint on watch or at in the control room jerked me back to the stinking, claustrophobic reality of submarine warfare.

Motivated by a desire to make my Alaskan dreams come true someday, I took great pains to keep up my self-taught English lessons. One very regrettable day, I was practicing to say the word "queen" because the 'Q' consonant sound was particularly difficult for me to pronounce. A couple of my buddies overheard me repeating the word and immediately began calling me by that name. Even Lange called me "queen" a couple of times! I hated that nickname so much I almost stopped practicing my lessons. In the end, though, I continued with my lessons and eventually my crewmates tired of the joke. Needless to say, I took care to choose a different "Q" word to practice my pronunciation in the future.

The bad weather kept us busy more or less constantly, but once the weather calmed, we had more leisure time. To relax, I especially liked standing on the bridge at night, enjoying a quiet smoke and watching the star constellations sway back and forth in time with the rocking of the boat. Without a horizon to provide a reference point, it seemed like God was rocking us in a heavenly cradle, infinite in its size and beauty.

Of course, such moments of carefree whimsy were a rare luxury aboard a U-boat in 1944. It was sobering to remember that my few minutes of leisure were only possible because four other sets of eyes were there on the bridge, busy at work scanning the horizon for danger. Who knows how many young sailors, lost in the beauty of the nighttime ocean sky, let their minds wander away from their duty, and as a result never returned home to their family?

At any rate, the skipper was very good about letting us have a breath of fresh air whenever possible. He understood how important a few minutes topside can be for a submariner's health and morale. In comparing Lange to Zschech, it was clear to us that the Old Man's experience as an ordinary seaman was more valuable in making for a good skipper than all of Zschech's years in the Naval Academy.

During those days, I sometimes volunteered to help my buddy Toni finish washing the dishes early so he could enjoy a few minutes topside, too. He would inevitably fall asleep in the warm tropical breeze, exhausted from cooking for a crew far larger than our small galley was designed for. In appreciation for his breaks from the galley, Toni would often save me an extra scoop of dessert. The monotony of submarine food made an occasional cup of pudding with raspberry syrup poured on top, my favorite, seem like the most luxurious dish in the world. At night, Toni would often bring the bridge watch a hot pot of sweet coffee mixed with a little rum. Only someone who has lived and fought aboard one of those old submarines can truly understand the comfort and joy such simple demonstrations of comradeship could provide.

Remembering the sense of brotherhood we felt for each other in our crowded little steel cave makes me angry to hear thoughtless people refer to us today as "Nazi submariners." Who were the Nazis aboard our submarine? I never met one. When we were on duty, we followed the course set by our skipper. When we were off duty, we tried to enjoy ourselves, read letters from our loved ones, and dreamed of the day peace would return to our homeland. In this way, we were identical to the sailors from every nation who faced the hazards of war and the sea during those years. Party members or not, we performed our duties with professionalism and honor. America Admiral Chester Nimitz knew this when he put his career on the line to defend the Kriegsmarine's wartime conduct during the Nuremberg Trials.

Of course, many lies have been told about the men of Germany's armed forces during World War II. Some of these storytellers are Germans themselves who surely know better, but who, for their own motives, perpetuate these lies. They create the impression that there were a few "bad" Germans—inhuman Nazi monsters who wanted to conquer the world, and the "good" Germans—gentle little lambs who were against the Nazis and wanted peace, but were forced to fight against their will. Naturally, they always happen to be members of the second group.

All of this is pure self-serving fantasy! Whether one was a Party member or not didn't matter a bit. Everyone I knew, without exception, was willing and eager to fight. The reasons were quite simple. First and foremost, our country was literally in a life or death struggle with Soviet communism. Depending upon our success on the battlefield, our nation was "to be or not to be." Like Admiral Dönitz told us many times, we were fighting to save our country, not for a particular leader or political party. Second, almost everyone had family members who had been killed in the bombings or on the battlefield. We wanted to avenge ourselves against the gangsters who had brought about their deaths. Lastly, and perhaps most importantly, a depth charge exploding over your head did not care about your politics or religion. So, doing your duty to the best of one's ability was the best means of self-preservation.

These were the reasons we fought on, united as a crew and as a nation against impossible odds. It never entered our minds for a moment whether this one was a Nazi or that one was not. We considered ourselves patriots, pure and simple. Ideology at that point in the war was irrelevant!

On April 1, we remembered the anniversary of our first crossing of the equator under our old skipper Axel Löwe. It was hard to believe that it had been two years since we celebrated the exotic rituals of Neptune. So much had happened since then. It seemed as if an eternity had passed. How easy and simple those earlier days seemed, when targets were plentiful and attacks from enemy planes were the exception rather than the rule! Lange was a skillful U-boat veteran, and we had high hopes for this patrol.

*   *   *

As we entered the warm waters off Africa, the waves took on a different character. Gone were the tall, violent breakers of March. Instead, we experienced enormously long swells that alternately pushed our boat forward then pulled her astern. Progress in these seas felt like riding on a child's swing. The greener members of our crew were not used to these new motions and went through another serious bout of seasickness. For the next several days, they could be seen with their heads in buckets or leaning over the rails, offering their meals to Neptune.

We received an *FT* from headquarters in the early hours of April 4. The whole boat buzzed with speculation regarding its content. Lange guessed what all the murmuring was about and broke the news to us: we had been directed to a rendezvous with *U-123* at Sea Square DG9179. Lange was a wise old fox to let us know what was going on. The tropical heat was beginning to irritate us and the skipper didn't need any unfounded rumors making the rounds.

Three days later, *U-123* came into view. She was the former boat of Reinhard Hardegen, now skippered by his Executive Officer Horst von Schröter. The anti-aircraft crews on both our boats were on full alert during the brief meeting. Our Exec, Paul Meyer, paddled over to the other boat to pass some secret codes over to them. One-half hour later, we waved goodbye and departed.

Later that afternoon, we heard two dozen depth charges exploding in the distance. We hoped the noise was not signaling the demise of *U-123*. That was one big difference between U-boats and the surface ships we fought: a ship almost always had time to radio an S-O-S to rescuers before sinking. On the other hand, U-boats often sank without being able to broadcast their fate to headquarters or any potential rescuers. After several days of anxious waiting, we were usually left to assume the worst after a boat failed to radio-in as scheduled.

As it turned-out, *U-123* wasn't sunk in the depth charge attack we heard. Indeed, like our own boat, she was one of the very few German submarines to survive the war. When the Allies overran France later that year, Admiral Dönitz ordered all operational boats stationed on France's Atlantic coast to sail immediately for German-controlled ports on the Baltic or North Seas. *U-123*, however, was left stranded in Lorient's dry docks, unable to sail because of a lack of batteries for her electric motors. After the war, the French Navy found the boat, repaired her, and re-christened her *Blaison*. She stayed on active service until 1953 when, regrettably, she was scrapped. It is a shame that this valiant and historic boat was destroyed for a few hundred dollars of scrap metal.

It was around this part of the war patrol that we had a memorable incident aboard the old *U-505*. Looking back, the entire affair was rather disgusting, but at the time it passed for high entertainment. It all started when we noticed that Gerd, one of the diesel mates, was spending much of the day holding and gingerly rubbing the front of his pants. Well, this didn't surprise any of us because this particular fellow was notorious for his lack of discrimination in choosing his bed mates. Every single time we had set sail on a patrol, he was found to have contracted some sort of disease from the ladies in port.

Because of our critical shortage of manpower, contracting one of these diseases during wartime was considered a serious offense in the German military. For instance, sailors who got gonorrhea were sent to a special hospital near Paris called the *Ritterburg*. Once the agonizing treatments for the disease were completed (these were the days before the advent of penicillin), the sailors were promptly court-martialed and thrown in prison for three or four months. Gerd had obviously caught one of these diseases while we were in Brest. According to regulations, he should have been immediately transferred to a homebound U-boat and arrested upon his return.

Well, no one wanted Gerd to be court-martialed, so with the skipper's permission, we decided to treat him onboard *U-505* ourselves. After a cursory examination, our quack doctor decided that an immediate operation was required. My friend Otto Dietz acted as a medic and made all the preparations. The mess table in the petty officers' quarters was transformed into an operating platform. After the doctor gave Gerd an injection to relax, Otto cut a hole in a blanket for the poor guy's penis to protrude through during the operation. Otto, ever the clown, wanted to make sure the hole was the right size, so he stuck his own joystick through the blanket and began parading it around for the benefit of us crewmen in the front torpedo room quarters. His crazy antics made everyone curious about what was going on, and soon the whole crew was jammed against the hatches to "the operating room," straining to get a glance of the procedure.

But when the doctor tried to poke Gerd's penis through the blanket, he found that the hole wasn't nearly big enough. Our eyes almost popped out of our heads when we saw why. The poor guy's member was a dark blue, almost black color, and had swollen to the size of a horse's penis. Otto had to cut the hole quite a bit larger to make it fit. Then, using a special pair of pliers, he pulled the swollen organ through the blanket.

At this point, Gerd was screaming at the top of his lungs in pain and fear. The white blanket with that huge black monster sticking out of it looked for all the world like a chimney in the snow. Then came the moment of truth. The doctor made a single slice with a scalpel and, to our immense amusement, a great spurt of hellish fluids flew from Gerd's member.

The organ was wrapped tightly with a bandage and then taped upright against Gerd's belly. Needless to say, this particular arrangement gave rise to countless more jokes. Some of the crew even gave it a squeeze when the poor guy walked past. Gerd's loud, anguished yells confirmed that his member was still quite tender several days after the operation. Eventually, the thing returned to normal size, though the jokes continued for quite some time afterward.

*   *   *

Predictably, as the weather heated-up, so did the tempers of the crew. Submerging did not bring us relief because the cooler deep water caused the moisture in the air to condense, subjecting us to a sort of Chinese water torture. Soon, we began to see an increase in arguments and scuffles. We knew this was another onset of the well-known *Blechkoller*, the mild sort of madness that gripped submarine crews when boredom and overcrowding became unbearable. By now we were used to this sort of thing, so minor disturbances were usually handled informally by us "bilge rats" without resort to higher rank. We were often able to nip trouble in the bud. For instance, as soon as someone started to get out of hand, everyone around him would shout, "Shut up!" right into their ears. That usually sufficed.

We looked out for each other in other ways, too. Around the 13th of April, I was performing some maintenance on the diving valves when I was suddenly struck with an intense migraine headache. The pain was absolutely unbearable. These sorts of headaches were a common symptom of CO_2 poisoning, but it was the first time I had ever experienced anything like it.

I reported my condition to the ship's doctor, but the quack refused to give me any medication for it. He was obviously still angry that I had not been adequately punished for disobeying his crazy diving order several months ago. Hearing what had happened, my friend Otto and Chief Navigator Reinig conspired to "organize" some medicine for me without permission from the doctor. Within minutes, a few bitter-tasting drops of medicine had me feeling fine. The doctor kept smiling at me, sure that he was leaving me in misery. I just smiled back at him, reveling in his ignorance of my complete recovery. I was thankful that, once again, we men of the crew were willing to take care of each other, despite the risk. It was this kind of bond between us that allowed us to work as a team, even in the worst situations.

* * *

Throughout April we ran on the surface as often as we dared. Lange clearly wanted to reach our patrol area as quickly as possible. Luckily, the skies were strangely empty of enemy aircraft, so we were able to make relatively good time. Toward the end of the month, however, we entered the shipping lanes west of the Cape Verde Islands and began to spend more time submerged. Occasionally we would stop altogether, lurking silently underwater, listening for the telltale sounds of a ship's propellers. Unfortunately, all our efforts were in vain. The shipping lanes were totally barren of traffic.

Lange decided we should move closer to the coast. He thought it was possible the Allies were aware of our presence and were redirecting their ships closer to the shoreline. Of course, the Old Man was very familiar with these waters because of his experience in the merchant fleet before the war. Armed with his knowledge, we would sometimes cruise within a stone's throw of the shoreline, the water so shallow our depth finder registered zero clearance under our hull. To our frustration and dismay, we didn't encounter any enemy ships close to the coast, either.

I remember we were cruising slowly along the shoreline one night at periscope depth when I heard the skipper call me into the conning tower. He pointed to the periscope and told me to have a look at something funny. At first, all I could see were some small bubbles around the spray shield.

"Turn the scope slowly, then you'll be able to see those lazy fellows," he told me.

I had no idea what he was talking about, until suddenly I saw them: two young sharks were hitching a ride on our sub, using their mouths to hang on to the bridge railing!

"Those boys have been with us for two days. I suppose they're hanging around in order to have a free lunch whenever we throw our garbage overboard. In the meantime, they just hold on with their teeth until we begin to surface. Let's hope they never find something better to eat . . . like you or me!"

I laughed at the skipper's dark humor and returned to my post.

* * *

An entire month passed without us sighting a single enemy vessel. For weeks we zig-zagged back and forth across the sea lanes off Freetown, searching in vain for targets. Several times we heard depth charges exploding in the distance, but failed to spot any enemy escorts or aircraft. Only once did we encounter a ship, but after a lengthy chase it turned out to be a 9,000-ton Portuguese passenger liner. Even though Portugal was neutral, Lange prudently decided to stay out of sight. We did, however, take the opportunity to surface about 35 miles behind the ship in order to test our new *FuMO* radar device. We raised the large radar antenna we called "the mattress" out of its protective housing and turned the device on. To our distress we found that, even in this perfect weather, the damned thing could not pick up this large target.

As we entered the last week of April, the Old Man decided to move our patrol area southeast of Cape Palmas, the bottom of Africa's "elbow."

Surely there, we thought, we would run across some traffic coming up toward Britain from the Horn of Africa. Lange usually ordered the engines turned off so we could slowly and silently drift along with the current, listening intently for propeller noises. Every hour or so we would surface to take a peek with the periscope. Meanwhile, we were ordered to quietly lay in our bunks whenever off duty in order to minimize noise and to conserve oxygen.

It was about this time we experienced another mechanical difficulty, and this one was extremely dangerous. The rear torpedo room reported that the outer hatch for Torpedo Tube #2 would not close completely. As a result, we were incapable of diving deeper than 20 meters. In those clear waters, that meant we were almost sure to be spotted by a prowling enemy aircraft, even when submerged. To make matters worse, the flooded tube was loaded with one of the temperamental *T-5* acoustic-homing torpedoes. As noted earlier, these complicated beasts had to be dried and serviced on a daily basis or else, the torpedo mechanics warned us, the moisture could detonate their complicated electrical firing fuses. Nothing we tried freed the stuck outer hatch, so we just said our prayers and continued with the mission, stranded near the surface like a sitting duck with a time bomb stuck up our rear.

On the afternoon of the 27th, we drifted past the Liberian capital of Monrovia. We were only two nautical miles offshore and every detail of the city's port was clearly visible to us. The harbor was filled with about twenty small, single-masted fishing boats, but nothing of military significance was anchored there. Our echo sounder often indicated only a few meters of water depth under our hull, but Lange knew these waters like his own face in a mirror and we did not run aground. The shallow water almost didn't matter anyway, since we were still unable to dive more than a couple dozen meters deep because of the stuck torpedo hatch.

That night, after the lights of Monrovia had sunk into the distance, the Old Man finally ordered the diesels cranked up. By long flat zig-zags, we followed the general course of the 100-meter depth line southward along the coast toward Cape Palmas. Still there were no targets! A few weeks previously, *U-66* had sunk a couple of ships in this exact area. As a result, the place now looked as if it had been swept clean by a broom. We reckoned that, while *U-66* got the credit, we would end up reaping the consequences.

The month of May welcomed us with a heavy thunderstorm. Spectacular lightning displays flashed around us all day long. Some of us were worried a nearby lightning strike might set-off the *T-5* torpedo still stuck in our flooded Tube #2. When the storm finally cleared, nothing but yawning openness greeted the searching eyes of our bridge watch. Lange used some pretty salty language from his old days as a merchant sailor to describe his frustration at the lack of targets.

Two days later, our *Naxos* device failed, as did the cable mechanism used for raising our front periscope. I was assigned to work on the periscope. When we finally got it working, I was allowed to take a peek through the device. I was surprised to discover how close we were to the coast. I was also surprised to see the bright trail of lime green phosphorescence we were leaving in our wake.

The phosphorescence convinced Lange we had to do something right away to solve our torpedo hatch problem. Some of the boys donned artificial lungs and dove down three meters to manually work on the hatch. After more than 20 hours of labor, they finally freed the hatch mechanism and we were able to pull the *T-5* out of the tube.

For the next several days, we prowled back and forth like a hunting dog sniffing for the scent of its prey. Still, no enemy targets. We were all very nervous and frustrated. I was filled with so much anxiety that I stopped practicing my English lessons.

Finally, on the afternoon of May 10, we spotted a very large British freighter off our stern. For the first time in a long time we felt the hunter's blood rise in our veins. The ship was well over 10,000 tons and would put our total tonnage sunk over the magic 50,000 mark. We had traveled more than 4,300 miles so far on this patrol, and we were absolutely mad to sink this enemy vessel. Lange wheeled us around and we gave chase. The freighter, however, was a very fast one. Even at top speed, our diesels could only give us a 2-knot speed advantage over her.

Our diesels seemed to be running fine, but the starboard engine must have been burning some oil because it was blowing a cloud of blue smoke out the exhaust. Well, someone else must have noticed the smoke the same time we did, because our skipper spotted a destroyer coming up over the horizon toward us at great speed. A quick check with the silhouette recognition book showed her to be an *Atherstone*-class escort, one of the Royal Navy's most modern and dangerous types. There was no time to maneuver out of the way, so Lange ordered us down to periscope depth and prepared one of the *T-5* "Destroyer Killer" torpedoes for firing.

The escort's skipper was clever, too. Instead of barreling in straight for us, the destroyer began employing the "sprint and coast" method of submarine hunting. This tactic consisted of short, high-speed runs followed by minute-long coasts with the engines switched off. This allowed the escort's sound detection gear to better locate a submerged sub. At the same time, he would get no closer to us than five miles, so we had no opportunity to fire our torpedo. After a couple of hours of pinning us down underwater, the escort suddenly moved off at rapid speed to rejoin the freighter, now at a safe distance from us. It was a fine display of seamanship by that escort's commander.

After all the excitement of the chase, the disappointment of another missed opportunity hit us very hard. Even Lange missed some sleep that night, fretting about our miserable luck. For the next several days we sailed up and down the African coast between Cape Palmas and Cape Three Points, but with no luck. We even poked our noses into the harbor mouths of some ports on the Ivory and Gold Coasts—still no enemy ships. At one point, the officers even discussed hitting some targets on shore with our anti-aircraft guns, but we couldn't even find any worthy targets ashore. We eventually turned tail and returned to deeper water. Neptune marked our departure by granting us another hair-raising encounter with "St. Elmo's Fire."

We sailed back up the coast towards Monrovia, the capital of Liberia. We had several close shaves with bombers and flying boats before we realized both our new *FuMO* radar device and our *Naxos* radar detector were totally out of order. We had a couple of other mechanical breakdowns, too. We weren't sure whether it was more sabotage or just the declining quality of war materiel that was causing our difficulties. Luckily, the technical boys partially repaired our *Naxos* radar detector, so we still had some measure of warning of approaching enemy aircraft, at least on some wavelengths.

The next couple of weeks passed monotonously with no sightings of enemy shipping. Finally, near the end of May, the Old Man decided he had had enough. Hanging around in this African backwater with no targets to attack was a waste of a valuable U-boat. He turned us north, intending to dog-leg our way across the Allied shipping lanes back to Lorient. We were pretty disappointed, but still held out hope that we would stumble across targets on the way back. How could it be that, in an ocean full of thousands of ships, we had not had the chance to fire one torpedo?

*   *   *

On May 30, after several quiet days, we were inundated with almost non-stop radar warnings. A hornet's nest of enemy aircraft had suddenly descended upon our heads. That night, we heard several depth charges exploding in the distance to the west. This many aircraft so far away from any major Allied airbases convinced our skipper that an anti-submarine search group, one of the so-called "Hunter-Killer" task forces built around an aircraft carrier, was operating in the area—or on our tail. Lange was absolutely right. A carrier task force, one that had sunk our sister boats *U-68* and *U-515* just a few weeks earlier, was hunting for us.

We knew we were in a very tight spot. For three days, we couldn't surface for more than a few minutes before our radar warning gear let out its scream of alarm. The air inside the boat grew so stale we were forced to don the hated personal re-breathing devices to stay alive. Even worse, our battery charge was reaching a critically low level. We had to get out of the area, but how? It was one thing to avoid destruction at the hands of destroyers escorting a convoy, because eventually they must move on with the rest of the ships. But the diabolical aircraft carrier groups almost always meant the destruction of any U-boat unlucky enough to be cornered by them, because our subs simply didn't have the underwater range to escape the carrier's airplanes. We knew if we were caught in the web of one of these "Hunter-Killer" task forces, all hope would be lost.

The situation called for something clever, and our crafty old skipper came up with just the right plan. He knew the enemy was well acquainted with our need to regularly surface, as well of our habit of doing so under the cover of night. As a result, we noticed that enemy radar vigilance sometimes relaxed a bit once the sun rose. After all, what U-boat would be crazy enough to run surfaced in broad daylight?

Well, that's exactly what Lange ordered us to do: make a high-speed run back toward the African coast during daylight hours. We made our move on the afternoon of June 3. Blowing our tanks, we surfaced to find the sky empty of clouds and planes. The Jumbos roared to life and we began our dash away from the bright setting sun. We saw a few Allied aircraft passing high overhead during the next couple of hours, but none of them took any notice of us.

We submerged after we had traveled what we considered a sufficient distance. We were a very happy crew that night! The next day, we resumed our usual routine, cruising underwater during daylight and surfacing under cover of night. For the first time in a long time, we were able to surface without immediately being sent to the basement by a *Naxos* alarm.

Heavens, how proud we were of our foxy old skipper! Our mood was almost giddy. Talk began to center on our return voyage to Lorient, and what we would do when we got there. With the carrier group off our backs, we boasted, we might even put a couple of freighters in the bag before we got back.

Unbeknownst to either side, we and the American "Hunter-Killer" group, composed of an aircraft carrier and five destroyer-escorts, were unwittingly headed on intercept courses. Fate decreed that we would meet the next day.

Chapter 15

Captured!

*J*une 4, 1944, began like any other day. Indeed, there was nothing that set it apart in my mind at the time except that it was a Sunday. We were low on oxygen, so everyone not on duty was confined to their bunks to conserve air. I laid there in that stinking bunk, whispering prayers from the little black Bible my mother had given me when I joined the Kriegsmarine. In her dedication to me on the inside cover of the Bible, she had noted the passage from Romans 13:10:

Love worketh no ill to his neighbor;
Therefore love is the fulfilling of the law.

The tender message she held so close to her heart seemed bitterly ironic given the life or death struggle we faced here at sea.

By noon, I was back on duty in the control room. The smell of hot coffee wafted through the boat and I remember wondering, rather absentmindedly, what was for lunch. It was a this moment our hydrophone sound man reported faint propeller noises coming from several distant points off our stern. The skipper thought a convoy might have blundered across our path. It never occurred to any of us that the damned carrier task force might have accidentally intercepted us. After a quick word with the Exec, Lange ordered us up to periscope depth to investigate the noise.

We rose toward the surface very slowly, anxious not to cause too much turbulence in the water with our periscope mast. As we neared periscope depth, the order went out for torpedo battle stations. After weeks of frustrated waiting, we were all very excited at the prospect of finally drawing blood. Lange climbed up to the conning tower to take a peek through the scope at our targets.

No sooner had the periscope breached the surface than we heard the Old Man's booming voice shout out, "Destroyer!" In fact, as he scanned back and forth, he counted three enemy destroyers, all virtually on top of us and roaring in for the attack. He yelled out that there were also planes overhead and a vessel that was probably a small aircraft carrier in the distance. Our underwater sound equipment was obviously faulty, which allowed the "Hunter-Killer" task force we thought we had escaped to creep right up on top of us. Our most dreaded fear had come true.

We blindly fired one torpedo in the general direction of the carrier, more to create a distraction than in any hope of actually hitting the target. Then the skipper ordered us to dive for the basement. Our only chance of survival was to get down to our maximum depth and hope we could once again ride out another prolonged beating from depth charges.

As we began to leave the surface, we heard the unmistakable sound of a destroyer's high-speed propellers approach, louder than we've ever heard them before. A few seconds later, and at point-blank range, the destroyer fired a full salvo of "Hedgehogs," the Allies' deadly anti-submarine mortars. Somehow the shotgun pattern of Hedgehogs missed us as we started a series of violent evasive maneuvers to throw off our attackers.

We were beginning to think we might have a chance to escape when we suddenly heard a loud metallic "clinking" noise coming from above our heads. Everyone in the compartment looked at each other in puzzlement, trying to guess the meaning of such a sound. We were quite familiar with every underwater noise a wartime submarine was ever likely to encounter, but this one was completely new. The majority opinion thought it sounded like the links of a heavy chain being dragged across our hull. When I heard that suggestion, a cold chill ran through my blood and I instinctively grabbed for something to hold on to. Surely the noise meant we had snagged the mooring chain of a mine and that a fatal wall of water would come crashing through the hull any second.

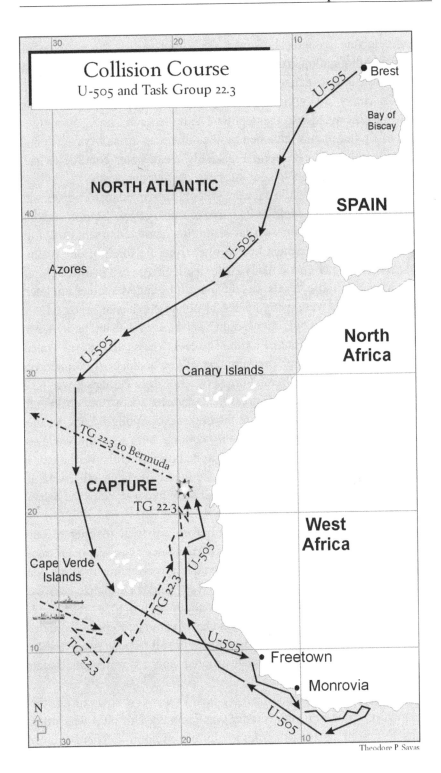

Collision Course
U-505 and Task Group 22.3

Brest

Bay of
Biscay

NORTH ATLANTIC

SPAIN

Azores

North
Africa

Canary Islands

TG 22.3 to Bermuda

CAPTURE

TG 22.3

West
Africa

Cape Verde
Islands

U-505

TG 22.3

TG 22.3

U-505

Freetown

Monrovia

U-505

N

Theodore P. Savas

After a few seconds, however, the sound ceased. In my blissful ignorance, I thought the danger was over and I allowed myself to relax a bit. What we didn't realize at the time was that the sound was actually caused by heavy .50 caliber machine gun bullets hitting the hull of our boat as we descended into the depths! The bullets were being fired by a couple of fighter planes launched by the American aircraft carrier lying just a few miles off our stern. Freakishly clear water conditions had allowed the enemy pilots to spot our boat, despite our depth.

A short time later, while we were still only about 60 meters deep, the depth charges began to explode. The first few charges were close, and the next few even closer. Then, two ear-shattering detonations sent us flying off our feet. The boat almost keeled over from the force of one of the blasts. We had experienced many close depth charge explosions before, but the impact of those devils was the biggest by far. We found out later that the Americans were using giant 600-pound depth charges on us.

All the lights went out, but we didn't need our eyes to tell us we were taking on water in the control room. The leak was small, but the water coming in was at such high pressure that, if you accidentally blundered into the stream, it felt like being burned by a hot iron. Perhaps it was just fear, but I began to feel the air pressure squeezing against my chest and ears as I imagined seawater filling the control room bilge. Luckily, the leak was manageable and was probably coming from a sprung valve or pipe because the pressure hull seemed to be holding up. Nevertheless, I prayed our pumps could catch up with the intake of water; otherwise, it was only a matter of time before our boat sank like a stone to the ocean floor.

When the emergency lighting came on, we tried to operate our equipment, only to discover that all electrical devices were dead. Despite the gravity of the situation, everyone stayed relatively calm, awaiting our skipper's orders. After all, we had survived Sillcock's attack, and we were still confident we could handle just about anything.

A moment later, however, more bad news came in. Reports from the rear compartments told of severe flooding in the aft torpedo room. Lange ordered the compartment to be evacuated and its watertight hatch clamped shut.

No sooner was that done than we heard the worst news of all: the helmsman reported our main rudder was jammed. Our boat was stuck turning in a tight starboard circle, totally out of control. There was an emergency method for steering the boat manually, but the auxiliary rudder control hand wheel could only be operated from the evacuated aft torpedo room.

When word got around that we had lost steering control, we knew for sure that our beloved *U-505* was doomed. Lange ordered us to surface. The Old Man didn't have to tell us that, one way or another, the war would be over for us in just a few more minutes.

*   *   *

The only question on our mind was when the skipper would order us to abandon ship. But to abandon ship, we first needed to get back to the surface. No one except those of us in the control room knew our sub was still plummeting toward the bottom in an uncontrolled dive. We frantically worked the controls to pull us up, but we discovered the diving planes were jammed in a downward position and that some of the ballast tank valves were not responding. We desperately tried every trick in the book to pump enough air into the tanks before we passed our crush depth. Something must have worked because our boat's descent finally stopped, and we began to rise to the surface. I am unsure how deep we had sunk.

Everyone assumed we would get the "abandon ship" order as soon as we got to the surface, but there was always the chance our skipper would order "battle stations surface" instead. Of course, we had heard several stories about damaged U-boats that had been forced to fight it out on the surface with single escorts, but not many of those stories had happy endings for the U-boat crews.

In our situation, we were facing a half-dozen enemy warships supported by war planes. Those were impossible odds—even for a U-boat in perfect condition. The *piece de resistance*, of course, was that we were in far from perfect condition. We had no steering or diving control, no rear torpedo tubes, and already had a breach in the hull to boot. Even the greenest midshipman could tell we had zero chance of victory. Only a madman or a butcher of a skipper would have even considered ordering his crew to fight it out under these conditions. Still, it was Lange's decision to make, and we control room mates considered it a matter of honor not to move to abandon ship until the skipper gave the word.

Our electric motors were working fine, but because of the jammed diving planes, the old *U-505* seemed sluggish in returning us to the surface. It probably only took a minute or two or so for us to get back up, but it seemed like forever.

No sooner had the top of our bridge poked itself above the waves than we began to hear the bell-like clang of enemy bullets slamming into our conning tower. A moment later, the heavy stuff started arriving. Our whole boat shook with the concussion of cannon shells and depth charges straddling our hull. I'm not ashamed to admit that I was scared. I felt like a trapped rat—terrified to face the hail of fire hitting us on the outside, but knowing that in another minute our boat and anyone in it would be heading on a one-way trip to the bottom.

In a dire crisis like this, there is only one man who can break the inertia of fear and indecision that can grip a crew: the skipper. Lange was never one to ask anybody to do something he wasn't willing to do himself, so he didn't hesitate one second. Pushing the watch crew aside, Lange made sure that he was the first one up the ladder to the bridge to assess the situation, despite the danger.

It seemed like certain death for anyone to step out into the firestorm of bullets out there, but the Old Man knew it was his duty to check the situation for himself and decide whether we should fight or immediately abandon ship. He popped open the hatch and bravely climbed out onto the bridge, followed closely by our Exec Paul Meyer and the members of the bridge watch crew.

Within the blink of an eye, our skipper was cut down by shrapnel from a shell that hit our upper deck. A moment later, a swarm of fighters swooped down and sprayed the conning tower with heavy machine gun fire. Most of the bridge watch were wounded, but some boys still managed to make it to the anti-aircraft guns and fire back at the planes. Paul Meyer had tried to man one of the guns, but he too was hit and fell to the deck, blood streaming over his face.

Despite frightening leg wounds, Lange crawled back to the conning tower hatch and shouted down to us the order to scuttle and abandon ship. That was all the Raccoon, our Chief Engineering Officer, needed to hear. He was standing right next to me when he started screaming, "Out, out! We're sinking!"

A great mob of men from the aft end of the boat suddenly stampeded through the control room to scale the ladders to the bridge. I could clearly hear the cries of men being wounded by gunfire as the crew poured out on to the deck.

Most of us control room mates stayed at our posts to make sure the scuttling order was carried out. We kept looking around for Hauser, our Chief Engineering Officer, because we needed to know if he had set the demolition charges. He was nowhere to be found. We quickly learned the Raccoon had already jumped overboard. Wonderful, we thought, he was busy saving his own worthless neck instead of carrying out his final and most important duty aboard our boat. (NOTE: After the war, Hauser's son told me his father claimed to have single-handedly saved *U-505* on three separate occasions, and that he deserved a great medal for his bravery. In my opinion, he deserved a medal from the Allies, because that guy did a lot more harm to us than good.)

Unfortunately, for security reasons, only the skipper, the Executive Officer and the Chief Engineering Officer knew how to set the timer for the demolition charges. Since all three of them were already wounded or had evacuated the boat, it was obvious it was going to be up to us enlisted men to devise another plan for scuttling *U-505*. In the absence of any officers, Engineering Petty Officer Holdenried assumed control of the situation. He ordered us to open up the diving tanks once the rest of the crew was safely overboard. That would give us about 30 seconds to get out of the boat before she slipped under the waves.

We waited for the last of the men to evacuate the compartment, which seemed like an eternity. The very second they were clear, we tried to open the valves to let water into the tanks. All went well except for forward main diving tanks #6 and #7. Something was preventing the relief valves on those big tanks from opening. We tried again and again to open those damned valves, but with no luck. We even tried to push the controls by hand, but the operating shafts had been bent by the force of the depth charges and wouldn't budge. We knew the air bubbles hanging in #6 and #7 might prevent the boat from going down, but no one could think of an alternative. We finally gave up and made a dash for the conning tower ladder, hopeful that the holes in the hull would flood the boat with enough water to send her down.

I had already started climbing the ladder to the conning tower when I suddenly remembered the sea strainer located on the deck close to my duty station. The sea strainer is a filter mechanism for the main pump, with a bucket-shaped removable sieve set inside a 12-inch steel housing.

Acting on impulse, I ran back and unlocked the four clamps and removed the heavy steel cover of the sea strainer. A dinner plate-sized stream of water started gurgling out of the main pump line into the boat. As the water flowed back toward the stern, I felt sure this would be enough to sink our beloved *U-505*.

Then, in a move that I would regret for the rest of my life, I tossed the sea strainer cover down onto the deck plates in the corner of the control room. If I had thrown the strainer cover down into the bilge where no one could reach it, *U-505* would have had a very different ending.

*   *   *

Having done my duty (or more precisely, the Chief Engineering Officer's duty), I decided it was high time to get the hell out of our sinking boat! I was small but very strong back in those days. My crewmates said I could move through the confines of the submarine with the agility of a weasel. But on this occasion, I broke all my previous speed records getting back up that ladder.

The bulkheads of the conning tower were resonating with the metallic clang of bullets and shrapnel when the rush began to abandon ship. From the inside of the sub, the hits on our boat sounded like a group of boys throwing rocks at a trash can. I was terrified by the thought of what was happening to my crewmates out there, but not as terrified as I was to be the only man left inside that sinking boat! By the time I began climbing to the conning tower, however, the bursts of fire had subsided. The shouts of men outside on the deck began to get louder than the blood pounding in my ears from my racing heart. My head swam from adrenaline and the fresh, oxygen-rich air pouring into the boat.

When I got to the top hatch on the bridge, I stuck my head up to survey the situation. It took a moment or two for my eyes to adjust to the brightness of the sunlight. When they did, the first thing I saw was poor Gottfried Fischer, one of the radio room crewmen. His body was torn and twisted, and he was obviously dead. The whole bridge deck was slippery with pools of foamy brine tinted red from the blood of wounded men. I made my way over to the leeward side of the conning tower, the one area of the boat shielded from enemy fire. Everything seemed to be moving in slow motion.

I took a quick glance around at the long, gray hulls of the enemy destroyers. They were circling in for the kill like a pack of jackals. I could also see my crewmates floating in the sea, clusters of them strung out in a long line behind the boat. I climbed over as quickly as I could to the lee side of the conning tower. There were a few other men huddled there, trying to deploy a large inflatable life raft. I lent a hand for a moment, then joined them in the raft.

We were afraid the destroyers might be preparing to ram, so we paddled frantically away from the boat. When I glanced back at her, however, I realized U-505 was still fully under way with her electric motors. Before we knew it, she was hundreds of meters away, barely visible above the waves. I remember to this day how hard I tried hard to get one last glimpse of our battered old boat before she joined her many sisters at the bottom of the Atlantic.

Our attention quickly shifted to staying afloat in the water until, hopefully, we were picked up by the Americans. Some of the boys thought the airplanes were strafing survivors in the water. I thought the planes were shooting the water between our boat and us to prevent anyone from re-boarding her. If they were, they could have saved their ammo, for none of us was crazy enough to want to get back aboard U-505 because she was slowly but surely going down.

We were scattered along a fairly extensive arc of ocean. The water was warm, but choppy. We tried to gather ourselves into groups and get the more heavily wounded men out of the water to stop their bleeding. Word spread that our skipper was badly wounded in the legs and we were particularly concerned about him. The big raft in which I was sitting was soon filled to overflowing with men. With all the blood in the water, we were very fearful of sharks. Even those of us who were not wounded were very reluctant to leave that raft.

At this point, my story intersects that of my friend Wolfgang Schiller, one of the forward torpedo room crewmen. What follows is his recollection of the capture, as told in an excerpt from a letter he wrote to me last year:

> In an atmosphere of intense anxiety, I was standing in the forward torpedo room at the communication tube and heard the voice of our commander as he looked up and down with the periscope. Each

direction he looked, he called out what he saw, 'destroyer! Destroyer!'

Looking all around, he saw the hopelessness of our situation and gave the order to dive deeper. After a short time, the first water-bombs exploded. The glass covers of the manometers burst. After it was reported to the Old Man that water was breaking-in and that the rudder was damaged, he ordered us back to the surface and to abandon ship.

I forwarded his order to all the comrades in the torpedo room. In a short time, I was all alone. I did not want to leave my wristwatch, which was hanging on one of the pipelines, so I was a little late in getting to the control room. On my way through the officers' rooms, I saw a lamb's wool sweater laying there, so I put it on, thinking that the water might get cold after a while. I was only wearing a pair of navy shorts and a civilian shirt. I had sailcloth shoes without socks, one of which I lost in the water. I put on my emergency breather gear over the sweater.

After a little while, I got to the escape hatch. Wilmar, who was from Berlin, held me back. He was timing our escape in between the rhythms of the aircraft strafing passes to prevent casualties. As I came out into the dazzling sunlight, I became blinded. Then I saw a plane coming up from starboard, and I tried to take shelter behind the shield of the anti-aircraft gun. But because I could not make it in time under the hail of bullets, I just jumped onto the starboard side of the deck. It was at that point that I was probably grazed by some bullets, because later when I opened the oxygen bottles on my breathing gear, I found two burned bullet holes on the left shoulder and left wrist of the thick wool sweater.

I drifted quickly away from the boat. A destroyer came toward my direction, yielded a little, and a sailor threw a rope to me. I was lucky I didn't catch the rope because it would have pulled me into the propeller. I then swam to a big life raft that was loaded with so many comrades that it was almost under water. One of them was scooping water out of the raft with an empty food can.

Someone, I think it was Fricke, asked me if I was still strong enough to swim over to Becker. Becker was a great distance away from us and was calling for help. I answered, 'Yes, if someone will come with me.' Hans Göbeler volunteered to come with me to rescue Becker.

I kept feeling something brush against my naked leg as I swam, so I asked Hans if he saw a shark following me. He said 'Yes, swim faster, there's a shark right behind you!' There were reflections of the sun on the waves, so I couldn't see for myself. Later, I found out that in my hurry, I had forgotten to fasten the belt of the breathing gear. It was the belt that I felt rubbing against my leg, not a shark.

When we got to Becker, we found that he was not wounded, so we didn't need to carry him. He swam under his own power with us back to the raft.

(NOTE: Schiller was a slow swimmer, so I told him there was a shark behind him to make him swim faster.)

*   *   *

While we bobbed in the surf, we watched with amusement as the Americans chased our still-circling boat with motorized whaleboats. Eventually they managed to board her, but we were still confident it was only a matter of time before she slipped beneath the waves. After all, only a sliver of her bow and conning tower was still above water. We joked to each other that old *U-505* might take more Americans down with her all alone than when she was crewed.

Our amusement slowly turned to concern, however, as more time passed. The boat, while still barely above water, stubbornly refused to sink. I told a few of my mates that I had uncovered the sea strainer. Was it possible that one of the Americans had found the cover and replaced it? It seemed impossible.

Of course, as we now know, that's precisely what happened. Captain Daniel V. Gallery, the commander of the "Hunter-Killer" task force that forced us to the surface, had specifically trained a prize crew to board and capture a U-boat in just such circumstances. The Americans managed to enter our boat just before she sank and replace the sea strainer cover. The cover had lost its gasket and was therefore still leaking a little, but not dangerously. A little later, they used a sailor's tee shirt to seal the gap completely. Over the course of the next couple of days, they took *U-505* in tow, recharged her batteries, and blew her ballast tanks to equalize her surface trim. In doing so, our boat became the first enemy vessel seized on the high seas by the U.S. Navy since the War of 1812.

Climbing down through that hatch into the dark conning tower of a sinking enemy submarine is the most heroic act I've ever heard of. The courageous American sailor who found his way into the control room and replaced the sea strainer cover was Zenon "Luke" Lukosius. Luke and I became good friends during *U-505* reunions I later organized in Chicago, and we even appeared together in a television special about the capture.

Under American control, two salvage parties work on the afternoon of June 4, 1944, to keep captured *U-505* afloat. Gasoline bilge pumps were put into operation inside the boat. The stern was completely submerged, and only some of the bow and the top of the conning tower was dry. As a result, equipment was brought aboard there and transferred by pulley up the antenna cable to the tower. *Author's Collection*

What he and those other American sailors did to salvage *U-505* is the very definition of bravery. Once the shock and shame of having our sub captured wore off, we were compelled to congratulate Gallery and his gallant men on their audacity and courage. Some of this, of course, we did not know until much later.

At any rate, after an hour or so of anxious waiting, we finally got fished out of the drink by one of the enemy ships, the destroyer escort *Chatelain.* U.S. Navy photographers with motion picture cameras recorded much of our rescue. Chicago's Museum of Science and Industry's film on the capture of *U-505* shows several crewmen, including me, being herded onto the deck of the destroyer. All of us are wearing the same wide grins. We were happy-happy-happy to be alive!

Salvage and boarding crews set up gasoline-powered pumps to remove water from *U-505*. The first tow line broke that night and left *U-505* on its own until a stronger tow line was hooked up. *Author's Collection*

We believed we had done our duty and put down our share of enemy shipping, and now were one of the few U-boat crews to survive the sinking of their own boat. Besides, even then in the summer of 1944, we still had confidence Germany would eventually win the war. We knew about the fabulous new U-boats being built and were confident that the smug grins worn by our American guards would someday be on our faces.

Our treatment at the hands of the Americans was fairly good. Several of our crew had been wounded during our evacuation of the boat, and they were given immediate medical treatment. The more seriously wounded were taken to the sickbay, including our skipper Harald Lange who had to have his leg amputated. (NOTE: To this day, I can't believe poor Fischer was the only fatality on either side during the engagement. Our low casualties were all the more remarkable when one considers the weight of firepower thrown against us. For instance, according to U.S. Navy records, the *Chatelain* alone fired one torpedo, 14 depth charges, 24 Hedgehogs, 48 rounds of 3-inch cannon, 328 rounds of 40mm cannon, and 955 rounds of 20mm heavy machine gun ammo at us. There were too many rounds fired by .50 caliber machine guns to count. And that barrage was just from one ship!)

Once the wounded were attended to, the rest of us were searched, stripped, and herded together under close guard by sailors armed with enormous looking Thompson sub-machine guns.

Every once in a while, we got a glimpse of *U-505*. There were still several whaleboats moored to her, and American sailors were crawling all over her decks. At one point, the destroyer *Pillsbury* pulled right along side her. To our immense satisfaction, we learned that our boat's bow diving plane cut a long slash into the hull of the American ship, almost sinking her. That gave us something to cheer about, at least momentarily. I felt especially jolly about the incident, because the control shaft to that diving fin was the one I had picked up in Bordeaux.

At the time, however, a sick feeling was growing deep in our stomachs because of the failure of our boat to sink. The presence of several highly classified documents left aboard was a particular concern. I was obsessed with trying to remember whether the sea strainer cover I removed had fallen into the bilge where it couldn't be recovered. Of course, the Americans really didn't need the cover, because all it took was a wrench to shut off the valve and stop the inflow of water.

Nevertheless, my spirit sank into a private kind of hell as I mentally relived my last moments aboard our boat, over and over again.

*   *   *

We were eventually moved to the aircraft carrier *Guadalcanal* for detention. Once there, we were showered with seawater to wash off the diesel oil that had leaked from our boat's ruptured fuel lockers. Our crew was then split into two halves. My group was thrown into a big cage-like compartment located right below the flight deck. The compartment was adjacent to the carrier's engine exhausts and the heat radiating on us was truly frightful. Over the course of the next couple of weeks, we each lost 20 or 30 pounds from sweating. One American sailor eventually took pity on us and moved a fan so that it blew cool air toward us. An officer came by and angrily ordered it to be pointed away from us. Once the officer left, though, that good seaman turned the fan back toward us. It just goes to show that there are always some people who remembered that one's enemy is still a human being.

Grinning, gum-chewing American sailors kept telling us that they had captured our boat with all of our secrets intact. We did not want to believe them, and suspected the story was just a ruse to elicit information from us. But every time we glimpsed *U-505* with a big American flag flying from her bridge, we knew our brave old boat had indeed been captured intact—including our code books. As if that wasn't enough, a little while later, our captors told us the Allies had landed in France and that the long-awaited invasion of Europe had begun.

The story about the invasion didn't worry me much. Even if true, I was confident our comrades in the *Wehrmacht* could handle any invasion, just as they had at Dieppe. But the idea that we had allowed our boat to be captured was a devastating blow. My role in the attempted scuttling of the boat made me feel particularly bad, especially when I learned they had indeed replaced the sea strainer cover that I had removed. It's not an exaggeration to say these were the worst few days in my life. Our depression over *U-505*'s capture was probably what gave the American commander, Captain Dan Gallery, the mistaken impression that our morale had been broken by our experiences under Zschech.

Over the next few days, we found several Morse Code messages scratched into the metal bars of our prison cage. The messages had been left by crewmen from our sister boat *U-515*. They said their boat had been forced to the surface by depth charges, then sunk by gunfire. Forty-five men had survived, including their skipper *Kapitänleutnant* Werner Henke. The messages also said Henke was being held separate from them, and that they suspected he was being tortured for secrets.

As it turned out, Henke was not physically tortured, though Captain Gallery did employ every manner of psychological pressure and trick in order to extract information from his prisoners. For Henke, this took the form of a false accusation of war crimes. Using forged documents, Gallery convinced *U-515*'s skipper the British had accused him of ordering the machine-gunning of helpless survivors from the passenger liner *Ceramic*.

The accusation was absurd, of course, but Henke believed Gallery's assertion that he would be hanged once he was turned over to the British authorities. Nevertheless, the *Kapitänleutnant* steadfastly refused to reveal any secrets in order to save his skin. When he arrived in the United States, Henke was notified he would indeed be handed over to the British (the American authorities didn't want to make a liar out of Gallery). Still convinced he would be put on trial, the day before his transfer to England this winner of the Knight's Cross purposely drew the fire of a prison camp guard, preferring a soldier's death to the dishonor of unjustly hanging for war crimes.

Gallery knew all along the accusations against Henke were without basis, but still allowed him to believe he would be hung. I met Dan Gallery after the war, and he seemed like an ethical man. But I find it difficult to forgive him for what he allowed to happen to Werner Henke.

The reason I mention all of this is because I ended up personally involved in some of Gallery's psychological shenanigans with *U-505*'s crew. Naturally, we were all repeatedly questioned regarding technical details of our sub, but we refused to give the Americans any information. Every one of us, regardless of rank, said our only duty aboard the boat was emptying the diesel room shit bucket. I could understand much of what our interrogators were saying to each other, and they were getting pretty frustrated at their inability to get any of us to crack.

The Americans found out that one of the boys in our crew, Ewald Felix, was half-Polish. They tried to use that fact to get him to talk. One of the members of the American boarding party that had captured our sub struck up a conversation with Ewald in Polish. Once they confirmed his mother was indeed from Poland, Captain Gallery had Ewald separated from us and interrogated him personally.

Gallery promised Ewald that if he told them what they wanted to know, he could spend his captivity unsupervised in a luxury hotel in America. After the war, Gallery said, he would have an easy, well-paying job assigned to him. Ewald had only made two war patrols with us, but he was still a good, trustworthy lad. He didn't fall for the bait and only gave the Americans a few useless or inconsequential details about *U-505*. Gallery wasn't about to stop there, so to add a bit of psychological pressure to us, he kept Ewald sequestered incommunicado from the rest of us.

Because I was the best English-speaking crewman from *U-505*, I was called to Gallery's wardroom to convey some information back to the rest of the crew. Gallery told me that we should hold a Catholic funeral ceremony in honor of a certain Ewald Felix because he had just died of tuberculosis. Well, I knew damned well Ewald was healthy as an ox, so I told Gallery that if he really was dead, someone would be held accountable after the war.

Gallery sent me back to report the news to my comrades nonetheless. To this day, I don't know if Gallery was merely trying to scare us, or if he was deliberately using such an implausible cover story to create the impression that Ewald had collaborated and was being kept separate from us for his own protection. In any event, we never saw Ewald Felix again.

After the war, some German magazines reported that Felix had indeed provided the Americans with valuable information. They said he went into hiding after VE-Day and was now living in Poland. I never believed those stories, and tried for several years to track old Ewald down. I eventually found him living a quiet life in West Germany, just south of Hannover. In lengthy interviews with him, he swore he never told our captors a thing. Later, at a *U-505* reunion in Chicago, I talked to an American Ensign who had been an electronics expert in Gallery's task force. He confirmed they never learned anything of value from Ewald. I hope this book helps set the record straight about this unjustly maligned man.

After a couple of days, another ship took over the towing of *U-505*. It was a very bittersweet moment as our beloved boat disappeared over the horizon toward an unknown fate. We never saw her again, at least not until she was placed on display at Chicago's Museum of Science and Industry long after the war.

As far as we were concerned, the next three weeks were a hot, depressing hell as we slowly cruised westward. The heat coming from the *Guadalcanal*'s engines was unrelenting. We pressed against the bars of the windward side of the cage in a desperate attempt to stave off heat exhaustion.

One day, I found a little stub of a pencil no bigger than a thumbnail next to the bars of our cage. A little later, a piece of paper blew against the bars of our cage and I grabbed it. I finally had the materials I needed, at least mentally, to escape from my prison. I started to while away the hours by drawing tiny sketches of my home and of *U-505*. An American sailor I knew only as "George" saw the sketch of our boat and asked me to draw another one for him as a souvenir. The next day he brought me more paper and pencils, and I started a secret little cottage industry, trading sketches for cigarettes and extra bits of food. This barter system reached its zenith when we got to our prison camp in Louisiana, when almost every one of us spent our free time making little handicraft souvenirs for trade with the guards.

*   *   *

In late June, we finally made port in Royal Bay, Bermuda. Getting out of that cage and setting foot on dry land was a moment of unbridled joy for us. We were officially processed as prisoners of war, then moved into a detention camp. My new dog tag read "LANT 13 GNA." Over the next several days, cool breezes and good food restored much of our health that had been lost in that hellish cage on the *Guadalcanal*.

In the U-boat service, no news was always bad news, so our main concern at that point was contacting the International Red Cross in order to notify our families that we were safe. It soon became clear however, that the U.S. Navy had no intention of allowing word of our boat's capture to find its way back to Germany by notifying the Red Cross, even if it meant ignoring the Geneva Conventions. Our morale sank to a very low level.

Once our entire crew was reunited in the prison camp, questions began to be raised regarding whose fault it was that our boat had been captured. I initially came in for some criticism because I had not tossed the sea strainer cover down into the bilge where it could not be retrieved. That conclusion was quickly dismissed, however, since what I did was on my own initiative without orders from anyone. Besides, such an improvised action would have never been necessary if our Chief Engineering Officer had done his duty in the first place. After some discussion, I ended up being commended for my independent action.

The questioning quickly turned to our Chief Engineering Officer, Josef Hauser. In his defense, the Raccoon protested that he thought the boat was sinking, and therefore considered the setting of demolition charges superfluous. In the end, it was agreed that although it was unforeseeable that the Americans would attempt to board our boat, the Chief Engineering Officer was still negligent in his duty to scuttle the boat, as per our skipper's order. There was never any intention to punish the Raccoon on our own, though a formal military proceeding once we were released was held out as a possibility.

Unwarranted as it was, the Raccoon was beginning to fear for his safety and complained to the Allied authorities about it. He was eventually transferred out of the camp, an occasion that aroused little disappointment on my behalf.

In time, we were moved from Bermuda to Texas, and then to a large prison camp in Ruston, Louisiana. In every respect it was a normal prisoner of war camp, but we U-505 crewmen were kept in a separate compound apart from all the other prisoners. The American government maintained the cover story that it was a special sort of detention area for prisoners that were anti-Nazis. By labeling it a camp for political detainees rather than prisoners of war, it was exempt from obligatory inspections by the International Red Cross. Once again, no word of our capture would reach Germany. Our hearts sank at the anguish we imagined our families going through, assuming we had been lost.

Being incarcerated in a so-called camp for anti-Nazis was a funny joke for us because we had lost none of our patriotic ardor for a German victory. For instance, one night, we mixed some cleaning chemicals together to produce hydrogen gas. We then filled some cellophane bags with the gas to make little lighter-than-air balloons. These balloons floated over the perimeter fences and showered the neighborhood with our paper Iron Crosses proudly proclaiming, "U-505 lives!" Another time, we snuck through the perimeter fences and hung a German war flag

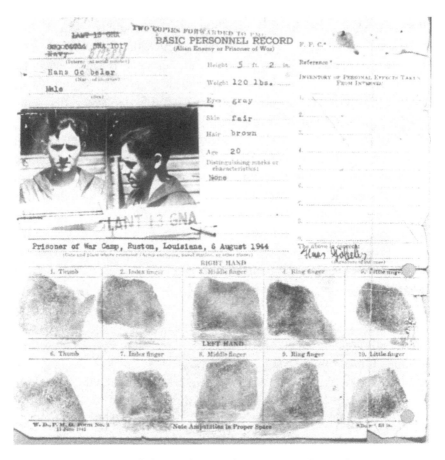

Hans Goebeler's prisoner of war personnel record.

---

from the top of the American's water tower. That really made the guards angry!

Inside the camp, we maintained strict military discipline and allegiance to our country. The guards considered us "hardcore Nazis," but what we were really demonstrating was professionalism and patriotic pride. Even after we realized the war would be lost, we resolved never to lose our dignity as military men.

After a while, we were put to work clearing forests and picking cotton for local farmers there in Ruston. The farmers were very happy to have us, proclaiming that we Germans worked much harder and meticulously than the people they usually hired. But as far as I was concerned, the backbreaking labor cured me of all my Jack London-inspired fantasies about the romantic life of lumbermen. The strange creatures of the Louisiana woods were a special terror to me. Big wasps we nicknamed "Stukas" stung us as we worked, and snakes often dropped down onto our heads when we chopped at trees. Picking cotton was even more odious. The cotton flowers tore at one's fingers like knives, and the constant stooping and bending was agonizing.

At one point, we helped the residents of Ruston repair some nearby dikes during a hurricane. They said we had made the difference in saving the area from being flooded. In May of 1984, the mayor of Ruston presented me, on behalf of the entire *U-505* crew, the keys to the city in appreciation for our efforts during that storm.

I spent most of my time clearing trees and brush for a local farmer, William Simington. Mr. Simington was a fine old gentleman and we became quite good friends. In fact, he told me that if I returned to Ruston after the war, he would adopt me as his son! He didn't have anyone to leave his farm to, and he said I would make a fine farmer and would be a credit to the community. I was deeply touched by his offer, but I told him I had a family back in Germany and that they would need my help to get through the tough times ahead.

*   *   *

In early May 1945, we learned the war had finally ended. Though not entirely unexpected, we were still shocked and thrown into depression when the terms of the surrender reached us. Once again, the penalty for Germany losing a war would be the dismemberment of our country. We were particularly horrified with the prospect of millions of our women and children falling into the bloody hands of the communists. The one bright spot was that, with the war now over, the Americans finally allowed us to mail letters to our families and tell them of our survival.

Each hour of our captivity now lasted an eternity as we waited to rejoin our loved ones at home. In December, we were transferred back to Europe, but we still could not go home. We had been sold to the British for forced labor in Scotland. My departure from the good Mr. Simington's household was a sad occasion for both of us.

The work in Scotland was hard, but our living conditions were comfortable. In many ways, we were better off than the civilians in Germany. My immediate family had survived intact, but just like the aftermath of the First World War, hunger and misery abounded. For two long years we toiled in Scotland. Finally, in December of 1947, we were released to return to our homeland.

I was torn by conflicting emotions as I traveled back home. I was naturally ecstatic to be rejoining my family, but the thought of going through the required "de-Nazification" program upon reentering Germany deeply disturbed me. When I took my solemn oath of allegiance upon enlistment into the German Navy, it was for life. I was revolted by the idea of being forced to swear another oath to an enemy-imposed regime.

During the ferry passage across the English Channel, I made my decision. Like my father before me, no matter what the cost imposed by our conquerors, I would refuse to renounce my beliefs.

When the ship arrived, I was put on a train filled with hundreds of other former prisoners of war. Just before the train reached the German border at Duisburg, I jumped off. Sympathetic smugglers helped me cross the border and I made my way back to my hometown. The occupation authorities never did manage to "re-educate" me.

*   *   *

Life was very hard in my devastated homeland during those first few years after the war. German military losses had numbered more than three million dead. Our civilian losses during the war were even higher, due mainly to the carpet bombing raids on our cities. Most tragically of all, more than three million more of my countrymen died in the years immediately after the war from disease and the starvation rations imposed upon us by the victors. Not many remember, much less mourn, the innocent victims of this genocide.

Although my hometown of Bottendorf escaped damage from the bombings, we were flooded with refugees from the east, all desperate to escape extermination at the hands of the Soviets. These pitiful victims of "ethnic cleansing" put a terrible strain on our land as we tried to feed and find work for the exiles.

The journey to Chicago. *U-505* is being towed in 1954 on her way to the Chicago Museum of Science and Industry, where she can be seen and toured. *Author's Collection*

Eventually, I found employment as a welder and started a family. The healing began, for both my homeland and me.

* * *

In 1954, I heard the thrilling news that *U-505* was being installed as a permanent exhibit at the Museum of Science and Industry in Chicago. As the years passed, I found my thoughts returning more and more to those days I spent aboard her. With encouragement from my wife, we moved to Chicago after my retirement in order to be near my old boat. Once in America, I began to organize *U-505* reunions for the German and American crews involved in the capture. I also began writing this book as a record of our experiences.

* * *

Author Hans Goebeler played a key role in bringing together former enemies. Here, members of the USS *Guadalcanal* Task Group and *U-505* reunite in 1982. German crewmen are seated in front. Hans (with cane) is on the far left. Earl Trosino, *Guadalcanal's* engineer who led the salvage team, can be seen over Goebeler's right shoulder. For the Germans, this was the first formal visit to *U-505* since her capture in June 1944. *Author's Collection.*

Hans Goebeler standing on the deck of his beloved *U-505* once again—this time in the 1990s in Chicago outside the Museum of Science and Industry.

Author's Collection

My story has thus come full circle. Like many of the Hessian soldiers from my province who decided to stay and raise families in America after the Revolutionary War, I too have adopted this wonderful land of freedom and opportunity as my own country. Health permitting, I visit that lucky old boat, *U-505*, every chance I get.

In talking with my former crewmates about our experiences, I have come to realize that people can witness the same event and come away with very different impressions of what actually happened. I do not insist that this book is the full story of what happened aboard *U-505*. It is only what I can personally attest to having witnessed and experienced. The final judgment must be left to historians who can combine all the various impressions, like the pieces of a puzzle, into something approaching the complete truth.

Setting the historical record straight about World War II is a very important goal. After all, as George Santayana once said, "Those who forget the past are condemned to repeat it." But what good is studying history if all one reads are one-sided fairy tales written by the victors? It seems clear to me that only if we know the whole truth about the past, can we determine the right solutions for the future. This is crucial for everyone, not just for those whom history has cast into the role of villain.

INDEX

U-510, 162
U-514, 69, 138, 140
U-515, 244
U-523, 146
U-533, 138, 139
U-534, 54-55

Vanzo, John, Introduction, xv-xvii
VonFriedeburg, Hans-Georg, 182
VonGortzen, skipper of *T-25*, 196-197
VonSchröter, 219
Vowe, Bruno, 92

Wanze radar detector, 155, 195
West Irmo, British freighter, 30-31
Willi (crewmate), 115, 118, 132
Wintergarten, 133, 163, 180
Wolfbauer, Leo, 56

Z-27, German Destroyer, 194
Zschech, Peter, 60-77, 81-106, 108-112,
      129, 140-143, 147-149, 151, 153-154,
      174-175, 215, 243, suicide, 168-173,
      181-192